THE GROWTH AND DEVELOPMENT OF SPORT IN COUNTY TIPPERARY 1840–1880

THE GROWTH
AND DEVELOPMENT
OF SPORT IN
COUNTY TIPPERARY
1840–1880

PAT BRACKEN

CORK UNIVERSITY PRESS

First published in 2018 by
Cork University Press
Youngline Industrial Estate
Pouladuff Road, Togher
Cork T12 HT6V, Ireland

British Library Cataloguing in Publication Data
A CIP catalogue record for this book is available from the British Library.

ISBN- 978-1-78205-274-6

Typeset by edit+ www.stuartcoughlan.com
Printed in Poland by HussarBooks

CONTENTS

ACKNOWLEDGEMENTS

The inspiration behind my desire to chronicle the sporting history of Tipperary was Dr Tom Hunt. Having got to know Tom through various sporting queries, I was enthralled by his study of Westmeath and discussed with him my desire to do something similar for Tipperary. This is the end product of a long journey. It is a journey which could not have been achieved without the great support and backing of Professor Mike Cronin who was lead supervisor during my PhD research. Mike's wide knowledge of sport was, and continues to be, a joy to behold. Professor Tony Collins and Professor Dilwyn Porter provided insight and encouragement along the way and all three taught me new ways of looking at things. Dr Conor Curran, a fellow student along the journey, lent a willing ear on many occasion as I teased out one problem or another. Dr Dónal McAnallen was always ready with support and was a great source of friendship also. Dr Sean Reid, though residing in England, provided sound advice and support and to him I am very thankful. I also greatly acknowledge the support of Dr Denis G. Marnane during my PhD research and his interest in my work.

I wish to thank those at the National Library, Kildare Street and in the National Archives in Bishop Street for their help during my research. The staff in Tipperary County Council Library Service were always supportive and I thank them all and in particular my colleagues Mary Guinan-Darmody and John O'Gorman in the Tipperary Studies department. To Sally Wilson at the Turf Club in the Curragh for access to the library there and Audrey Crowley for her help in accessing Córas Iompair Éireann records at Heuston Station. My thanks to the late Lord Waterford for permitting me access to Curraghmore House and the hunting diaries of the 3rd Marquis. I am also grateful to the present Lord Waterford for his interest in and support of my work.

To Mike Collins and Maria O'Donovan at Cork University Press, I thank them sincerely for their willing support of my work and their constant assistance with my queries. I greatly appreciate the work they put in, guiding me to bring a manuscript through to publication. This could not be achieved either without the guidance and input of my two peer reviewers and I sincerely acknowledge, with heartfelt thanks, the work they put in and the welcome advice and comments which they made on the draft manuscript. Thanks also to Stuart Coughlan of edit+ and Daniel Brown for design, setting and assistance with maps and graphs.

I have been engaged in research in one way or another for the past twenty years and through it all there has been one ever constant behind it all, my wife Norah. She has had to endure countless days and nights of isolation as I ferreted away in books, papers and press cuttings. Then came into our lives our wonderful son and daughter, Kevin and Ellen, and they have given us great joy and friendship during their young lives. But there have been sad times too, the loss of my parents and a brother. Their absence helps to put a lot of what I have done into perspective. I dedicate this work to their memory, Kitty, Jimmy and Jimmy Jnr.

ACRONYMS

CC	*Clonmel Chronicle*
CC	Cricket club
CG	*Cashel Gazette*
FLJ	*Finn's Leinster Journal*
FJ	*Freeman's Journal*
ICAC	Irish Champion Athletic Club
IT	*The Irish Times*
KM	*Kilkenny Moderator*
MCC	Marylebone Cricket Club
MFH	Master of Foxhounds
NC	*Nationalist* (Clonmel)
NCO	Non-commissioned Officer
NG	*Nenagh Guardian*
Pers. comm.	Personal communication
RIC	Royal Irish Constabulary
TA	*Tipperary Advocate*
TAA	*The Argus* (Australia)
TC	*Tipperary Constitution*
TE	*Tipperary Examiner*
TFP	*Tipperary Free Press*
TL	*Tipperary Leader*
TLI	Tipperary Light Infantry
TV	*Tipperary Vindicator*
TWN	*Tipperary Weekly News*

FIGURES

TABLES

INTRODUCTION

Victorian Ireland was a time of great change, of emancipation, famine and emigration. In tandem with these changes a sporting evolution took place that included the codification of games and an enhanced awareness of sport. The 1840s was a watershed decade in the history of Ireland as the Great Famine changed the lives of many people forever. The years which followed brought much change to both urban and rural Ireland. In the context of sport there was also great change. New games emerged and older games were codified. County Tipperary is chosen as an area for examination to explore this issue in greater detail. The growth and development of sport, between 1840 and 1880, is used to illustrate the changes that took place and the agencies which were instrumental in this change. All sports in the county are looked at in greater or lesser detail, depending on how widely they were played and the availability of relevant sources.

Sport and society were much more fluid than arbitrary lines on a map. What happened with sport elsewhere in Ireland was important to the development of sport in the county, as were individuals who lived outside of the county, but who had a significant impact on the direction and patronage of several sports within Tipperary. Sport in mid-nineteenth-century Tipperary was often haphazard. This book starts at a time when sport, for the most part, was unregulated. Over the course of the next fifty years a lot changed in the world of sport. Paul Rouse, in his book *Sport and Ireland: a history,* has shown how, in an

1

Irish context, this can be dated to the late 1870s and early 1880s with the organisation and codification of Association football, rugby football and Gaelic games.[1] Some sports fell out of favour and became but a memory; these are documented in this book as a means of illustrating how the popularity of various sports came to prominence and then faded. In this context the term 'popular' is used to imply the degree to which it was popular among a specific section of society. Not all members of society participated in sporting activity.

The temporal boundaries of this study have been carefully chosen. A commencement date of 1840 was chosen so that sport in the famine era is included. Pre-Famine sport in Ireland had until 2014 received little attention. When it did, it was part of a widespread assessment of a sport as viewed in a national context.[2] In writing *Sport in Ireland, 1600–1840*, James Kelly has clearly demonstrated how the sporting environment of the country was shaped during this period.[3] The analysis of Kelly complements the findings of this book. The findings presented here also support the work of Paul Rouse, in arguably the finest general history of sport in Ireland yet written.

The terminal date of 1880 is chosen as it coincided with the onset of widespread land agitation inspired by Michael Davitt's campaign for low rent, free sale and fixity of tenure for tenant farmers.[4] This led to civil unrest which impacted on all aspects of social life, including sport. Stopping the hunt became a feature of this unrest. During the Land War, landlords and tenant farmers were pitted against each other. Hunt packs were prevented from entering land. However, as the chapter on hunting demonstrates, the period immediately prior to widespread land agitation was one of the most prolific for hunting to hounds in the county's history.[5] The terminal date is also four years prior to the foundation of the Gaelic Athletic Association (GAA). The period leading up to the foundation of the GAA and the organisation itself have received much attention from both a national and local perspective.[6] Consequently, the evolution of sport in Tipperary, and indeed for much of Ireland, in the preceding forty years has not been assessed at a micro level except for the study of County Westmeath by Tom Hunt, which had a start date of 1850.[7]

CLASS-BASED

The growth and development of sport is examined with a focus on some central themes. Firstly, sport in mid-Victorian Tipperary was class-based. The landed elite, businessmen and military officers were the principal agents through which sport in Tipperary developed. In a county devoid of industrialisation and urbanisation, sport developed in Tipperary's rural setting quite differently from how it developed in the urban centres of Dublin, Belfast, London, Manchester or Liverpool. In those cities, sport could draw on a large industrial population for support and participation. A growing Victorian interest in sport, which was evident in England, was soon replicated in Ireland as the codified games ethic, which was in vogue across the water, quickly became apparent here too, through diffusion and emulation. Also, in the post-Famine period Ireland experienced a period of relative calm, following the unrest, death and emigration of the 1830s and 1840s, while the estate system too enjoyed a period of sustained economic certainty, although some estates did experience difficulties.

Resident Magistrates and Justices of the Peace were scattered throughout the county, with some of these holding large estates. The High Sheriff, Sir John C. Carden, of Templemore Abbey, had an estate of over 6,680 acres, while the sub-sheriff, Samuel M. Going, had an estate of over 2,522 acres.[8] While there was a social status associated with owning an estate, there were also benefits to be had if one was a member of parliament, a member of the grand jury, or a poor law guardian.[9] Taking a mid-range date of 1860, there were ninety-two county families recorded for County Tipperary.[10] 'County families' was a term used by Edward Walford in his study of such families resident in the United Kingdom in 1860. They were families of means that had lived in a particular county for several generations. Walford in his book derived much of his information on Irish families from Thom's Directory. Cork, the biggest county in Ireland, had 164 families, while Dublin had 111 families listed.[11] Other counties had smaller numbers of such families: Limerick had seventy-one; Antrim had sixty-five; Kilkenny had fifty-two and Kildare had forty-one. This gave Tipperary a range of county families at the higher end of the scale.[12] Forty-nine families had a demesne attached to the main residence, ranging from eighty acres, at Woodville, near Templemore, up to the 2,500-acre demesne held by Viscount Hawarden at Dundrum. The extent of his estate was 15,272 acres, making him the third largest landowner in the county, behind Viscount Lismore (34,945 acres) and the Marquis of Ormonde, whose Tipperary estates totalled 15,765 acres.[13] These three gentlemen were also peers in the House of Lords.[14] In 1878, in a return of landowners, there were a total of 389 men who held estates valued at £100 and over in Tipperary.[15] Of these, 122 estates were valued at between £100 and £500, while 141 were valued at between £500 and £1,000, with 109 valued at between £1,000 and £5,000.[16] The remaining seventeen estates were valued at £5,000 or over.[17]

Tom Hunt has shown for County Westmeath that it was a number of wealthy individual farmers and estate proprietors who invested some of their finance in the patronage of sport.[18] A similar situation occurred in Tipperary, where the presence of such estates and the patronage of their owners were critical to the emergence of sport in the county.

Sport at this time was strongly gender biased but participation was not solely a male preserve. Female participation was centred around the country house setting. The limited role of women is also assessed, particularly among the hunt community, on the archery field and the lawn tennis court.

THE MILITARY

Class alone is not the sole reason for the growth of sport. Key to understanding how sport developed in Tipperary was the large-scale presence of military personnel in the county, many of whom were born outside of Ireland. They were instrumental in the promotion, advancement and support of various sports, with the officer class taking a lead role in the promotion of sport throughout Tipperary. It was the social network of the officers commanding the garrisons and the landed elite which encouraged sport to take place. They also had control of one of the essential requirements which allowed sport to happen – access to land. The role of the landed class and their association with military officers is central to how sport took off and developed in Victorian Tipperary.

HURLING

New sporting recreations, which were popular in Great Britain, became popular in Ireland too, marking a transition from the traditional games of hurling and local versions of football. Hurling however, did not disappear, and this book argues that in fact the opposite was the case. Central to this argument is the evidence provided by previously underused Petty Sessions records which identify references to heretofore unrecorded hurling matches. A key feature of this book is that it challenges the widely perceived notion that hurling was in decline in the post-Famine, pre-GAA era and on the cusp of oblivion. The Petty Sessions records and documentary evidence from the local press show that such was not the case in Tipperary. When this evidence is combined with this writer's research into hurling played in Australia, in the 1870s and 1880s, there can be no doubt that the game was still relevant prior to the foundation of the GAA and was played far more extensively than previously realised.[19]

LITERACY

The period between 1840 and 1880 also witnessed the emergence of commercialised sporting journalism, which came on the back of an increasingly literate society. This was underpinned by the presence of eleven local newspapers, though some were of short duration. This growth of the popular press spread countrywide in the second quarter of the nineteenth century. In Tipperary, there were, by 1840, two bi-weekly newspapers printed in the county, each representing a different political standpoint. These were the nationalist *Tipperary Free Press*, established in 1826 and published in Clonmel in the south of the county, and the *Nenagh Guardian*, established in 1838, printed in the northern end.

The founding proprietor of the *Nenagh Guardian*, John Kempston, set the stall out for his paper as one which was 'strongly Conservative'.[20] Similar to the *Tipperary Free Press*, its content featured meetings of the various Poor Law Unions, meetings of the various government bodies, and accounts of 'army news'. Both devoted similar amounts of space to what was termed 'sporting intelligence'. Newspapers were a key element in the promotion of sport.[21]

The growth in the range of local newspapers complemented the development of the education system in Ireland. The new national school system set in motion a structure which, for the first time, gave all children an opportunity to learn how to read and write.[22] Education, even if school attendance was erratic, gave people the ability to read the local newspaper or letters home from relations who had emigrated. It also began a process whereby a popular culture characterised by belief in fairies and dedication to holy wells was replaced by a culture which was 'literate, anglicised and politically aware'.[23]

BUSINESS

There was a clearly defined take-off period for sport in the county in the mid-1860s, when there was a transition from occasional fixtures and contests to a more frequent 'calendar' of competition in a range of sports. This coincided with a steady growth in the business surrounding sport, which included the shopkeepers who carried sporting goods to meet an emerging market. Sport was a promoter of commercial opportunities from the outset, as local landowners and businessmen were receptive to the appeal of sport and the business and money they could accrue from it. Business acumen was not the sole preserve of the business elite. The book also illustrates that people were willing to travel long distances to sell wine, beer and spirits at sporting events. In a local context, a whole range of trades and industries sprang up around the country house estates as farriers, caterers and gamekeepers serviced the needs of those in authority.

PROMINENT SPORTING INDIVIDUALS

The growth and development of sport in Tipperary relied on the support of many people. However, key individuals emerged who were instrumental in promoting, organising or participating in sport. Some of them, such as Maurice and Pat Davin, gained national and international success. Others, because of their social status or the means by which they indulged their sporting passions, were also significant, with their presence at an event enhancing not only the general attendance, but also the sporting occasion. The 1870s witnessed the introduction of professional sportsmen into the county to assist club development, notably with the Clonmel Rowing Club. The roles these men had in developing competitive clubs are also explored.

Most sports had an individual who was a lead agent in its promotion or advancement. With the military this was a member of the officer class at Cahir barracks who supported hunting to hounds; Adjutant Maitland at Nenagh barracks, who promoted horse racing; or Lieutenant Carr, also at Nenagh barracks who outlined the laws of rugby to a team of local players in 1875.[24] One man who loomed large in the hunting and horse racing scene was the 3rd Marquis of Waterford, Henry de la Poer Beresford. He was very influential in both activities in Tipperary, though he resided at Curraghmore House in County Waterford. John Bagwell, landlord and Conservative member for Clonmel borough, with his provision of land for sport, was also instrumental in the support and backing which he gave to various sports, notably cricket, though he was never an active participant in the way that the aforementioned gentlemen were.

TOPOGRAPHY AND POPULATION

Tipperary, the sixth largest county Ireland, is 430,519 hectares in extent. It was similar to many other parts of Ireland in that the population of the county declined for many decades in the aftermath of the Great Famine, principally due to emigration. The topography of Tipperary is such that the third longest river in Ireland, the Suir, bisects the county north–south, flowing 183 kilometres to the sea at Waterford city. On its western border is the River Shannon, which flows into Lough Derg before entering the Atlantic Ocean at Limerick. The Galtee Mountains to the south-west of the county are the primary mountain range in Tipperary, with Galteemore peaking at 917 metres, making it the sixth highest mountain in the country. There are some other hill ranges such as the Slieveardagh Hills, encompassing the Killenaule and Ballingarry districts to the east, and the Slievefelim and the Silvermines Mountains which extend from Upperchurch to Kilcommon and Rearcross to the west. Both the Shanbally estate near Clogheen and the Glengall estate at Cahir encompassed much of the Galtee Mountains. Game preservation notices for the estate lands featured regularly in the local press.[25] While the effects of the Famine ensured great hardship for many, within the county there were thousands of people who emigrated in the wake of the distress. Of those who emigrated from 1 May 1851 to 31 March 1881, 154,802 gave Tipperary as their county of origin.[26] Yet, despite the failure of the potato crop, along with death and emigration, much general agricultural activity continued within the county.

While there was untold distress caused by the Famine, Tipperary did not fare as badly as counties in the south-west and west of Ireland. Galway and Mayo, in the west, and Cork and Kerry, in the south-west, were the four counties which endured higher mortality rates because of starvation. Between 1846 and 1851, when compared to the rest of the country, Tipperary came in twelfth highest in relation to average annual excess death rates per 1,000.[27] Mayo at seventy-two, and Sligo at just over sixty-one, were the counties with the highest mortality rates per 1,000 of population. The mortality rate for Tipperary was thirty-five per 1,000 persons.

By 1855 'as many as two and a half million people had departed Ireland'.[28] As Table 0.1 demonstrates, the population was in continual decline after the 1841 census. In fact this decline continued until 1961, by which date the population of the county was 53,696. This was 73.3 per cent less than that which was recorded in 1841. Up to 1901, the net emigration rate from Ireland was in double percentage figures, with 'the outflow about four million between 1850 and 1914'.[29]

Table 0.1 Population change in County Tipperary, 1841–1881

Census date	Population	Male	Female	Decrease	Percentage decrease
1841	201,161	100,558	100,603	-----	-----
1851	147,164	71,049	76,115	53,997	26.84
1861	109,220	53,967	55,253	37,944	25.75
1871	93,617	46,405	47,212	15,603	14.29
1881	86,331	42,773	43,558	7,286	7.78

Sources: *Census of Ireland returns 1871* (Dublin, 1872); *Census of Ireland returns 1881* (Dublin, 1882)

Cormac Ó Gráda has observed that there was a 'common perception of nineteenth-century Ireland' relying heavily on agriculture.[30] The evidence from the 1821 census suggests otherwise, with 'two-fifths [of the population] declaring an occupation ... chiefly employed in trades, manufactures or handicraft'.[31] Tipperary was a rural-based economy with strong ties to the land and agriculture. In 1859, 'flour milling was in the zenith of prosperity ... in every part of the county. The tillage lands were used largely for wheat-growing, and many fortunes were made by mill-owners.'[32] Cahir, in 1866, was described as 'a thriving town ... a great place for flour mills, an immense lot of wheat being sent annually to Waterford.'[33] However, once the Corn Laws were repealed, Irish milling declined. A fall in the export of corn through Waterford port was an indicator of the decline in Clonmel and the south-east.[34] Throughout much of Ireland, there was a general move away from corn towards livestock. Corn growing and milling continued in some regions of Tipperary, with 'nearly all the extensive farmers' around Thurles dividing their 'attention between the raising of young stock, dairying, sheep fattening and tillage'.[35]

Tipperary was typical of most other counties of Ireland in terms of urban growth and population density. Its strength lay in its pastoral agricultural base. But it also had market towns located throughout the county. In 1841, there were seven significant market towns: Cashel,

Carrick-on-Suir, Clonmel, Nenagh, Roscrea, Thurles and Tipperary. This made Tipperary comparable to County Cork with towns of this status.[36] Twenty years later all the main towns in the county had a population threshold above 2,000 persons. For comparative purposes, a mid-range date of 1861 is chosen to indicate population levels in the post-Famine era. Clonmel had the highest population figure, 11,646; Carrick-on-Suir, 6,536; Nenagh, 6,204; and Tipperary town, 5,864 persons.[37] The other towns had population levels below 5,000.

In relation to religion, the majority of the population were Roman Catholic, with Church of Ireland / England, Presbyterian, Methodists and other denominations following to a much lesser extent. On average, Catholics accounted for 94 per cent of the county's population. Table 0.2 gives a breakdown of the religious denomination for the years 1861, 1871 and 1881.

Table 0.2 Religious denomination of the population of Tipperary, 1861–1881

Census date	Roman Catholic	Established Church	Presbyterian	Methodist	Other
1861	234,881	12,800	498	572	355
1871	203,227	11,855	607	642	382
1881	188,115	10,211	487	574	224

Source: *Census of Ireland 1881. Part 1, area, houses and population* (Alex Thom & Co., Dublin, 1882, p. 851)

INFRASTRUCTURAL DEVELOPMENTS

The single most important infrastructural development in the county during the nineteenth century was that of the rail network. The development of rail allowed for the cheap and easy construction of sporting networks, was good for sport and was a critical feature in its growth in the county. The railway permitted the easy movement of people, animals and goods. It also assisted in the diffusion of sport, especially horse racing. The railway had great economic, social and sporting benefits for Tipperary business people and residents. The Tory Prime Minister Robert Peel, who commenced his political career as a Member of Parliament for Cashel in 1812, after his father purchased this seat for him, kept a watchful eye on the various rail networks proposed for Ireland.[38] It has been suggested that Peel sought to open up the countryside outside of Dublin to 'make Tipperary amenable to work and policing'.[39] Work on rail lines commenced. Progress was rapid and at a time of Famine, the construction of the railways gave huge employment to local communities. In May 1847, work on the line to Thurles was well advanced, with many men employed in its construction.[40] On 13 March 1848, the Great Southern and Western Railway (GS&WR) opened the connecting rail line between Ballybrophy and Thurles.[41] This effectively connected the county with Dublin. Under the initial 1844 Act, the desired terminal for the first section of the rail link was Cashel but 'the promoters had not yet decided whether the railway should run east or west of the Galtee Hills. In the following year the company obtained a second Act which prescribed the western route.'[42] Consequently the line stopped at Thurles. It was later extended to Limerick Junction and then to Cork. The new line opened on 29 October 1849. Dublin, Cork and Limerick were now connected by a rail link.

Further rail connections – from Ballybrophy to Roscrea, opened on 19 October 1857, Roscrea to Nenagh, opened on 5 October 1863, and Nenagh to Birdhill, which opened on 1 June 1864 – brought the railway to the north of Tipperary. When the rail connection between two other cites – Limerick on the western seaboard and Waterford on the south coast – was completed, its route had crossed much of south Tipperary. The connecting link between Tipperary town and Clonmel, opened on 30 April 1852 as part of the Waterford and Limerick Railway, gave the south of the county a connection to not only these two cities but also to Dublin and Cork where it met the GS&WR at Limerick Junction.[43] Because of the central position of the county, the connecting routes serving four of the seven principal cities in the country – Dublin to Cork, Dublin to Limerick and Limerick to Waterford – passed through it. By 1870, south of a line drawn from Dublin to Galway the rail network was reasonably extensive but north of this line it was virtually non-existent.

Over the course of sixteen years, from 1848 to 1864, the introduction of the railway into Tipperary effectively saw all of the main towns in the county serviced by a rail connection. The landlords whose land it cut through were handsomely rewarded. In November 1846, Sir Henry Carden was paid £4,650 by the GS&WR for lands it procured as it crossed his Templemore estate.[44] A branch line from Clonmel to Thurles, opened in two stages, on 23 June 1879 and 1 July 1880, connected the east of the county with the GS&WR and also the Waterford and Limerick Railway.[45] A proposed connection between Templemore and Nenagh, much vaunted in the local press, never came to fruition.[46] Like County Westmeath and the other regions of Ireland which had a rail network, its introduction was 'the most important infrastructural improvement to take place within the county'.[47] But the rail network greatly facilitated the transportation of not only people but also animals and specifically horses. The railway was to prove of great benefit to the horse racing fraternity in Tipperary.[48] In September 1850, the tender of seven purpose-built horse boxes to be supplied to the Great Southern and Western Railway by Joseph Wright, at a cost of £78 10s each, was accepted by the company, emphasising its requirement to transport animals for whatever purpose, including horse racing.[49]

The rail network also permitted the transportation of adolescent boys and girls to boarding schools around the country. While there was nothing unusual in this, the Tipperary Grammar School did make note of the fact that the school stood within 'five minutes walk of the railway station, and is completely secluded from the town'.[50] Some eleven years later, the walking distance had miraculously come down to two minutes.[51] The education sector was an important medium through which children were introduced to sport. St John's College, Newport, boasted that the house was most favourably situated, 'remote from the temptations of a large town' and that it had twenty acres of playing grounds attached to the premises.[52] While the development of the education sector was an integral feature of the early Victorian years, with new national schools erected all over Tipperary, just a few second-level schools participated in regular sporting activity.[53] These included Tipperary Grammar School, Rockwell College, St John's College, Newport and Roscrea school.

But the railways were also a means by which children were transported away from Tipperary to educational institutions elsewhere. Typically, this meant public school education, either in Ireland or Great Britain. Some of the sons of successful Tipperary landowners and businessmen attended public school, such as Harrow, Stoneyhurst and Winchester in England. For others St John's College, Waterford; Blackrock College, Dublin; or Clongowes Wood College, Co. Kildare, were likely destinations. The attendance of boys at public schools in Great Britain and the degree to which they were either knowledgeable of, or active participants in, public school games is featured throughout this book.[54]

RELEVANCE OF THIS STUDY

Following on from the research conducted by Tom Hunt for County Westmeath, this book adds to the knowledge of the growth of sport in Victorian Ireland. The book is inclusive, encompassing as it does the patronage role of lords and gentlemen and the participation of the lower classes in various sports.

The thematic approach to the growth of sport in Tipperary allows for analysis between sports where there was a common theme, such as the military, horses, stick or racket and ball, athletics and the various football codes. The fluidity of society and how sport in Tipperary adapted to fashions of sport, as they became popularised, more usually among the middle and upper classes throughout the British Isles is also demonstrated. The role of the public schoolboy in this respect is a new area of study in the historiography of Irish sport. It is new insofar as the schools and colleges were in England and not grammar schools in Ireland or Trinity College Dublin.

This study from Tipperary, 1840–1880, illustrates how sport in rural Ireland moved from being an irregular ritual to one which became codified and recorded, to paraphrase Allen Guttman.[55] In its entirety, it explores the emergence of modern sport in one Irish county. It shows that the seeds of modern sport were sown by the promotion, interest and enthusiasm of the gentry and the garrison in the decades before sports were codified and regulated. The book makes a major contribution to sports historiography as it concentrates on the pre-modern era, where participation in sport has been understood as limited. It challenges the overarching narrative that sees the emergence of modern sport as predominantly an urban process and explores instead an alternative model in which patronage and the social stability of the post-Famine economic boom can be used to understand how organised sport came into being.

CHAPTER STRUCTURE

The chapters are set out thematically, though some items are held over from specific chapters to maintain a particular theme. Chapter 1 looks at the role of the military in the promotion of sport countywide. This was especially noticeable in the towns and surrounding communities where there was a military barracks. Among the military it was specifically the officer class which was instrumental in the advancement of specific sporting recreations and this is demonstrated throughout the chapter. Chapter 2 examines the role of the country house setting in the overall promotion of sport in Tipperary. It was behind the demesne wall where much sport took place, especially lawn games, and through the nurturing of these games the men and women who played here were replicating what was happening on the British mainland. Though there is no tangible evidence left to indicate the variety of events which took place, the country estate was the de facto playing arena for much of the period under review.

Chapter 3 continues the country house theme, but in a much broader sense. It examines the relevance of hunting to the social and sporting life of many people countywide. The support of various individuals was key to the success or failure of a particular hunt and the chapter shows how there was a move away from private packs to subscription packs, often to the financial disadvantage of the Master of the Hunt. Chapter

4 is also associated with horses, in this case the growth and development of horse racing. It outlines the gradual move from locally organised meetings to those which had support from Turf Club officials at the Curragh. The involvement of some important Turf Club personnel at many meetings helped shape the future direction of racing in Tipperary. Horse racing at Cashel is explored in detail to illustrate all that was involved in organising a successful meeting. However, success did not equate with longevity, and reasons for the decline of racing in Cashel in the 1870s are also explored.

Chapter 5 looks at the twin sports of athletics and rowing. Athletics is used as an all-embracing term for the various events which constituted a typical meeting in Tipperary in the 1870s. Once more, individuals who were important in terms of participation and organisation are highlighted. Also highlighted are issues around amateurism in the true sense of the word and those men who competed for monetary prizes. To this end, some of them earned a good living, travelling around the county and winning various events. The spread of athletics throughout the county is also explored.

Rowing took place on the River Suir at Carrick-on-Suir and Clonmel. The history of the Clonmel club is assessed in detail, looking at professional trainers brought in to aid in the development and success of the club. Once again there were issues around amateurs and professional trainers. This brings in to question the issue of amateurism, and the merits of what it meant to be an amateur sportsperson in Tipperary in the 1870s is also addressed.

Ball games are the subject of Chapter 6. The term 'ball games' is all-embracing for games played with the hand or foot and those played with a hurley, bat or racket. Cricket and hurling are looked at in detail. Using evidence from the Petty Sessions reports, hurling is shown to have been more widespread in the post-Famine era than what had previously been believed. This is backed up with fleeting reference to the development of hurling in Australia in the latter half of the 1870s. Cricket was the most widespread team sport in the county before the foundation of the GAA, and distribution maps and graphs help to demonstrate this. The various forms of football played are then investigated, including local versions of football, rugby and Association football. Those instrumental in promoting these games are also identified. There is also analysis of the Kilruane Football Club. An account book of this club has survived and it provides an insight into the organisation and finances associated with the club. The chapter concludes with an overview of handball and evidence for ball courts around the county. Handball was one game which attracted gambling and this is also highlighted in the account of the game during this period.

CHAPTER 1
SPORT AND THE MILITARY

INTRODUCTION

To understand the growth and development of sport in County Tipperary it is necessary to look at the agencies which were responsible for much of the initial impetus for sport. The first of these was the military. Military personnel stationed in the county played a critical role in the developement of sport across Tipperary. The willingness of officers to become actively involved with cricket matches, race meetings and hunting to hounds was very important to the development of these sporting recreations. Race meetings associated with a specific barracks were those to which soldiers naturally offered the most support. These meetings, in terms of patronage, required sponsorship, so it is no surprise to see that the prizes on offer were contributed by the officers. This was especially so with the races at Cahir barracks, which was the principal cavalry barracks in the county.

While the role of the military in sport, chiefly in England, has been analysed from 1880 onwards, the forty-year period prior to this in Tipperary adds a new perspective to how military personnel were instrumental in introducing and supporting sporting recreation, wherever they were stationed.[1] Tony Mason and Eliza Riedi have shown how the sporting life of the military took on a new significance with the commencement of the 'Army Athletic Meeting, held annually since 1876'.[2] Using information taken mainly from the Tipperary press, it is clear that the military had a major impact on the growth and development of sport in Tipperary between the years 1840 and 1880.

Not all of the military sporting activity in the county during this period is included here, as later on in the book there is a discussion of the military's role in the promotion of athletics meetings.

Levels of military personnel garrisoned throughout the county are included so that there is a reference base from which to demonstrate how the military were, by sheer volume of numbers, able to provide an input into the sporting calendar of Tipperary. After all, many of them were single men with often a lot of time on their hands. The population of the towns in which there was a military barracks is also given. Military numbers, where they can be isolated from specific urban returns, are also given. These give an indication of the strength of the military in a particular area.

In 1830, there were 40,979 Irish non-commissioned officers and other ranks in the British army, representing 42.2 per cent of the army as a whole.[3] Though the actual numbers of men enlisting in 1868 (55,583) and 1873 (42,284) were above the 1830 figures, the overall percentage of Irishmen enlisting in the army continued to decline. In 1898, the figure was 26,376 men, or 12.9 per cent of the army. Of ninety-five military barracks in Ireland, in 1837, eleven of them were located in Tipperary. This was the second highest concentration in the country after Cork, which had thirteen barracks.[4] Seven of those in Cork had accommodation for 500 men or more, compared to just three such barracks in Tipperary.

At Templemore, Richmond barracks was opened in 1812 'with accommodations for 54 officers, 1,500 men, and 30 horses, and a hospital attached for 80 patients'.[5] Apart from serving a military function, this barracks played a huge role in the promotion of sport, not only in the town itself where it was located, but throughout much of mid and north Tipperary. Similarly in Clonmel, Cahir and Tipperary town the military had a significant presence. Clonmel had a mix of infantry and cavalry and consequently the barracks brought to the local town and hinterland many officers and enlisted men from a variety of backgrounds, both in Ireland and Britain. The presence of the military brought economic benefit to a town. Many of the army personnel were active participants in various sporting recreations.

OVERVIEW OF MILITARY STATIONS IN TIPPERARY

In 1837, there were eleven military barracks in County Tipperary. These were comprised of cavalry barracks at Cahir, Clogheen and Fethard; an artillery barracks at Clonmel; and infantry barracks at Carrick-on-Suir, Cashel, Clonmel, Nenagh, Roscrea, Templemore and Tipperary. In that year, in south Tipperary, Cahir had accommodation for twenty-three officers, 346 non-commissioned officers (NCOs) and privates, and 292 horses.[6] Clogheen had two troops of cavalry[7] while Clonmel, a parliamentary borough, was described as having an 'extensive barracks for artillery, cavalry and infantry'.[8] Carrick-on-Suir, initially a cavalry barracks, with accommodation for eight officers and 140 NCOs and privates, was then occupied by infantry.[9] Cashel, the other parliamentary borough in the county, had barrack accommodation for one field officer, six other officers, 146 NCOs and privates, and stabling for three horses.[10] Fethard was described as having an 'extensive barracks at present occupied by infantry'.[11] This barracks later acted as a backup cavalry barracks for Cahir. Tipperary town had a temporary barracks, with accommodation for 100 men.[12]

In the north of the county there were three military barracks. Nenagh could accommodate one field officer, twelve other officers, 208 NCOs and privates, and four horses.[13] Roscrea barracks could accommodate seven officers, 106 NCOs and privates, and four horses.[14] Templemore, the largest of all the barracks at that time, had accommodation for fifty-four officers, 1,500 men, and thirty horses.[15] In total, where specific figures are available for six barracks, there was provision for at least 112 officers and 2,454 NCOs and privates, in addition to '100 men' at Tipperary and 'two troops of cavalry' at Clogheen. The presence of a larger number of barracks in the south of the county may be linked to a communication which Colonel Sorrell, secretary to the commander for the forces in Ireland, had with the under-secretary, William Gregory, in 1822, where an 'anxiety [was] expressed by magistrates and gentry in Tipperary to have military protection'.[16] Much of the civil unrest in pre-Famine Tipperary was caused by the activities of secret societies, notably the Whiteboy movement. The collection of tithes was a constant cause of friction. The movement created great unrest as the 'Whiteboys imposed their own irregular and highly idiosyncratic system of rough justice on those they deemed guilty of damaging the common welfare of the peasantry'.[17] Agrarian violence resulted in countrywide agitation and assault against the person. Similar troubles were also affecting families in County Offaly, where it was reported that 'not a night passes without an outrage being committed in the county which bids fair to out rival – in deeds of blood and savage barbarity – neighbouring Tipperary'.[18]

1848 was a year of rebellion in Ireland, and especially in Tipperary, as the Young Ireland movement sought to break the Union. An infantry barracks at New Inn, erected 'about 1815', was, at that time, occupied by the police.[19] Yet while Templemore did have the capacity for a large force of men, the evidence suggests that it was rarely at full capacity because of the amount of military accommodation elsewhere in the county. In 1847–48 the 64th Regiment of Foot had eleven officers and 300 men present in Templemore. The 70th Regiment, which shared the barracks at that time, had 500 men, of which 300 were recruits.[20] Though it was a large military presence in an Irish market town, it was still well below full occupancy. But such were the vagaries of military life there was no guarantee that military numbers would be maintained at any given time. In the early 1840s, 'to the great displeasure of local businessmen and politicians, no regiment was based in Clonmel'.[21] Things did improve, however, and over the remainder of the century the total number of troops in Clonmel, despite some dips, 'was seldom less than 350'.[22] When the Tipperary Light Infantry (TLI) departed Clonmel for Tralee in 1855, twenty-one officers, three hundred and sixty-four men, thirty-nine women and thirty children boarded a special train to Killarney.[23] These numbers imply that the barrack accommodation level was quite high, with separate married quarters.

That the war in the Crimea was raging at this time must be factored into these figures, as on the return of the soldiers from the war, militias raised locally were stood down. That the TLI had such large numbers suggests that it was a means of deriving income locally, with accommodation and food included. In Tipperary, troops from Clonmel garrison headed to the Crimean battle front in late 1854.[24] Captain Morton, from that barracks, had to embark for the Crimea as soon as the

6th Dragoon Guards (Carbineers) received orders to head to the east.[25] Not only that, recruitment was once more on the agenda as 'on average, 100 [men] a week enlisted in Clonmel'.[26] At the end of the war in 1856, festivities were held in Templemore to honour the successful return of Major Carden and Captain Willington after they were 'exposed to all the dangers and sufferings of the entire campaign of the Crimea'.[27] By 1857 it was reported that there were 'no military at Carrick-on-Suir, Thurles, Nenagh, Roscrea and only a few at Clonmel'.[28]

In 1865, the removal of troops from Templemore led to 'an important meeting' of the Town Commissioners 'for the purpose of adopting a memorial to his Royal Highness the Commander-in-Chief, praying that Her Majesty's troops might not be removed from the garrison of that town ... as the inhabitants felt that the removal of the troops must prove injurious to the commercial interests of the town'.[29] This was a core fact of the military presence in a community. There was no heavy industry, as in England, no large-scale mill or factory enterprises which would sustain some of the Tipperary towns. In their place were large numbers of, primarily, single men dependent on service industries, whose presence was an economic boon to a local economy. Along with the added benefit of having the cavalry at Cahir barracks, where equine care was paramount, the military presence generally was advantageous to the town of Cahir and its hinterland. It is little wonder that the businessmen of Clonmel and Templemore were aggrieved when military numbers were low, or that a threat of their removal was seen as detrimental to the economy of the respective towns.

The 1861 census returns for Ireland were the first in which specific military data was recorded. In 1841 and 1851 the numbers of army and navy personnel had not been included in the census tables.[30] The number of military included in the population of County Tipperary in 1861 amounted to 1,715, and in 1871 the figure was 1,833. Of the latter figure 1,217 were natives of England and Wales; thirty-one of Scotland; twenty-nine were born abroad; and one was born at sea. What these figures clearly demonstrate is that of the 1,833 soldiers in Tipperary in 1871, 1,278 (69.7 per cent) were born outside of Ireland. This was a large body of men who brought with them new ways of doing things, as well as new sports. The remaining 555 men (30.3 per cent) were born in Ireland and what this figure shows is that not all the Irishmen serving in the army were sent abroad. Many of them were garrisoned in Ireland.

It was in Tipperary town, Templemore and Cahir that the military had a significant presence, when viewed as a percentage of the town population at the time of both the 1871 and 1881 censuses. When the number of military and their dependants are viewed as a percentage of all those in County Tipperary the returns are very low, at below 1 per cent.[31] In 1871 there were 1,833 military men and their families in the county (0.84 per cent of a population of 216,702), while in 1881 the figure was 1,563 (0.78 per cent of a population of 199,602). It was only Tipperary town, Templemore and Cahir, in 1881, where military numbers were far above the county average, at 22.15 per cent, 18.46 per cent and 16.64 per cent respectively. The level of military personnel in these and other towns had a strong economic bearing on the communities where they were garrisoned.[32] The economic prosperity of these market towns and the surrounding communities was due in no small part to the year-round interaction with military personnel. Similarly, the military were also instrumental in the participation in and promotion of various sporting activities. There was no part of the county that was not within close proximity to a military barracks, which provided security to landowners, specifically those whose loyalty was to a United Kingdom of Great Britain and Ireland.

SPORT AND THE MILITARY: CRICKET

The examination of the role which the military played in relation to cricket is not intended to be a roll call of the various regiments and personnel who took part, but rather an assessment of the contribution which the military made to the sporting environment of Tipperary. Though other aspects of cricket are examined in greater detail later on, the focus here is to explore the role of the military.

Between 1840 and 1880, whenever a regiment was transferred to a barracks in Tipperary, sport quickly became part of the life of many of the personnel associated with it. At an early stage cricket was a sport popular among the officers and other ranks. A note in the local press in 1840 indicated that the Board of Ordnance had directed that cricket pitches were to be laid down in Cahir, Fethard and Templemore for the use of troops.[33] Officers, NCOs, men and civilian players regularly participated together on the cricket field, though there were times when officers from one company took to the field against the officers of another company, particularly when the garrison was large enough to accommodate such numbers, as was the case in Templemore and Clonmel.[34] It was not that the military were wholly responsible for the transfer of cricket to the local communities but they were primary facilitators and promoters of the game.[35] At this time the civilian participants were principally drawn from among the gentry in Tipperary, although men from the various localities were also used to make up numbers as required.[36] These men were often employed on the estate of some of the gentlemen players.

Cricket was unique in terms of ball sports, in that it had codified laws dating back to 1744.[37] It had a regulating body, the Marylebone Cricket Club (MCC), and it was a game which, by 1840, was widespread in Great Britain. It began to make inroads as a popular sporting recreation in much of Ireland in the pre-Famine years. As Con Costello has shown in his study of the Curragh Camp, 'sporting fixtures brought not only the military and civilians together, but the cricket pitch also encouraged the officers and other ranks into a social mix'.[38] Initially, it was the officer class alone that featured in early reports. Cricket was somewhat different, as reports regularly referred to a mix of officers and rank-and-file members appearing on the same team. That said, Mason and Riedi in their work have observed that 'cricket was an officer's game [and that] an ex-NCO commented on the discomfort of private soldiers included in officer dominated teams'.[39]

In 1843, one of the earliest references to cricket in Tipperary featured the Cahir club which played the officers of the 15th Hussars, a fashionable regiment.[40] In this instance the Cahir team was composed of the principal residents of Cahir and its hinterland. The officers were drawn to them as much by class association as by sport, in this instance cricket. The fact that there was a cricket team in existence in Cahir, established around 1841, indicated that the area was receptive to the development and spread of the game. Here was a group of men, drawn mainly from the public-school-educated officer class that could interact, socially and sportingly, with a similar number of Cahir gentlemen. The local Cahir men, in the manner of their social and sporting activity, were not that far removed from their social equals in Great Britain or other parts of Ireland. An opportunity arose for sporting relations to develop between them, and it was cricket which was to the fore in this respect. Cricket was to remain part of the sporting landscape of Cahir until 1963.[41]

Unlike Australia and the other colonial territories which comprised the British Empire, Ireland was not a colony; it was integral to the United Kingdom of Great Britain and Ireland under the terms of the 1800 Act of Union.[42] The role of the military in Ireland was no different to that in any other part of Great Britain – in theory. Officers, cavalry men and other ranks were as likely to be stationed in Ireland as they were any part of Great Britain. An example of this deployment may be seen at Templemore, when Lieut. Harry Loft and the 64th Regiment of Foot arrived there, in May 1847. Upon arrival and after settling in, one of the first things they did was to establish a cricket team, which, Loft noted, had 'a capital field close to the barracks'.[43] That same year, officers from the garrison featured on the Templemore team which competed against the Ashbrook Union CC, from Durrow, County Laois.[44] In July 1862, the Templemore garrison team defeated the Templemore town team, which, the *Tipperary Advocate* commented, 'was no great victory; the latter being but two seasons in existence and most of the opponents being professionals, formerly belonging to the Surrey and other crack clubs'.[45] Names that appeared in this match report could not be located in the Surrey Cricket Club records of the period.[46] Be that as it may, sporting challenges were a common feature of military life, especially, as Mason and Riedi note, in 'those far flung parts of the Empire where soldiers had a lot of time which was hard to fill'.[47]

The military were involved in 228 of the 921 cricket matches identified in Tipperary between 1840 and 1880, representing almost 25 per cent of all matches for this period (Table 1.1). Twenty-five of these

Table 1.1: Military team participation in cricket in County Tipperary, 1840–1880

Year	Total	Military Total	Percentage of Total	Year	Total	Military Total	Percentage of Total
1840	0	0	0.00	1861	2	2	100.00
1841	0	0	0.00	1862	13	6	46.15
1842	0	0	0.00	1863	13	5	38.46
1843	1	1	100.00	1864	21	9	42.86
1844	0	0	0.00	1865	22	5	22.73
1845	0	0	0.00	1866	27	6	22.22
1846	4	4	100.00	1867	33	18	54.54
1847	2	0	0.00	1868	55	23	41.82
1848	2	0	0.00	1869	44	9	20.45
1849	14	8	57.14	1870	35	12	34.29
1850	5	3	60.00	1871	26	8	30.77
1851	11	6	54.55	1872	47	15	31.91
1852	8	8	100.00	1873	86	12	13.95
1853	0	0	0.00	1874	77	5	6.49
1854	0	0	0.00	1875	84	7	8.33
1855	0	0	0.00	1876	81	9	11.11
1856	1	1	100.00	1877	52	2	3.85
1857	2	1	50.00	1878	56	5	8.93
1858	2	0	0.00	1879	37	7	18.92
1859	2	2	100.00	1880	49	26	53.06
1860	7	3	42.86	**Total**	**921**	**228**	**24.75**

Sources: *CC, CG, NG, TA, TFP, TWN* 1840–1880. Ashbrook Union CC score book 1846–8

matches involved military teams playing home and away, for instance Templemore barracks against Nenagh barracks, or Clonmel barracks against Cahir barracks. The overwhelming majority, 202, featured military teams against civilian teams, indicating consistent levels of interaction between the military and the sporting middle classes and the gentry around Tipperary. Con Costello has argued that on occasions such as these 'the officers and men experienced a rare social mixing when they also met up with teams from the civilian clubs'.[48] The data for Tipperary seems to challenge this, however, suggesting that the military's cricketing interaction with local communities was anything but rare and that military teams constituted an important cohort of those active in cricket in Tipperary.

Military teams were prominent in the early diffusion of cricket-playing in the county. As the game expanded, so too did the participation of the military teams of non-commissioned officers and lower-rank soldiers. Of the eighty-nine matches identified between 1840 and 1863, a military team participated in fifty. This represented just over 56 per cent of the total number of matches recorded. Between 1864 and 1880, military teams were still a feature of cricket matches in Tipperary. Of the 831 matches recorded for this period, a military team participated in 178, or 21.41 per cent.

That the military integrated quickly with the local communities may be observed in the case of the 79th Cameron Highlanders, when stationed at Nenagh in the late 1840s. They soon established their own cricket team after taking up residence in the local barracks. Several of the officers also turned out for the Nenagh club, prominent among them Lieut. Maitland.[49] An important degree of intermingling between the military and the civilian population was apparent on the cricket field, and latterly on the rugby field. It has not been possible to identify if these meetings resulted from prior social engagements between officers and the local middle class, or if they were arranged simply as a sporting occasion. Essentially the British class structure was replicated in Ireland and the army functioned the same way in both places, except in terms of religion. While there was scope for intermingling on the cricket field between civilian teams and military selections, this intermingling was reserved for the officers when club functions took place. In September 1875, officers of the 50th and 53rd Regiments were among a long list of the upper- and middle-class community of Dundrum and its hinterland who received invitations to 'a ball and supper, on a very extensive and fashionable scale', which was hosted by Dundrum CC.[50] Occasions such as this reinforced and underpinned class association with the military officers. This was but one aspect of the social life of the officer class while stationed in Tipperary, or indeed during any posting in Ireland.

While the military men, principally the officers, did not set out to be pioneers, the knowledge and support of the game which they brought with them coincided with its development in the county. It was a sporting symbiosis, one which greatly assisted in the promotion and development of cricket up to the end of the 1870s. Military officers were key members of civilian teams in the communities in which they were garrisoned. They had a lead role in the promotion and diffusion of cricket throughout the county. The leadership qualities which they brought to the cricket field were also deployed in other sporting spheres. Foremost among them was horse racing.

THE MILITARY AND HUNTING TO HOUNDS

The hunt community were to also prosper from the level of support which the officer class gave to the various hunt packs. Those officers could, especially from the middle of the 1860s, afford considerable time for hunting to hounds, as well as racing and cricket. This suggests that society was stable and peaceful as the country was, in general, undergoing a period of relative calm. This calmness was to be abruptly curtailed by the onset of the Land War in the late 1870s, however, but the full rigours of the campaign to stop the hunt did not impinge on the hunt community of Tipperary until that time.

As far as the military were concerned, hunting to hounds in Tipperary was comparable to that of Westmeath where Tom Hunt found that 'hunting was central to the lifestyle of many members' of military regiments.[51] The sons of the Anglo-Irish gentry followed a career path in the military as a means of confirming social status. With limited career prospects in the civil administration in Dublin Castle, a career path in the army was a prudent choice, unless they wanted to join the church. Furthermore, in the army, 'they had plenty of time to indulge their passion for field sports', something they would have in common with officers of English origin.[52] In Aldershot, when a newly posted officer asked his commanding officer for leave to go out hunting, he was informed that 'as long as there is one subaltern left in the barracks to do the work on a hunting day, I do not want you to ask for leave.

Always go.'[53] This suggests that there was an acceptance among officers of a social obligation to follow the hunt in those communities where a hunt took place. An officer would have been hard pressed not to find a hunt pack in County Tipperary, especially after 1860. In December 1865, the *Nenagh Guardian* reported that the 11th Depot battalion in Templemore had been sent to Newry and Enniskillen, to be replaced by the 59th Regiment from Glasgow.[54] The reason was that it was strongly suspected that the regiment was tainted with Fenianism. As the 11th Depot prepared to depart Templemore the report continued:

> ... the removal of the Battalion is a source of much regret to the inhabitants of this town and neighbourhood. The officers were justly respected by all parties, as no gentlemen could do more to create amusement, and not one of the least losses felt will be that of their splendid pack of harriers, which afforded such capital sport during the past few years.[55]

All aspects of hunting – fox, stag and otter hunting – were integral parts of the life of an officer in rural Tipperary. While several officers followed the hunt with one of the many packs that were established in the county, the garrisons at Cahir and Templemore supported their own packs of hounds. For these to be successful, they needed the support and compliance of the local landowners and this, it would appear, was something which was readily given, especially near Cahir. Captain Poyntz ran his hounds from the Templemore garrison in 1840 but there is insufficient evidence to determine whether the various regiments there maintained hunt packs more than occasionally. At Cahir the situation was very different. The regiments stationed there were regular supporters of hunting to hounds and especially the hunting of hares. Hunt packs were maintained at the barracks for a few seasons between 1840 and 1860, but between 1861 and 1880 the regiments there sent out a hunt pack each winter, irrespective of which regiment was resident. Data compiled for these packs indicates that hunting was most common in the season 1879-1880, with fifty-six meets scheduled. In October 1879 the 19th Hussars Harriers was the pack which hunted out of Cahir barracks. From November 1879 they were replaced by the 7th Hussars Harriers. This pack continued to hunt around Cahir for the next couple of years. The Tipperary Foxhounds were well established as the primary fox hunting pack in south Tipperary. The military in their pursuit of the hare were never in opposition to the fox hunting community and neither were they a threat to them.

As has been shown previously, there were very amicable and friendly relations between the military officers and the inhabitants of Cahir and its vicinity. On the departure of the 12th Royal Lancers from the town, after a period of almost twelve months, an address was presented to Col. Oakes, CB and the officers, noting the regret of the people of Cahir at the departure of the regiment.[56] When news of their impending removal was announced it was observed that 'in the racing field – during the hunting season – and though last not least, as will be admitted by our neighbouring *elite* [sic] in the ball-room, the 12th left nothing undone to spiritedly uphold the well-known hospitable and sporting character of the regiment'.[57] A similar address was presented to Lieut-Col. Somerset J.G. Calthorpe and the officers of the 5th Dragoon Guards when they departed Cahir in 1864.[58]

HAWKING AND OTTER HUNTING

While fox and hare hunting were not novel aspects of the Tipperary sporting scene, some military officers were active in two other types of hunting, that of hawking and otter hunting. In late 1856, Captain Salvin, late of the York Rifles, visited south Tipperary and he brought with him his hawks and John Barr, his falconer. Each time the hawks were set to flight their exploits received complimentary reviews in the local press. Not only that, they also attracted many people 'from the booted Meltonian to the brogued countryman, whose stout galloway was taken from the plough to join the ardor [sic] of the chase'.[59] Such was the desire to keep up with the chase that 'ladyes fayre [sic] quitted their equipages, and on foot, proceeded through the fields'.[60] Captain Salvin departed Clonmel in January 1857, but not without emulation. His falconry exploits drew admiration, which resulted in Henry Langley acquiring 'some splendid birds' to keep the amusement going once it was revived owing to 'its introduction here by Captain Salvin'.[61]

In both the north and south of the county there is some evidence of otter hunting. Though the Remondstown Otter Hounds were active in the summer of 1868, there is little evidence that they lasted much beyond this.[62] Similarly, Mr Hill brought his otter hounds to Dromineer and Youghal-Arra, in the north of the county, for the summer of 1870.[63] Also in the summer of 1870, Lieut. Greene, 70th Regiment, joined the detachment at Nenagh barracks where he brought with him 'a splendid pack of otter hounds'.[64] His stay was brief, but on the departure of his regiment the *Nenagh Guardian* noted that it was a long time 'since the removal of soldiers awoke such a strong feeling of regret in the civilians'.[65] One of the principal causes of regret was that Lieut. Green had afforded 'genuine sporting excitement' while stationed in the town.

The involvement of military officers with the hunt communities of Tipperary was primarily focused on the community around Cahir barracks where several harrier packs were maintained by successive regiments from 1860. While the country hunted over often overlapped other hunt packs, the choice of quarry was different, and as such there was space for packs to operate independently of each other. Invitations extended to estate owners and retired military personnel to hunt with military packs strengthened the bond between military and community. These bonds were further cemented with reciprocal invitations offered to military personnel to attend country house activities, such as sporting events, dances and entertainment evenings.

THE MILITARY AND HORSE RACING

While matters associated with the Turf feature in a chapter of their own, specific reference is made here to the military involvement. Sport and the military, as the evidence from Tipperary and elsewhere shows, was something which did not remain within the confines of the garrison. Officers from various regiments appeared on the list of stewards and featured in the accounts of the fashionable people who attended. For the Nenagh races in April 1850, Lieut. Adam Maitland doubled up as secretary and clerk of the course.[66] A report of the races which appeared in the local press observed that much credit was due to 'the clerk of the course Adjutant Maitland, 79th Highlanders, for his untiring and active service in preparing the ground, having the "leaps" erected, and preserving regularity in the starting of the horses'.[67] The report suggests a close relationship between the military officers and the landed and professional classes in Nenagh and its hinterland. This relationship was reinforced a short time later, as prior to their departure from Nenagh, the officers of the 79th Highlanders were treated to a banquet 'by the members of the Ormond Hunt Club and the gentry of Nenagh and its vicinity'.[68] The banquet was 'to testify their warm esteem and heartfelt regard towards them [the 79th Highlanders], to appreciate their noble conduct and exalted character, in every point of view while stationed amongst us, and as a token of respectful regret at their intended departure'.[69]

At Cahir barracks the cavalry regiments regularly hosted their own regimental races. In the 1870s alone the XIV Hussars, Inniskilling Dragoons, 4th Dragoon Guards, 7th Princess Royal Dragoon Guards, 5th (Princess Charlotte of Wales's (PCW) Dragoon Guards, Queen's Bays, 3rd Dragoon Guards, and the 7th (Queen's Own) Hussars all hosted regimental race meetings on military grounds associated with the barracks.[70] Irrespective of the regiment involved, the continuity and consistency of the race programme remained the same. The races took place in April at the end of the hunting season. After a busy winter season out with the hounds, the races gave the various regiments an opportunity of affording thanks to the owners and leaseholders of the lands over which they hunted. The 5th (PCW) Dragoon Guards organised the 1876 races with exemplary efficiency. Major George Waller Vesey, Hon. Secretary, appeared to have covered all areas of interest. Vesey, a native of County Tyrone, subsequently held the office of High Sheriff of his home county in 1879, where he was also Deputy Lieutenant.[71] For the Cahir Garrison races, apart from taking race entries, there were several other tasks the officers had to perform, leaving 'nothing undone to render the meeting successful'.[72] One may infer that representations were made to the Waterford and Limerick Railway Company to make allowances for prospective travellers to Cahir on race day. The company advertised return fares at single rates, from both their Waterford and Limerick offices, including all intermediary stations to Cahir.[73]

The races themselves proved successful. The staging of horse races had financial implications for officers in the garrison. Race purses were supplemented by contributions from officers of the regiment. As such, while not only facilitating race meetings, the officers were also net contributors to the races themselves. It was a regular aspect of officer and non-commissioned officer career paths, as entertainments in their respective messes were also 'financed from members' subscriptions and mess funds'.[74] J.D. Campbell has noted that 'during the nineteenth century … British Army officers were of primarily upper-class origins, with a majority coming from landed families'.[75] At one level, the life of an officer in Tipperary was no different to that of an officer in any other barracks in Great Britain and Ireland. On another level, however, there were issues relating to religion and political affiliation. Officers were likely to associate with families who were supportive of British administration in Ireland. Though prize money at races, to which officers contributed, could vary from £20 given as prize money for a farmers' race to 'three magnificent challenge cups', these figures demonstrate that when one was an officer one was expected to evince a certain largesse.[76] This generosity in supporting local sporting events allowed officers to fit in very well in society life in mid-Victorian Tipperary.

At Cahir, perhaps the most telling aspect of the 1876 race meeting was the list of 'those invited to the luncheon at the Garrison races', published in the days that followed. That the 'attendance was large and highly aristocratic' is seen from the names listed. Lords and Ladies from counties Kilkenny, Tipperary and Waterford featured prominently. This was supplemented by other landed gentry from these and other counties, demonstrating the wide reach of the military social network and the level of support which was afforded them by those in attendance. For the officer corps, field sports 'went beyond mere leisure pastimes. They were professionally important as well.'[77] If proof were needed that the army presence in Tipperary was appreciated, these people showed it in the way they supported the race meeting, which was also a very sociable occasion. The evidence suggests that were it not for the military officers there would have been few, if any, race meetings in the district of Cahir. From 1860 to 1880 inclusive, the only years for which no evidence of military races near Cahir has been identified are 1868, 1869 and 1870. During the winter months of those years, the garrison hounds hunted as regularly as in previous years, indicating that sporting diversions were still taking place.

The provision of horse racing, while primarily centred on regimental races, still catered for farmers' races. In February 1841, the 17th Lancers held steeplechases near Cahir.[78] This was followed up, in October, by another local meeting, though on grounds north of the town, at which one of the stewards was a lieutenant colonel with the 5th Dragoon Guards. From late 1841 to 1860 the pattern of horse racing in Cahir was one of civilian and military meetings on an infrequent basis. There is no evidence to suggest that there was racing each year. Fifteen meetings have been identified between 1840 and 1859. Both military and civilian personnel were involved in setting up these meetings. When meetings were not specifically organised by military officers the list of stewards still included leading officers from the Cahir garrison.[79] These serve to indicate the administrative sporting role which the officers held within the local Cahir society. Similar roles were also held by officers at Clonmel, Nenagh and Templemore.[80] With their promotion of local horse race meetings, the officers, especially the cavalry officers with their riding expertise, were to the fore in the advancement of these meetings. This was especially so at Cahir where their support of racing in the two decades after the end of the Crimean War made them a welcome feature of societal life in and around the town. Fields used for the races were often 'kindly lent to [the military] by the farmers without any charge whatever'.[81] There was a close relationship here, one which benefited the town of Cahir, where for almost twenty years the military provided an annual race meeting. The races gave the military officers an opportunity to meet socially with the gentry and create social bonds. These bonds were very important when the daughters of the Tipperary gentry sought out marriage partners.

THE MILITARY AND COUNTRY HOUSE LAWN GAMES

The officer class essentially mixed in their own social sphere, as has been shown. This was reflected in the level of officer attendance at country house functions. Other aspects of country house sport are examined in greater detail in Chapter 2, but here the military involvement in terms of patronage, support and participation is outlined.

As far as outdoor pursuits were concerned, and specifically those which could take place behind estate or garrison walls, archery proved very popular for the mingling of officers and various members of the local landowners in Tipperary from the late 1850s. Officers were in regular attendance at 'archery prize meetings' in Templemore, Nenagh, Clonmel and Cahir.[82] In May 1858, at a meeting of the Templemore Archery Club, which opened the season's shooting on the cricket ground at the Priory, officers from the town garrison joined the members.[83] Later that month, the *Nenagh Guardian* noted that 'a large party, consisting of the elite of the town and surrounding country, assembled on the Military Parade Ground, to practise the justly favourite and interesting amusement of archery … The sport was excellent … This being over, there was a capital race between the horses of Colonel Irwin, Captain Triton, and Dr. Manfold, the Colonel's being the winner … and the amusement was brought to a conclusion by a grand ball and supper given by the officers of the garrison to the surrounding gentry, and the officers of the Limerick garrison'.[84] One year later in Nenagh, the Ormond Archery Club held meetings in a field adjoining the military barracks. Once more it was reported that 'the attendance included a large array of the elite of the surrounding country and the officers of the Templemore garrison were also present'.[85] Commanding officers at Templemore and Nenagh facilitated the growth of archery meetings by permitting these events to take place on parade grounds. Reciprocal invitations were then issued by the officers to country estates where archery and other lawn games took place.

Similarly, the emergence of lawn tennis as a sporting recreation in the mid-1870s saw many members of the local officer corps invited to various meetings. Officers at Clonmel barracks competed against each other in March 1878, with the victors 'warmly congratulated by the numerous spectators of the game'.[86] Some of the newly arrived officers also brought the latest sporting fashions with them. This occurred with lawn tennis in Clonmel where the military officers stationed there were responsible for the diffusion of the game, though its growth was slow. However, the officers were principally spectators rather than participants. In north Tipperary local military officers were not part of the summer circle of lawn tennis parties associated with 'this aristocratic amusement'.[87] Name lists of those in attendance are included in lawn tennis reports. The names on these lists suggest that it was only those military officers who had received personal invitations who were present.[88]

Accounts of various sporting events with which the military were associated often refer to luncheons and dinner tables. In this regard, the evidence for Tipperary is similar to that noted for Limerick, where Tom Hayes found that 'eating, drinking and refreshments continued to be integral to the sporting experience'.[89] One of the most telling aspects of military participation and attendance at such meetings was that the officers were gravitating towards those people whom they identified as belonging to the same social class. Sport was once more a medium through which such associations were maintained and, in the case of country house games and recreations, it brought officers into the environment, enhancing matrimonial prospects for the daughters of the home owners. Examples of matrimony between Tipperary ladies and military officers, as recorded in Burke's account of the landed gentry, demonstrate the importance of such associations. Archibald James Lamont, of Lamont, Argyll, formerly an officer in the army, married Adelaide Massy Dawson, Ballynacourte, County Tipperary, in September 1839.[90] Similarly, Anna Lidwell, Dromard, Templemore, married Capt. W.J. Hoare, 7th Royal Fusiliers, in 1853.[91] Charles Morant, Brokenhurst, Hampshire, and late of the 11th Hussars married Malvina Elizabeth Hemphill, of Cashel.[92]

Conviviality and recreation intertwined on these occasions, which afforded military officers opportunities to interact with county families in the same way as has already been observed with regard to horse racing. Essentially, the nucleus of people involved regularly numbered less than two hundred, while, typically, many of the same family names recurred at the various sporting events.[93] That this was so indicates that these people moved in the same social circle and that the critical mass of individuals who promoted such activities was quite small when compared to the size of the local communities. At a joint meeting of the Kilcommon Archers and South Tipperary Bowmen 'about two hundred and fifty persons were present', with officers from various regiments amongst those recorded as being in attendance.[94] Though military numbers and those of the leading families in the county were but a fraction of the county's population, they were essentially the fraction that mattered. These were the people who shaped the sporting landscape of Tipperary.

THE MILITARY AND RUGBY

The military played an important role in the growth and development of rugby football in Tipperary. Rugby was a new football code, and the military were to the fore in introducing it. When reports of rugby started to appear in the Tipperary press they featured play between the military and local teams. It is almost certain that military officers introduced rugby football to Nenagh.[95] Reminiscent of the 79th Highlanders before them, the departure of the 50th Regiment from Nenagh was also lamented in the *Nenagh Guardian*, where it was remarked that 'no corps ever left the town more deservedly regretted, as a most cordial relationship existed since the football matches of last season, and the courtesy of the officers on these occasions ... made them well worthy of the compliment paid them yesterday on their departure'.[96] Not all football games in which the military participated were reported in the local press. However, the surviving records of the Kilruane Football Club for the period 1876 to 1880 indicate that matches were played against the 53rd Regiment.[97] Moreover, the 53rd Regiment played rugby in Tipperary town against both the Clanwilliam club and the local grammar school in 1879.

The military as a whole greatly contributed to the growth and development of rugby in Tipperary. Their participation in it led to emulation among the civilian community. It is likely that the military introduced Association football to south Tipperary in 1879. A report in the local press noted the features of the 'association game' when describing a match between two military teams at Cahir barracks.[98] Similar to other activities, the military played a key role in the promotion of ball games. This was more by way of a dissemination process than one calculated to be injurious to any sporting recreation then played in any local community at the time. That they did so with the compliance, cooperation and participation of local residents suggests that there was local support and a local appetite for these new sporting activities.

OVERVIEW OF THE IMPACT OF THE MILITARY ON SPORT IN COUNTY TIPPERARY

There is no doubt that many military personnel were instrumental in the introduction and spread of sport in Tipperary in the years between 1840 and 1880. Specifically, they introduced rugby and Association football, while they were leading figures in the promotion of cricket, both in terms of playing the game and providing grounds on which to play, as was the case with horse racing and hunting to hounds. The military, especially the officers, came to know their social equals in Tipperary, and they quickly integrated. This sociability was a key component in the relations between the military and the communities in which they were stationed. When the South Tipperary Bowmen met at Marlfield, in late July 1868, appended to the list of those in attendance, including the military personnel, was a note stating that 'all officers are considered honorary members of the club'.[99]

The evidence also indicates that some regiments and some individuals were more active, in sporting terms, than others. When the 7th Queen's Own Hussars were garrisoned in Cahir and Fethard in 1879, reports of their activities while engaged in football, cricket, horse racing or on the hunting circuit with their harrier pack regularly appeared in the Tipperary press, most notably in the *Clonmel Chronicle*. Indeed, the activities of the harrier pack appeared regularly with a list of landowners from Cahir and its hinterland on whose land they were permitted to hunt. In the various press reports, one name is common to these four sports, Thomas Hone, a former pupil of Rugby school and a member of the Hone family renowned for their role in the early development of Irish cricket.[100] A regular on the Hussars cricket team, he rode his horse Walmer to victory in the Tally-Ho Challenge Cup at the Hussars steeplechases in 1880.[101] He also appeared in angling reports during the salmon-fishing season. In August 1886, the then Capt. Thomas Hone, 7th Hussars, was part of the Hurlingham Polo Club, which competed against the Westchester Polo Club, in Newport, Rhode Island.[102] While Hone was active in various sports, this activity was exceptional. The degree to which he participated was not reflective of the military as a whole, let alone in Tipperary. What Hone does represent, though, is the enthusiasm of the officer ranks to be sportingly active in the communities in which they were stationed. It was as if there was a sporting evangelism associated with their posting. The military were a critical link between the successful development of codified sport in Tipperary and its British inspiration. Sport was practised and promoted primarily through the landed gentry with whom the military officers easily associated. The military were maintaining links, sporting and social, which helped keep the Empire, as they saw it, together. These links would later see military officers prominent in the emergence of polo (at Cahir barracks, in 1887)[103] and golf (at Templemore barracks, in 1890).[104]

In India, when the 'European soldiers played cricket on the northern end of the Esplanade, with bats and ball imported from England … they soon found their imitators. Parsi boys were playing cricket here as early as the 1830s.'[105] In Tipperary, the local people were exposed to the games of the Empire by the military, either directly, by playing with or against them, or indirectly as in India, by observing the military at play. An imprint of the various sports on the native psyche was being established. In spite of later protestations from the Roman Catholic hierarchy and nationalist supporters, the games of the military were, by and large, here to stay.[106] A similar claim could be made for the teams at Carrick-on-Suir and Kilcash copying garrison teams when playing Association football. This interaction between communities fostered the growth of football among them.

When the officers promoted sport at a barracks, whether it was archery, cricket or athletics, great attention to detail was the norm. Permission was sought from commanding officers to have a regimental band perform. On occasion, the day concluded with a festive ball, which was held in the garrison, and on the whole a great rapport developed between the landed and professional people from the surrounding town and hinterland. These activities helped to cement the positive relationship which officers had with a proportion, albeit minor, of the local population. But the commanding officers also granted permission to the non-commissioned officers and privates to play in sports of their own, notably football. In this respect the spread of sport outwards to the local communities of Tipperary is an example of military-related activity with other social classes.

If Mason and Riedi can 'emphasise the sheer quantity of sport in the British military between the 1880s and 1960',[107] then the activities of the military in Tipperary show that it was not something which suddenly started in 1880. It was a process which commenced almost as soon as a regiment arrived in town and a cricket pitch was laid, a horse race was arranged, or a ball court was erected. The evidence from Tipperary shows that all these components were quickly put in place and sport soon became a vibrant aspect of the military presence in the county. It was a presence which greatly assisted the growth and development of sport in Tipperary between 1840 and 1880.

Yet, military participation at various sports in Tipperary cannot be viewed in isolation. The participation of officers has to be seen as part of a growing movement among the upper and middle classes for the advancement of those sports and recreations which were of interest to them, and which acted as a means of facilitating and maintaining social contacts. The military greatly assisted in facilitating the continuance of sports – such as hunting to hounds, horse racing, archery, rugby football, cricket and athletics – and could make use of local farmland for hunting to hounds and horse racing while accommodating other field sports within the barracks. Many in the military, especially the officers, lived active lives in the locality to which they were posted and were an important, if not central, part of local social and sporting life.[108] The officers had a symbiotic relationship with their Tipperary social equals. It was a relationship which greatly assisted the sporting environment of Tipperary in the nineteenth century.

CHAPTER 2

COUNTRY HOUSE SPORT

INTRODUCTION

The country house estate setting was an important arena for the promotion and development of sport in Tipperary.[1] The term 'country house' is used to denote the house which was the main residence of people who were of independent means. They were professional men or landowners who had the financial resources to invite friends and associates to their home to play some form of sport. Sports played were archery, croquet, lawn tennis or cricket, all essentially lawn games. Cricket required more space but it too had a defined perimeter. These were principally summer games. They filled a void that was left after the hunting season finished. Yachting was another sport, in the north-west of the county, that was also keenly supported. It was closely associated with the residents of houses and estates that were on the foreshore of Lough Derg. Though hunting to hounds and horse racing often took place within estate confines, these are dealt with elsewhere.

It was within the estate setting that sport became firmly established. It was promoted by the owners and residents of estates and demesnes for their own enjoyment. For many, it was important that what they did on their estates mirrored what was happening within estate settings in Great Britain. Without patronage and access to estate land and parkland, sport would not have taken place in Tipperary on the scale that it did. The impetus would not have come from any other source and this was critical to its evolution and growth. In a book of essays on the history of the county, *Tipperary: history and society*,

Willie Nolan compiled a distribution map of 344 country houses in Tipperary, based on a minimum Griffith valuation of £10.[2] This map clearly identified the spread of these house types between 1840 and 1880. It is not intended here to investigate the size of the house or estate associated with it. The country house setting was central to the evolution of sport in Tipperary and the criteria identified by Nolan is used as a basis for assessing the level of sporting activity at these locations. These houses and estates were the *de facto* arenas for sport in the county. Nolan's map also ties in with the documentary evidence for sport on these estates. In some parts of west and south-west Tipperary no houses were identified by Nolan. This was also reflected in the absence of lawn games in these areas as much of this land was 500 feet, or higher, above sea level.

Another map by T. Jones Hughes, in the same book of essays, shows the distribution pattern of dwelling houses of the dispersed rural population, valued at under £1, around 1850.[3] In the west of the county there was a concentration of such houses specifically where there was no recorded evidence of elite sporting recreation. This does not demonstrate that the people living here did not have recourse to sporting recreation, rather that they left no documentary evidence in the local press of their deeds. Consequently, it was within the estate and demesne setting where sport left its imprint, and the evidence presented here reaffirms this.

Unlike the large cities of Ireland and Great Britain, where issues of crowd control were central to law and order, such a situation did not arise in Tipperary. The control element, in a sporting context, was one of access to exclusive areas of play. One was invited to attend. Similar to England, the houses and the estate grounds in which they were situated were important arenas for one to display their wealth and power in a local Tipperary context.[4]

Of the 344 houses recorded by Nolan, thirty-three had a valuation above £50, of which Marlfield, Knocklofty, Shanbally Castle, Knockeevan, Barne Park, Woodroof and Grove, all in the south of the county, were locations where much sporting activity took place, including hunting to hounds, archery and cricket.[5] The press reports also suggest that not every house or estate was associated with the sporting evolution that took place in Tipperary. Samuel Murray Going was vice-president of the Thurles Cricket Club and he resided at Liskeveen House, which was seven miles from the town.[6] Both he and his daughters attended cricket matches associated with the club.[7] Yet there were no press reports to indicate if his house or lands were ever used for sporting purposes. So while there were houses and estates which were active as arenas for sport, there were other locations which were not used. This is a trend that continued through the middle of the nineteenth century. The level of sport fluctuated at specific locations, principally on account of what was fashionable at any given time.

The principal feature in the development of sport in County Tipperary is that it was different from sport that took place in an urban context. The coming together of people for sport was one part of wider social networking. Music recitals and balls were occasions that also brought these families together. It is clear that this important phase in the evolution of sport occurred on private land, beyond the gaze of potential critics.[8] The houses were hidden behind parkland and demesne walls, emphasising the divide between the residents and the wider community outside of these private enclaves.[9] So the question remains, if sport took place among a privileged section of society in a private setting, how did it spread among the wider community? The answer is centred around class and one's position in society. Some games, such as lawn tennis, did not become universally popular until well into the twentieth century. However, cricket did make the transition and it did so because tenant farmers could play it on their own fields, in their own clothes, among their own friends. They didn't require the whites that were the order of the day for tennis or fashionable cricket teams.

Crucially, the country house setting was the only arena that provided women an opportunity to participate in sport, especially archery, croquet and lawn tennis. Another important factor was that it brought female members of families into regular contact with each other and allowed single people meet prospective spouses. Country house sport gave single women the opportunity to meet at varied locations, play sport and, hidden behind the estate wall, perform a role that was not afforded them in a public setting. Sport in the mid-nineteenth century was a masculine preserve.[10]

The importance of these various aspects of Tipperary culture and society adds to the existing knowledge of how pre-codified sport developed in Ireland. Apart from horse racing, no other sport in the country in the middle on the nineteenth century had a regulatory body. While the Marylebone Cricket Club (MCC) were the lawmakers of cricket, such was the parochial nature of the game in Tipperary that any disputes were resolved locally, as there was no administrative cricket body in Victorian Ireland. The landed estate setting provided the backdrop for all team and individual sports, apart from hurling, variations of folk football and athletics. It was the estate setting, allied to the role of the military and their parade grounds, that was the principal instigator of sport in rural Tipperary. This was sport in its infancy, pre-codification.

CRICKET

In its formative years as a sport in Tipperary, cricket was a game played by urban, rural and military teams, drawn from the middle and upper classes. The game had a stop-start introduction in the county, with the earliest reference to it found at Carrick-on-Suir in 1834, when Henry Mandeville allowed his lands to be used by the town club.[11] Cricket at this time was still something of a novelty in Ireland. It was a rare example, in an Irish context, of a team sport that had a defined set of laws, the oldest existing laws surviving from 1744, as noted in the introduction. Also in existence were 'articles of agreement' drawn up for a match between two teams which took place in 1727.[12]

Through the paternal support of some of the influential landowners, such as John Bagwell, Marlfield, Clonmel, who allowed teams the opportunity to play on his spacious demesne, it appeared that the game would prosper.[13] Several of the early matches in Tipperary involved a military team, as was shown in the previous chapter. As knowledge of the laws of cricket increased, the game started to expand, and it was not long before it became a sport that was played within the confines of the estate grounds, one which facilitated the associational culture between like-minded individuals within a community. One of the principal reasons for this was the provision of playing grounds. Unlike hurling, which many owners did not allow on their lands, cricket clubs, some formal and some less so, benefited from the patronage of benevolent landowners. This gave the game a key advantage over hurling and resulted in some teams incorporating the name of the local townland or estate in which the team was based into the club name. Gentlemen's teams such as the Priory CC, Sopwell Hall XI, and Beechwood Park XI took the name of the estate which the players represented.[14] In effect a patronage shift had occurred with these two field sports. Though landlord patronage was evident for the promotion of hurling in the eighteenth century, much of it for gambling purposes, this support ceased in the aftermath of the 1798 uprising and also the Peninsular Wars. Land agitation in the pre-Famine period, which featured bands of men often referred to as hurlers meeting for coercive purposes, only served to alienate the sport from potential patrons and supporters. Cricket filled the void left when the patronage of hurling declined.

In 1846, in Durrow, County Laois, the Ashbrook Union Cricket Club played on the local estate at Castle Durrow, which was at the centre of this small town. The estate owner, Viscount Ashbrook, was president of the club. He also opened the batting whenever he played for his team, whether in practice matches or in fixtures against a visiting eleven.[15] A surviving scorebook from the club is a fascinating read. It is a very early and important document relating to club sport in existence in Ireland. Starting in 1846 and extending to 1848, it records match details for all games played by the club, whether inter-club games or practice games between club members. At the start of each year the names of the club president, vice-president, secretary and club members are listed. The reports for 1847 reveal how carefully organised the club was. At this time the club was structured with a defined set of rules and regulations, which shows that a fledgling sporting economy had begun, even at this early date. Rule number one noted that each member was to pay £1 per annum subscription. Rule number three related to expenses for practice matches, for which each member of the losing team was to pay one shilling towards 'the ground fund of the club'. Lunches were available for 1*s* 6*d* on practice days. Rule number four stipulated that for matches against other clubs, each member selected to play had to pay five shillings per match, in addition to his annual subscription. Rule number five recorded the names of five men chosen as players of the club who were to receive two shillings for practice days and the same per day for matches against other clubs and their expenses.[16] Here was evidence of early professionalism in a sporting context at the height of the Great Famine in Ireland. While gentlemen paid to play cricket, rule number five clearly shows that estate workers were paid, demonstrating a desire by Ashbrook to field a strong team. It also provided very good employment for the men chosen to play. By extension one may infer that similar club rules existed among some of the country house teams in Tipperary.

In 1846 there were twenty-five members in addition to the three officers. Twenty-six matches were played between 25 April and September that year, of which only four were inter-club fixtures. These were home and away matches against Danesfort CC (County Kilkenny) and Carlow CC. On these occasions Ashbrook Union Cricket Club was used to identify the club. For each of the other twenty-two matches the name given was that of the gentleman who selected each team; gentlemen v. players, or a combination of both. In 1847 in addition to the three officers there were seventeen members listed. What differentiated the 1847 season from the 1846 season was that it included a list of rules and regulations for the attention of club members. Between 22 May 1847 and 18 September 1847 the club played twenty-one matches, of which nine were against external clubs: Kilkenny CC; Huntingdon CC (Laois); Carlow CC; Templemore CC (Tipperary); a Wexford and Carlow joint eleven; Castlecomer CC (Kilkenny) and a Phoenix and Garrison selection, Dublin. For the first two matches against Kilkenny CC and Huntingdon CC the club retained the name of Ashbrook Union CC. However, for all subsequent games it took the name of Durrow CC. There was no set day of the week when matches took place. Any day was likely to be used for play except Sunday. In 1848, along with the three officers there were eighteen members listed in the scorebook, along with the rules and regulations for the 1848 season.

The use of estate workers, non-commissioned officers and privates was important to the development of cricket. In September 1852, the meeting of military teams drawn from Clonmel and Waterford garrisons was looked forward to as there were many good players on both teams and consequently there was a large attendance of fashionable and local gentry at Marlfield, with people travelling from other towns and villages to attend as well as from Clonmel and its rural hinterland.[17] Across all realms of sporting activity the officer class were often seen as the best exponents of any game, and cricket was no different. They raised the standards. Yet the class distinction, which was common with cricket in England, was also apparent in Clonmel at this time. As the players adjourned for lunch the gentlemen players were able to dine in a marquee, while there was a second tent, where the non-commissioned officers and privates, who assisted as players in the match, had their meal. As detailed reports of matches started to appear in the press not only was the scorecard given but also a list of names of those in attendance. These lists announced to one's peers and associates that they were keeping up with the latest fashion by supporting and attending cricket. Though cricket had been played at various locations in the county from 1834, it was not until 1864 that the game spread to rural locations countywide, reaching a peak in 1876. To the fore in its promotion were the country houses of Tipperary as they facilitated clubs and their supporters. Indeed, in 1864, cricket in Clonmel was seen as another amusement which was 'added to those already enjoyed by our local aristocracy. That year a cricket club was started with Samuel Perry, Esq., J.P. [Justice of the Peace], Woodroofe, the hon. secretary.'[18] The fact that there had been a previous club in the town bearing the same name mattered little. In this instance, it was the 'local aristocracy' which gave the new club their imprimatur. This club was an example of a broadening awareness of sport which could take place within the confines of the estate wall.

At the Trant estate at Dovea, Thurles, a cricket team bearing the townland name competed against the Templemore garrison club in September 1865.[19] After play and dinner 'the spacious ballroom' of the Trant home was made available for dancing, with music provided by the Tipperary Light Infantry. Dancing and music added to the sporting experience. It was not something specific to cricket, however, as it was also an integral part of archery meetings. The newfound fashion for cricket and archery also made some businessmen aware that they could enhance their turnovers by providing the necessary sporting equipment. From a Tipperary perspective the earliest businessman to advertise as a 'cricketing outfitter' who could also supply 'articles connected with … other British sports' was John Wisden, Leicester Square, London. His advertisements appeared in the Tipperary press from May 1860.[20]

Mail order was a standard means of acquiring goods, of which the best items were obtained from London. The postal service gave many country families an opportunity to emulate their peers, neighbours and associates. It was not until 1866 that a Nenagh businessman advertised his wares in the local press. J.D. Harkness, a gunsmith by profession, stocked cricket, archery and angling supplies to accompany the gun wares which he had also 'on hands to meet the requirements of his numerous customers'.[21] All factors for the growth and development of sporting recreation were now in place. The local gentry had the capital to invest in these goods, they had the grounds on which to play, and local businessmen had the goods on stock or they could be acquired by mail order.

Despite this, however, sport could not take place without the consent of the owners of country houses and estates. And not only were the owners willing to allow sport to take place, many of them were active participants. This was a key element which was essential for any particular sport to flourish. This interest prompted Edward Bayly to establish a cricket club in Dundrum in 1866.[22] Another family member, John Bayly, played a key role in the club, but his duties as an officer in the Royal Navy ensured that he was often absent.[23] Still, the club continued to blossom. At the start of 1870 it had 'a pavilion erected capable of accommodating sixty persons at dinner'.[24] However, by 1876 the end had come for the club at a time when cricket was at the height of its popularity in the county. Commander John Bayly departed Dundrum in 1876 and with no member willing to maintain the 'crease and cricket implements in serviceable condition … the pavilion and implements were sold by auction'.[25] This example demonstrates the tenuous bond between sport and its advocates at this time. The club survived while there was patronage and someone willing to give it direction, but once this person departed, the very existence of the club was undermined and it folded.

Similarly in north Tipperary, the D'Alton brothers, Charles, St Eloy and John, were all integral members of the Ormond CC and also the Claremont XI, which was based on their home lands. All three gentlemen and their families emigrated to Australia and when they did, it brought to a close a cricketing association with Claremont which had commenced in 1864.[26] It was a scene all too familiar with other aspects of sport in the country house, as interest in a specific recreation came and went in accordance with what was fashionable at any given time. It also indicated that specific individuals or families were not fixed features on the landscape.

ECONOMIC SETTING OF THE ESTATES

All that aside, cricket remained a social occasion. Luncheons and dinners were important aspects of the sporting experience. The day of the game was as important as a social event, as it was for the sport it provided. If a landowner was not an active participant in the game itself the placing of land at the disposal of a team brought people into his circle. The Bagwell estate at Marlfield was a popular location for such matches. There is no indication that clubs were charged by John Bagwell – the elected MP for the Clonmel borough constituency from 1857 to 1874 – to play on his demesne. Rather, it was through his patronage that the demesne of Marlfield was freely given to the members of the Clonmel Cricket Club.[27] Neither was it a token gesture, as on occasion the grounds were thrown open to all, though who the 'all' were is open to debate.[28] That said, his estate had the appellation of 'The People's Park', so it is quite credible to infer that he opened it up for all classes in the community.[29] Bagwell allowed various clubs to use his estate for sport, of which cricket was the most popular. Yet while Bagwell's largesse may be considered as patronage, it was not altogether altruistic. The people invited onto his demesne lands were often his voters, so it was to his own benefit to have them present. Prior to the general election of 1874 his popularity waned as he would not support Home Rule or the demand for a Catholic university, losing his seat by a large margin to A.J. Moore.[30] Bagwell, having a net estate of 3,519 acres, accrued much of his capital from business interests in Clonmel and income from rentals on his property within the town and its hinterland. This gave his property a valuation of £8,480 in 1876. Edward Armstrong, at Mealiffe, Thurles, in the middle of the county, had an estate of just over 6,000 acres in extent but it only had a valuation of £1,920. This demonstrated the wide gap in income, between rural and urban contexts, in what was essentially a rural-based economy.[31] This gap also shows the dichotomy which existed within sport in Tipperary. It was no coincidence that sport flourished in those areas where both a capital-based economy and urban growth was strong. This was apparent in the north–south divide of some sporting recreations. For the majority of the estate owners in Tipperary their primary income was derived from land. This dependence on rent from land was an essential feature of the landlord system in Ireland.[32] There were more affluent houses in the south of the county than in the north and this was reflected in sporting recreation.

Income was a prime motivating factor in the successful operation of an estate or country house. Knocklofty House, for all its wealth and patronage of sport, was not immune to ill-fortune. John, the 5th Earl of Donoughmore, 'managed to run into considerable financial difficulties'.[33] This greatly impacted on the running of his estates, which were spread over eight counties. At Barnane, evictions on the Carden estate in the pre-Famine period led to great unrest.[34] The collection of rent was often fraught with difficulty. Landowners were entitled to collect rent but tenants, especially in the aftermath of the Famine, sought alleviation at every opportunity. Of the landowners in the county 'only 178, or less than half of the total number', were resident.[35] The management of their estates was entrusted to land agents, with much of the land 'held by tenants through a cumbersome web of leasing arrangements'.[36]

Another contributory factor was that the northern baronies of Tipperary did not have as many large leaseholders as those in south Tipperary. In the south of the county there were a large number of gentrified Catholic head tenants and many of these built country houses which were not unlike those of the landlord class.[37] In north Tipperary, in 1850, there was a concentration of houses which had a valuation between £10 and £39, of which sixty-five of these were in Lower Ormond.[38] These were important socio-economic indicators of how the county functioned, how money was made, and how people were then able to support the staging of sporting events. It was in Templemore where an estate comparable to that of Marlfield was located. It was comparable in the sense that the landlord derived much of his income from town and land rentals. The landlord, John Carden, opened the batting for the local cricket club. Carden was a playing member of the Priory CC.[39] His house, 'The Priory', was extensively renovated at a cost of £20,000, commencing in 1856 and completed in 1861.[40] He had property totalling just over 6,680 acres, which had a valuation almost equivalent to that of John Bagwell, standing at £8,344 10s.[41] His property, unlike that of Bagwell, however, was primarily rural in nature.

Apart from the house setting itself, which provided the means for sport to take place, the other important aspect was that these estates provided a means for cross-fertilisation of ideas, discussions and considerations about all aspects of life and society including sport. As the 1860s commenced Ireland was a decade removed from the Famine, though the period was not without its troubles for landlords. Difficulties in maintaining a standard of living comparable to that which they enjoyed in the pre-Famine era meant that many families had to resort to the Landed Estates Court. Expenditure exceeded income for many families and they could not sell land to pay off debts. With the introduction of Encumbered Estate Acts in 1848 and 1849 there was a mechanism put in place through which some families could free themselves from debt-ridden lands.[42] Tipperary families were among those who resorted to the Encumbered and later Landed Estates Courts as they sought to get out of financial and economic hardship. Between 18 May 1852 and 5 November 1857 nineteen Tipperary properties came before the Landed Estates Court, testament to the financial distress felt by many families unable to maintain their estates.[43] Of these, Noan House, sold in 1853, – featured in athletics; Garnavilla House, sold in 1857, featured as a meeting point for hunting to hounds, and Rehill House, sold in 1857, also featured as a hunt meeting point.[44]

PATRONAGE

Patronage of sport for the lower classes had not existed in Tipperary since the eighteenth century, when barony hurling was one of the favourite gambling pastimes of the wealthy.[45] Cricket, a game initially played by military officers and professional and landed family members, had spread countywide by the 1870s. All the classes played the game at this time but a critical social divide had been crossed. This commenced around 1864 when cricket spread outwards and it was played among tenant farmers, artisans and farm labourers. A press report of 1873 indicated that cricket was seen as 'a republican game', a game that was played by all the classes.[46] From this diffusion there commenced an appetite for sport among society outside of the estate wall which saw tenant farmers compete on the athletic field. They later began to organise themselves into football teams in the years prior to the founding of the GAA.

Table 2.1 gives a breakdown of sporting activity throughout the forty-one-year period covered by this book. Specific references to a sport have been counted and for the purposes of this chapter, the data shows that cricket was the only constant team sport, as it was the earliest one codified. While there was great support for archery, the specific numbers recorded are small, indicative of the narrow participation base. Similar claims may be made for croquet and lawn tennis, though the latter game continued to develop in the post-1880 period. The data from Table 2.1 also demonstrates that society in general was relatively stable in the 1870s, allowing for a growth in cricket and hunting to hounds. This decade also witnessed the arrival of new sports – croquet,

Table 2.1 List of references to specific sports in County Tipperary, 1840–1880

SPORT	1840 to 1844	1845 to 1849	1850 to 1854	1855 to 1859	1860 to 1864	1865 to 1869	1870 to 1874	1875 to 1880	TOTAL
Archery	1	0	0	6	23	20	16	0	66
Athletics	7	0	1	2	4	16	29	54	113
Coursing	0	22	42	10	8	7	1	1	91
Cricket	1	22	24	7	56	181	271	356	918
Croquet	–	–	–	–	–	5	4	6	15
Cycling	–	–	–	–	–	–	–	3	3
Football	1	0	0	2	3	5	1	11	23
Horse Racing	46	24	28	25	39	50	34	37	283
Hunting	746	297	336	810	859	1,186	1,453	1,853	7,540
Hurling	10	3	7	21	11	5	2	3	62
Lawn Tennis	–	–	–	–	–	–	–	41	41
Rugby	–	–	–	–	–	–	–	20	20
TOTALS	812	368	438	883	1,003	1,475	1,811	2,385	9,175

Sources: *CC, CG, IT, KM, NG, TA, TC, TE, TFP, TV, TWN*; *Hunting Journal of the 3rd Marquis of Waterford* (Dublin, 1901); Ashbrook Union Cricket Club scorebook, 1846–48; Ten volumes of Petty Sessions records from 1854 to 1860; Ms 9515. Account book and records of Kilruane Football Club, 1876–1880 (National Library, Dublin); Lawrence, *Handbook of Cricket in Ireland* (Dublin, 1865 to 1881)

lawn tennis, rugby football and cycling. There was no diffusion of lawn tennis, croquet or rugby to the lower classes in Tipperary. This just did not happen.

By 1865, there were several sports available to the gentlemen and ladies of Great Britain and Ireland. Of these, archery was the one which became very popular among residents of estates in Tipperary. Croquet and lawn tennis followed, and were also enjoyed in the relative comfort of the demesne setting. These sports also provided the opportunity for social discourse, lavish luncheons, band music and dancing. Though some gentlemen may have felt that summer got in the way of the hunting season, summer gave both sexes an opportunity to dress extravagantly and attend to that most important aspect of one's early life, finding a husband or wife.[47] This was a new twist on the season of social events. While the Georgians had favoured tea-drinking and sedate dancing, the Victorians were altogether more vigorous in their pastimes. Sport gave them the opportunity to watch and admire future partners. In May 1851, when the military and civilian cricket teams met at Marlfield, Clonmel, the lawn was 'graced by numbers of ladies in carriages'.[48] Occasions such as these further emphasised the social circle associated with sport where the dinners and dances, which punctuated the day, allowed for great interaction between different families and military personnel.

An examination of the various sports which the owners and residents of country houses pursued as they sought to keep up with fashion in Great Britain and the rest of Ireland shows that they did so with passion and fervour. It says much for the enthusiasm with which they undertook each particular pursuit. Occasions such as the hunt breakfast or evening ball were not cheap, and a certain degree of hosting was expected when one invited associates and friends to an 'at home' tennis party. Archery, croquet and lawn tennis afforded ladies the opportunity to exercise, compete and flirt. What the women of Tipperary did was no different from their middle-class contemporaries in Scotland.[49] Here too the attractions of archery, croquet and lawn tennis gave a platform for ladies to compete in sport and this was not perceived as in any way unusual.

The community of the country house residents was a close-knit social group. Many of the same family names and individuals reappeared at various sporting activities, demonstrating the ability of this social group to reinvent itself as necessity dictated. From the south of the county, Samuel Barton was an avid cricket supporter but he was also found at archery meetings. Similarly, Samuel Perry was involved with archery, cricket and the Suir Preservation Society. In the Ormond country of north Tipperary, Bassett Holmes was a dedicated yachtsman and official of the Lough Derg Yacht Club. He was also a committee member of the Ormond Tennis Club.[50] That this occurred was neither strange nor unexpected. In a small community of a few hundred individuals social intercourse where sport took place was not only commonplace, but expected. There was an onus to replicate what was happening in wider society and in this respect the owners of country houses and estates in Tipperary were not found wanting. There was enthusiastic support for the various sports as documented, though with varying levels of provision, reflecting once more the county's north–south divide. A regrettable feature is that no evidence has come to light to explain why the community of Clonmel and its hinterland took so long to establish a lawn tennis club or even why there appeared to have been no move among the country house residents to promote the game socially as their contemporaries in Cashel and Nenagh did. It depended on the actions of individuals.

Central to the success of country house sports was the interaction which the owners and residents of these houses and estates had with the military personnel stationed throughout the county. The military personnel were a key element in the local economy. For the country house and estate, military officers were, more often than not, the skilful opposition which their civilian contemporaries attempted to defeat. Victorian sport was constantly evolving and it was the military officers who were to the fore in this respect. As we will see in Chapter 6, the military introduced rugby football and Association football into the county and by competing against the landed, professional and business classes of Tipperary they provided the necessary competitive impetus for these sports. Cricket was the first game which effectively crossed the social divide. It gave the lower classes a taste for sport, which increased in the 1870s, the peak period in the history of the game in the county. Essentially, the other country house sports remained an exclusive pursuit for a minor proportion of the county's population. Cricket gave the lower classes a taste for competitive sport in a team format. Sports which followed later in the nineteenth century, such as hurling and the newly invented Gaelic football, were offshoots of the competitive element provided by playing cricket.

GENTLEMEN CRICKET ELEVEN

The gentlemen cricket eleven made its first appearance on the Tipperary sporting calendar in 1862.[51] Gentlemen eleven teams were a feature of the cricketing experience in the county, with the mid-1870s popular years for contests of this nature. In August 1869, Henry Munster, a parliamentary candidate for the Cashel borough and an able cricketer in his own right, brought his own eleven together to compete against Rockwell College 'on the beautiful demesne of William Murphy Esq., of Ballinamona'.[52] After the match, class distinctions were reinforced as Murphy 'hospitably entertained a numerous and respectable company of visitors, while there was an ample spread for the players and all comers upon the grass, provided by Mr. Munster'.[53] Munster attempted to gain election to parliament on the Cashel borough ticket and was keen to buy as much support as was within his means. Yet cricket, paradoxically, was the one sport that brought in all classes to the same sporting arena, no matter how divided they were politically and socially. Cricket was unique among all sports in Victorian Tipperary. While other sports such as archery, croquet and lawn tennis were class-specific, cricket evolved differently. Men were paid to bowl and bat at cricket, while typically the man who organised the team opened the batting or felt comfortable coming in after the fall of a few wickets. Bowling was not for him. Cricket was exceptional in this respect because of its inbuilt use of players from different classes. It would not be overstating it to say that it was the most democratic of all games.

The 'informal yet tightly knit social networks [which] were central to British middle-class male culture' were also found in rural Tipperary.[54] It was not unusual for a gentleman's team to appear bearing the name of a man who was better known for his association with a different sport. A team of eleven gentlemen was another conduit to maintain social networks and keep up to date with the latest gossip, as well as just whiling away the hours in sporting activity. Two men well known in the hunting field in the west of the county, Cooper Chadwick and Walter Ryan, put out two such teams in a match against each other in 1873. Mrs Ryan 'sumptuously entertained' both teams on the conclusion of the match.[55] Occasions such as this helped to reinforce a sense of community as the social networks were replicated across different sporting experiences.

It is no surprise to find that the country house environment facilitated cricket, especially in its capacity of providing grounds for new clubs and the gentlemen elevens. While cricket was a means of bringing people together, it was also another conduit through which social networks were maintained. Cricket provided the 'gentler sex' the opportunity to meet and the country estate gave them the setting where this could happen.[56] These matches brought together the social elites who reciprocated the welcome afforded to them by hosting similar events. This was a typical feature associated with the game. Though cricket provided a convivial setting for such gatherings, it was not the first country house sport or recreation to fulfil this function. Hunt meetings regularly commenced with breakfast at one house or another, before the hunt party moved off. Archery, the next sport to be considered, was the stimulus for subsequent sporting events to take place in a country house setting.

ARCHERY

Archery became fashionable in Great Britain in the latter part of the eighteenth century as it was a means 'to flaunt one's wealth and pass the large amount of time the leisured class had on its hands'.[57] A brief reference to archery, in conjunction with a pigeon-shooting fête at the home of John Power near Carrick-on-Suir in July 1844, does not constitute evidence that it was something that was widely practised at that time.[58] Though archery was popular in England and Wales from the 1780s, it did not become a fashionable pursuit in Tipperary until 1858 when a regular pattern of archery target-shooting became established.[59] This was twenty-five years after the Meath Archers were founded in County Meath.[60] The same may also be said of other archery societies throughout Ireland. It is likely that early archery went unrecorded as there was no reason to report it in the local press because it took place in a private setting – it was a more exclusive recreation than cricket. It was in the late 1850s and early 1860s that archery meetings became widely reported from locations throughout the country. This was a reflection of its increased popularity.[61]

Figure 2.1 Archery clubs in County Tipperary, 1858–1868

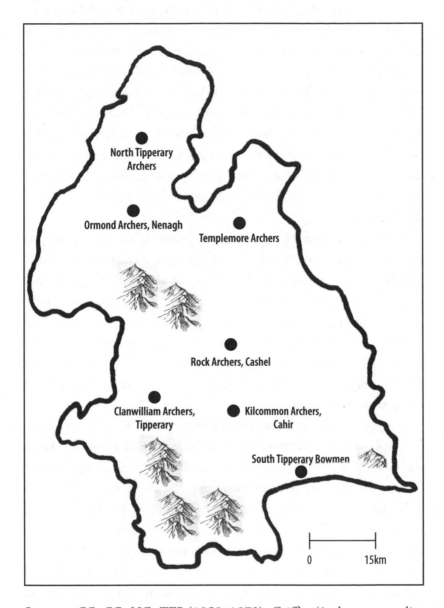

Sources: *CC, CG, NG, TFP* (1858–1872); Griffin, 'Archery as an elite pursuit' (Dublin, 2013), p. 164 (Note: a specific location for the North Tipperary Archers has not been identified)

In Tipperary, as elsewhere, archery was an easily administered sporting activity. Once it took hold among the residents of the country estates, it soon became another recreation that was essential for any aspiring socialite to participate in. Bourgeois society in Tipperary took it to their hearts once the sport became fashionable. The Templemore Archers (Templemore), the Ormond Archery Club (Nenagh) and the Clanwilliam Archers (Tipperary town) were all established between 1858 and 1861.[62] Of thirty-two active clubs in the 1860s as identified by Brian Griffin, four of them were found in County Tipperary (Figure 2.1).[63] Three further clubs have been identified, giving Tipperary a similar concentration in the 1860s to that of County Cork, each having seven clubs.

In 1861, a Clonmel businessman, S. Bradford, set about acquiring the necessary equipment to sell to an emerging niche market. He sold bows from twelve shillings while youth bows were sold from two pence to six shillings and nine pence each.[64] Four-foot targets were priced at eight shillings and six pence, six-foot iron stands were six shillings and six pence, while a dozen arrows for ladies were priced at twenty shillings. Gentlemen had to pay twenty-four shillings for the same number. Equipment prices indicate that it was a sport that was not cheap to play.

In common with meetings in England and Wales, an archery event in Tipperary was not complete without a dinner and a ball.[65] In 1858, 'upwards of eighty persons' who participated at a meeting of the Templemore Archers were treated to dinner by John Carden at his estate at Barnane, after which 'an accession of visitors took place [and] dancing commenced'.[66] This number was dwarfed at a combined meet of the South Tipperary Bowmen and the Kilcommon Archers when 'about two hundred and fifty persons were present'.[67] This was a feature of all archery meetings around the county. But unlike meetings of toxophilites elsewhere in Ireland, it was probable that those attending for dinner in south Tipperary had to pay a surcharge.[68] In July 1861, at the 'first prize meeting' of the year for the South Tipperary Bowmen, participants were requested to forward a charge of two shillings and six pence to the secretary prior to the meeting.[69] This enabled the Bowmen to pay Miss

Wade of Clonmel, the principal caterer for the society between 1861 and 1871, ensuring that dinners were served to members at various locations where the club met, including Knockeevan, Marlfield, Cahir and Knocklofty.[70] The club was not remiss in thanking and praising her for the service she provided. Through the medium of the local press, especially the *Clonmel Chronicle*, not only did correspondents glowingly recount the deeds of the various archery clubs but they used it to note the 'excellent repast' provided by Miss Wade.[71] On occasion she was assisted by her brothers David or William.[72]

Where meals were served on country house grounds a 'dining pavilion was erected and close to it a large tent, both supplied by P.J. Hynes, Blackhall Place, Dublin, together with the marquee which was placed close to the shooting ground'.[73] The Hynes family appear to have identified a market for themselves in this respect as they also supplied 'a spacious and beautiful tent' for a meeting of the Wexford Archers in 1850.[74] Hynes also took out an advertisement in the *Freeman's Journal* informing 'the Nobility and Gentry' of the 'pleasure marquees and tents' which he had for sale, while also noting that he would supply marquees 'for dejeuners and pleasure parties on the shortest notice'.[75] There was a great degree of sophistication and organisation associated with archery meetings, which ensured that everything went off smoothly and that all aspects of the day, both social and sporting, were covered. This included the provision of 'iced champagne and other sparkling wines, obtained at Mr. B.P. Phelan's establishment', Clonmel, which cost £5.[76] This show of strength, in terms of luncheons, dinners and accompanying drinks, was an aspect of the day. It clearly illustrated the degree to which money was no object, ensuring that meetings were of the very best order. Days such as these were a boost to the local economy. Sport generated an economy around itself.

Sport was another means through which established networks of people could meet. In 1864, at the commencement of the archery season, a report on the activities of the South Tipperary club noted that in no county 'in Great Britain or Ireland are sports and pastimes so universally patronised, encouraged and supported. In no other country are attempts made, more especially, to introduce and sustain an amusement, in which both sexes can take a mutual part.'[77] This is what archery, croquet and, latterly, lawn tennis did. But this aspect of sport was confined to the middle and upper classes in Tipperary and Ireland.

As far as archery was concerned, it gave women the first real opportunity to actively participate in sporting recreation. From the very outset, wives and daughters from the country house network competed. Records of the winning scores appeared in the local press and all clubs set about acquiring prizes to present to the winners. Prizes such as brooches, lockets and chains were purchased for the winning ladies. As the accounts of the South Tipperary club illustrate, the purchase of these prizes accounted for a significant proportion of club funds. In 1864, prizes awarded for the three club meetings accounted for £68 5s out of an income of 'little more than £80 for the year'.[78] In August 1861, a joint meeting of the Kilcommon Archers and the South Tipperary Bowmen was described as 'a truly splendid event', with the shooting ground 'festooned [with] the flags of all nations, conspicuous among them the insignia of maritime Britannia'.[79] The meeting was also remarkable for the presentation of a 'wooden spoon' to the lady who scored the lowest number of hits. From a Tipperary perspective, Lucy Quin, Loughloher Castle, was more than capable of holding her own among female competitors. At the first private meeting of the County Carlow Archery Club, at Kilmeany in July 1864, she carried off the Ladies' Challenge Cup. She also emerged victorious at the same venue later in October, after she was allowed to participate as an invited guest.[80] At that period the leading female archer in Ireland was Cecilia Betham, whom Miss Grubb, from Cahir Abbey, competed against at a meeting of the Irish Grand National Archery Club, in 1865.[81] But the Quins, and other South Tipperary Bowmen members, the Wise family, moved in the same circle as the Bethams. Cecilia's father, M.C.J. Betham, was a committee member of the Grand Leinster Archery Club, as also were Captain Quin and Captain Wise.[82] During the summer of 1866 the families headed for Dublin to participate in meetings of this prestige archery society.[83]

Though some evidence has been found regarding the cost of joining archery clubs in England and Wales, no such information is available for Tipperary.[84] It has been observed that an annual subscription of ten shillings, together with a one-shilling entrance fee, was levied on prospective members of the Kilkenny Archers in 1860.[85] This is somewhat on a par with the £1 annual subscription fee which members had to pay when joining the Ashbrook Union Cricket Club. South Tipperary Bowmen accounts for 1863 show that subscriptions for the year amounted to £89. This figure is not specific in terms of club numbers or individual subscription costs.[86] Miss Wade received £3 3s 10d for what were described as 'evening refreshments'. The *Clonmel Chronicle* also received payment of £3 8s, probably for notifications of forthcoming meetings. As such, fees for prizes and ancillary expenses were a draw on the club but that they were not in debt was perceived as a positive indication that the club was strong. Yet there was a desire that the club should have more members. As previously noted, it was not unknown for the club to impose a dinner charge, at the conclusion of a meeting, with two shillings and six pence charged for dinner in 1861.[87] Ten years later, charges for attendance at an archery meeting dance in Clonmel courthouse were seven shillings and six pence for gentlemen and five shillings for ladies, with morning or evening dress optional.[88]

In common with other clubs, such as those in Westmeath, female members of Tipperary clubs 'benefited from positive discrimination'.[89] In respect of annual subscriptions and other fees, women had to pay less than their male counterparts. Similar preferential subscription rates for women were found in Scotland.[90] But changes were on the way for supporters of archery in Tipperary. From 1863 attendance at the dance following an archery meeting was open to non-members.[91] But by this stage the fascination with archery had waned. No further reports or activities of the South Tipperary Bowmen appeared in the press. The club passed into oblivion, with no lamentations for its passing. There is no evidence to suggest that it was subsumed into a croquet or lawn tennis club, similar to that which occurred with the Rock Archery and Croquet Club.[92]

It has also been shown that the decline in archery was due in no small part to the appeal of more contemporary sports such as lawn tennis.

These sports were organised in a formalised club structure and they had a competitive element which was more appealing than archery.[93] Indeed, new lawn tennis clubs emerged from pre-existing archery clubs. In 1877, the Monkstown Tennis Club emerged from the County of Dublin Archery Club, while the Downshire Archers also played tennis in 1877.[94]

There is no doubt that the successful spread of archery occurred among a specific tier of people in Tipperary society; they were upper class, affluent and exclusive. Support of archery and the nature of the leading clubs in Tipperary mirrored other clubs around Ireland. That these exclusive clubs were able to restrict membership only to those deemed socially acceptable was indicative of self-regulation. Why should it be any other way? Archery was but a means to an end. It facilitated the coming together of a narrow strand of a local, or extended, community. It was an occasion 'for enjoyable socialising and group bonding … generous hospitality and social status at a local and wider level'.[95] Above all, archery gave women an early opportunity to not only attend but to actively compete in a sport. The value of prizes on offer was far in excess of that offered for those who competed in the athletics arena, as is shown later. Unlike the gentleman amateur, there were no problems associated with females receiving prize money at archery. As the appeal of archery declined croquet and lawn tennis filled the void. But there was a distinct geographical split in the county in relation to the location of these sports.

CROQUET

While croquet did not capture the imagination of the people to the same extent as archery, its appearance as a sport, which, like archery, was open to women, was indicative of how sporting fashions came and went. What differentiated croquet from archery was that it was a lawn game that did not develop into a network of clubs or societies as archery had. The only club to incorporate croquet into its title was the Rock Archery and Croquet Club in Cashel. Essentially, croquet provided not only recreation but yet another opportunity to spend time with friends and acquaintances of the same class while awaiting the arrival of the hunting season.

In July 1869, at the opening meeting of the Rock Archery Club, both croquet and archery were played. It was noted that 'the attractions of "croquet" seemed to have proved so thoroughly influential as to leave its sister sport rather under a cloud'.[96] Unlike other archery meetings at this time, those held in Cashel included both archery and croquet, with competitions for both male and female members.[97] Croquet, though obviously quite different from archery, fulfilled the same role. It was an activity that was played on a country house lawn and it invited the sexes to mix. It had none of the pseudo-medieval characteristics attributable to archery. It was an activity which brought the lesser gentry together in Cashel and in Nenagh. Though no evidence has been uncovered to indicate that croquet was played on the bigger estates, it is possible that it was played there but simply went unrecorded.[98] The South Tipperary Bowmen failed to reappear after the 1871 season ended. However, there is no evidence to suggest that the society re-emerged in another guise, nothing to indicate that it was reincarnated as a croquet club. Such was the frequency of archery reports in the local *Clonmel Chronicle* that an absence of croquet reports in this newspaper suggests that no croquet club or society was established. There is no clear reason why this is so. With the Rock Archery and Croquet Club this did not need to happen, as the club name featured both sports. The same thing occurred in north Tipperary with the Ormond Archery Club and the Ormond Croquet Club. The Ormond Archers were founded in March 1859, though the club had a short lifespan[99] – it was only in existence for two seasons.[100] When a list of those who attended a meeting of this club in late June 1859 is compared with a list of those who attended a meeting of the Ormond Croquet Club in September 1875, eleven of the same names appeared in both reports and there are other family names common to both.[101] This suggests that the Ormond Archery Club was reinvented as the Ormond Croquet Club in August 1875.[102]

Croquet afternoons in Ormond country required club members to attend at the residence of whichever member was hosting the reunion.[103] Not only did this have the advantage of spreading croquet, but it also encouraged other country houses to take up the sport. It also lessened the cost on one specific family having to entertain and provide refreshments and meals for guests. Though there was a good degree of support for croquet at this time, it was less than that afforded to archery. Another sporting evolution was about to take place and it was one which the Tipperary elite took to their hearts. It did great injury to the fledgling croquet circuit however. This sport was lawn tennis.

Croquet, in essence, was an intermediary between archery and lawn tennis. Croquet sets were purchased as a box game and played informally and it is likely that many games were played in such a manner and went unrecorded. There was no need for players to establish a club structure as the games played were a private activity, hence the absence of extensive reports on croquet in the press. Though it became popular among some residents of the country houses in Tipperary, it was more or less absent from the estate community network in and around Clonmel. At the northern end of the county the Ormond Croquet Club was about to undergo another reincarnation, this time as a lawn tennis club. For several people associated with this club it was a third change of sporting direction.

LAWN TENNIS

On 23 February 1874, Major Walter C. Wingfield patented a 'New and Improved Court for Playing the Ancient game of Tennis', which he called sphairsitke.[104] It is likely that 'a similar game had been played at Edgbaston', Birmingham in 1868.[105] Unlike other sports that had their origin in England, lawn tennis was remarkable for the speed with which it appeared in Ireland. If one bears in mind that archery took almost seventy years to cross the Irish Sea, lawn tennis took only two. Lawn tennis benefited from royal patronage and it was very popular throughout Great Britain. In essence, a lawn tennis craze took hold not only in England but throughout Ireland. With the establishment of lawn tennis clubs in Lansdowne, Dublin University, Limerick,

Monkstown and Fitzwilliam in 1877, and the establishment of an open lawn tennis tournament in Limerick, also that year, the building blocks of a new sport were put in place.[106] Though the Irish Lawn Tennis Championships were instituted in 1879, it was not until 1908 that the Irish Lawn Tennis Association was founded.

In September 1875, at an end-of-season meeting of the Ormond Croquet Club, the day's amusements were rounded off with lawn tennis and yachting.[107] This was four years ahead of the earliest reference to the sport in County Westmeath.[108] Lawn tennis quickly became popular with people living in and around Nenagh. During the summer of 1876 a specific pattern of tennis-playing developed which revolved around a circle of 'at home' meetings which took place at the residences of the local gentry in much the same way as archery and croquet previously did.[109] The Ormond Club was the most active in the county with meetings in the summer of 1876 taking place on a weekly basis, typically on Friday afternoons.[110] In Mullingar, County Westmeath, 'Thursday afternoons were devoted to public tennis events', suggesting that clubs had specific days set aside for practice and public matches in much the same fashion as cricket clubs had.[111] Such regularity gave clubs a sense of purpose, coupled with the sociability of the occasion itself.

Many members of the Ormond Club also shared an interest in yachting on nearby Lough Derg. This suggests that sport was for those who could afford it and, in this respect, lawn tennis was no different. Though playing equipment was relatively inexpensive when compared with that of hunting, it was the very nature of the game which made it a preserve of the country house scene. Lawn tennis required manicured lawns and tennis whites. By extension, some mechanised means of keeping the grass cut short was also required. This was not something which tenant farmers, let alone the labouring class, could afford. In September 1878, the club gathered for the 'first meeting of this aristocratic amusement' on the grounds of Henry H. Poe.[112] The club had become firmly established and lawn tennis was a popular summer activity to rival that of hunting in winter. Membership names of both the Ormond Tennis Club and the Tipperary residents of the Ormond and King's County Hunt were virtually identical. It was as if they removed their tennis whites at the end of summer and donned the red coat for the hunting season.[113]

Mirroring archery and croquet, female participation was high. However, it was the nature of the sport that was different. Unlike the other two recreations, lawn tennis was more physical and the game required ladies to compete in long dresses while also wearing some form of head cover, either a scarf or hat. To play matches or tournaments, the sport came with a price. It cost five shillings to compete in a match. Regularly these matches were associated with club tournaments.[114] To compete in a doubles match also incurred a five-shilling entrance fee. While initially tennis matches were private occasions, the advent of club tournaments attracted local interest. In July 1879, at a meeting of the Ormond Club, followed by a dance, there were over 120 people present.[115] One month later, at a 'lawn tennis party on a grand scale' at Inane, Roscrea, there were 150 people present.[116]

Similar to other sporting activities, there were local and national businessmen who sought to cash in on the new appeal of lawn tennis. Shopkeepers in Nenagh were prompt in advertising their wares in the local press. 'Mixed grasses for lawn tennis and croquet grounds' were available from Robert Hodgins in 1877.[117] In 1879, Day Brothers could offer for the 'summer season, [equipment for] lawn tennis, croquet, cricket and other amusing games'.[118] Also in that year, and once again on Castle Street, Nenagh, as were the previous two businesses, the curiously named 'India-rubber and Gutta-percha Warehouse' had on offer 'ladies' tennis shoes, best make, [with] corrugated soles'.[119] Local businesses were alive to the opportunities that sporting recreation could bring in terms of sales, and they promptly set about acquiring stock. This in turn assisted in advancing the game at a local level.

In County Westmeath there was a strong connection between romance and lawn tennis and this was also the case in north Tipperary.[120] Tea and other refreshments facilitated romantic encounters. Unmarried club members of both sexes could meet in what was still a confined and private setting. Reports of lawn tennis meetings were submitted by correspondents to the local press, an arrangement which seems to have suited the Ormond and Cashel clubs. But on one occasion in

1881, when a correspondent forwarded an account of a tennis meeting at Busherstown, 'the hospitable seat of that most deservedly popular landlord, George J. Minchin, Esq., D.L., J.P.', his actions were none too pleasing to Minchin,[121] who promptly wrote to the *Nenagh Guardian* 'expressing dissatisfaction at a private little tennis party' on his lawn which was reported in the paper.[122] This indicates that some private meetings were principally that and, as such, not for public consumption.

It seems likely that much lawn tennis took place in the south of the county in a private setting and as a purely social occasion but, unlike the activities of the Ormond and Cashel clubs, went unrecorded in the newspapers. This was similar to croquet. These were distinct from the club format, which had games organised around competition. In 1878, the officers of the Royal Artillery in Clonmel barracks, who were supportive of the game, put up prizes for ladies competitions. Those who entered were handicapped according to their skill level.[123] That the officers provided lawn tennis facilities suggests that patronage, once so commonly afforded to sport in the south Tipperary communities, was not yet as apparent as it was in the north of the county.

Clonmel businessman Charles Carrothers purchased the Clonmel Skating Rink and made it available for skating and lawn tennis matches in October 1878.[124] However, one year later, a report of a ladies' handicap meeting on the rink grounds illustrated the difficulties facing the supporters of tennis in the town. It was stated that 'the Rink (the only ground available) is a far from suitable place for playing tennis matches on, being too short for the regulation sized court, thus cramping the play ... On this account it is very much regretted that a club for the purpose of playing lawn tennis, cricket and football matches has not as yet been formed in so flourishing a town as Clonmel, and such a want of enterprise is much to be deplored'.[125] Yet, several of those present were the very people who openly and actively supported archery, including the Earl and Countess of Donoughmore, on whose grounds the archery club was based. Press reports show that there were lawn tennis tournaments in Clonmel in the latter half of the 1890s, with a club 'newly started' in 1897.[126] This era also predates the establishment of a lawn tennis club in the town around 1908.[127]

Essentially, lawn tennis in Clonmel failed to establish itself in the same manner as it had in the north of the county, mainly due to a lack of facilities. Elsewhere, at Cashel, Nenagh and Tipperary town the game established itself as a staple in the country house network; it was a game primarily associated with the Protestant members of the various communities. Inter-club matches and tournaments added to the local competitive nature of the game. The Irish Lawn Tennis Championships, which commenced in 1879, organised by Fitzwilliam Lawn Tennis Club in Dublin, further added to the appeal of the sport. With a national competition in place there was an opportunity for better players to entertain the prospect of honour outside of the Tipperary circuit. Though outside the remit of this book, such a situation did occur in 1890 when Lena Rice, Marlhill, New Inn became the first, and only, Irish winner of the ladies championship at Wimbledon.[128]

Coinciding as it did with the development of other sports in the county, lawn tennis provided another dimension to the range of sports then available to middle- and upper-class society. These were the classes that could afford adequate leisure time to pursue such activities. Yet what was strange about the growth of lawn tennis was that it did not mirror that of archery. Rather, it followed a similar distribution pattern to that of croquet. In 1877, croquet and lawn tennis were both adopted in the title of the All England Croquet and Lawn Tennis Club, further emphasising the close links between the two sports and their elite social location.[129] As the 1880s progressed, so too did lawn tennis. Unlike hunting to hounds, it did not suffer any ill-effects from land agitation subsequent to the founding of the Land League in 1879, principally because the games took place within the confines of the country house estate.

ANGLING AND GAME

The owners and residents of country house estates used their privileged position in society for their own benefit by utilising the rivers, lakes and countryside as another means to indulge their passion for recreation. Landlords, their agents and gamekeepers marshalled the rivers, especially the Suir, by means of the Suir Preservation Society and determined that only members were allowed fish on its waters. Similar controls extended over land, and prosecutions for trespass and hunting for game without a licence typified measures to counter the threat posed by poachers and unlicensed hunters. Local businessmen also fell foul of the Society as they used the rigours of the legislative procedures to prosecute mill owners whose sluice gates and weirs did not conform to specifications.

Children reared in country homes and estates regularly found themselves in the company of estate employees such as gamekeepers and servants,[130] who introduced the children to the vagaries of sport, especially field sports. These sports were the preserve of the landed classes and those found trespassing were regularly brought before the local magistrates.[131] In essence, it was a cosy arrangement, for the magistrates also took part in country house sport. Making use of the law against trespass and poaching often served to emphasise the disparity between the landed and landless members of a community. This entrenchment was even more apparent with the control of fishing rights. While salmon and trout were abundant in the River Suir, which bisected the county from north to south, the land on either side was private. This privacy allowed the owner to regulate who could and could not fish on the waters which flowed through his lands. Water bailiffs were employed to keep poachers off the rivers. It was not only the lower classes who ran into trouble with these bailiffs; some mill owners were also brought before the courts for trapping fish in mill races and weirs.[132]

Illegal fishing for salmon in the closed season regularly resulted in the appearance of men before the local courts.[133] Thomas Moroney charged Edward Jones for fishing for salmon with cross-lines without a licence.[134] In another such instance it was claimed that it was 'a law for the oppression of the poor and the amusement of the rich and proud'.[135] Taking that into consideration, the reality was that legislation relating to fishing was designed to protect river stock.[136] Licence fees placed a further restriction on the freedom of the lower classes to fish. The cost of a single salmon rod licence was ten shillings, while a cross-line and salmon rod licence was £1.[137] Such was the power of the Suir Preservation Society that they, as a body of landowners, resident magistrates and justices of the peace, were in a position to virtually control fishing rights for the length of the Suir and its tributaries. Established in 1857, the Society sought 'to aid and assist the conservators for the better and more effectually preserving and increasing the breed of salmon and trout in the River Suir and its tributaries'.[138] Water bailiffs were employed at a rate of thirty shillings per month, with four district committees appointed to supervise them.[139] Income for 1858, based on subscriptions and other funds, was £188.[140] The expenditure for 1859 was budgeted at £166. The Suir Preservation Society advised that directions should be given to gamekeepers to assist water bailiffs in their 'several duties'.[141]

Two issues arise here. Firstly, private property was safeguarded and the law of trespass was enforced to keep poachers away from rivers which ran through estate lands. Secondly, sporting stocks were controlled. Bailiffs were not only there to stop poaching, they also monitored the actions of mill owners and looked out for the presence of otters in the rivers. A small bounty was offered per head of otter trapped.[142] This reward was withdrawn in 1861 due to the 'state of the funds of the Suir Preservation Society'.[143] However, with increasing stocks there was scope for an enhanced angling experience in the south of the county.

In order for the stocks to be maintained at adequate levels the conservators required finance and this was principally derived from the licence fee.[144] With news of good catches made on the rivers of Tipperary appearing in the press, angling and fishing as a means of deriving income attracted 'the humble as well as the gentleman angler'. It was further noted that 'large hampers of fish ... are almost daily sent off by railway "to feed John Bull", who pays well for what he receives'.[145]

GAME SHOOTING

The names of men who held 'certificates to kill game' appeared in the local press in the latter half of the 1850s.[146] These certificates were essentially a membership card in all but name. Having paid the requisite fee, the holder of such a licence was at liberty to shoot game, provided there was no attempt to trespass on lands where he was not invited or permitted to shoot. Certificates were also granted to gamekeepers who were appointed by specific named individuals. It was further noted that rewards would be given to those 'who may supply information against persons sporting without certificates'.[147] Any person shooting snipe or woodcock without a game certificate was subject to a penalty of £20 under the Game Certificates (Ireland) Act, 1842.[148] In 1860, however, a change in the game laws displayed a marked difference as to how the law was interpreted in Ireland and Great Britain.[149] Under the terms of the Game Licences Act, 1860, it was called a licence in Great Britain but it was a certificate in Ireland. Furthermore, the penalty for taking game without a licence in Great Britain was £20, whereas in Ireland it incurred a fine of £50. Another anomaly was that in Britain one could kill rabbits without a licence, but not in Ireland. Though country estate owners and gamekeepers were a step above others in rural society in Ireland, they were still a few steps behind their contemporaries on the British mainland.

The varied interests of Nathaniel Buckley, of Ryecroft, Ashton-under-Lyme, as landowner, cotton mill owner and Liberal politician, did not prevent him from visiting his preserves on the Galtee Mountains.[150] In 1873, he brought to his Tipperary estates 'for the purpose of enjoying with his friends, Richard Shaw, Esq. M.P, Mr. Shaw, junr., and Edward Collier, Esq., the pleasures of the grouse shooting season'.[151] Due to the 'unceasing care of the keepers', the shooting season of 1874–75 yielded '23 pheasants, 235 partridges, 432 hares, 167 rabbits, 213 woodcock, 157 snipe, 5 royal bucks, and 414 grouse', with the 1875–76 season expected to surpass the previous one in terms of game bagged.[152] These men could sail into Ireland and shoot and bag any game they so desired. Viscount Lismore, Shanbally Castle, in the south-west of the county, also had game rights for that part of his estate that extended into the Galtee Mountains. Poison was also placed on Lismore's estate for the preservation of game.[153] Game preservation notices appeared with increasing regularity in the local press from 1851, with lands owned by various individuals 'strictly preserved', while any persons found trespassing 'in pursuit of game' were prosecuted.[154] In 1868, one such individual found trespassing with a dead rabbit in his possession appeared before the Tipperary Petty Sessions where he was fined £1 and costs.[155] Estate and farm owners were keenly aware of the threat of poaching and trespassing.

In February 1869, eleven guns shooting on the Dundrum estate of Viscount Hawarden bagged 60 woodcocks, 7 hares, 99 rabbits and one deer, and 'in accordance with the established custom of the family, the produce of the first day's shooting [was] sent to her Majesty'.[156] While the coverts were maintained with plentiful game, gamekeepers were busy bringing trespassers before the magistrates and also endeavouring to maintain an adequate stock within their respective preserves. A Game Preservation Association was established for the Cahir district in July 1870 to assist in this matter by ensuring that coverts were maintained.[157] At the meeting £42 was subscribed to assist the association with its efforts. This suggests that the rearing and management of wildfowl and game was well advanced, giving local employment to ensure that the coverts were constantly replenished to meet the needs of the game hunters and their associates. The use of gamekeepers was another example of the employment provided by sport. This, coupled with advances made in other elite field sports, such as hunting to hounds, shooting and fishing, indicates that a strong support network was required to underpin these activities. Blacksmiths, leather workers, farriers and dealers in sporting goods all assisted in transforming these recreations into more clearly defined physical sports. A tipping point had been reached whereby services were required to underpin their growth.

Throughout the 1860s and 1870s, the local press carried what can only be described as self-contributed reports of fishing and game shooting.[158] Col. Browne, 93rd Highlanders, killed two salmon, each weighing thirty-three pounds, 'on the portion of the Suir belonging to Colonel the Hon. and Lady Margaret Charteris' at Cahir.[159] A later report noted that Capt. W. Barton caught three fish 'on that portion of the River Suir belonging to Mr. Clibborn'.[160] Similarly, the angling deeds of Charles Langley, Cabra Castle, Thurles could not have appeared in the local press without him, or an associate, forwarding the information.[161] This self-reporting was a feature of sport in Tipperary at this time, but while team sports may have had a wider appeal, game hunters in Tipperary were not shy in forwarding data relating to their deeds.

Landowners maximised the resources of their country estates to the full and they used the law to ensure that fish and game were preserved for the sole use of their family, associates and friends. After a day shooting or fishing a full bag was the ultimate prize. Self-contributed angling reports to the local press mirrored those of archery, croquet and lawn tennis. It was a way of letting one's peers know how much one had shot or caught. The occupational role which gamekeepers had in attending to the needs of their employer by ensuring adequate game, coverts and breeding stock was central to the management of rivers and lakes. While estate owners satisfied their own sporting needs, there was also the issue of employment as gamekeepers, fowlers and water bailiffs maintained vigilance over their lands and waters.

YACHTING

There was one area outside the bounds of the estate wall, Lough Derg, which was an amenity area for people from the same social class to indulge their passion for yachting and sailing. Lough Derg borders three counties – Tipperary, Galway and Clare. It is the largest of the three principal lakes on the river Shannon, before it enters the Atlantic ocean at Limerick. In Victorian Tipperary it provided a means for the landowners in its hinterland to add another sporting recreation to the list of their amusements. While Lough Derg was a public place, the foreshore and jetties were not. The lake was the only location in the county where yachting could take place on such a scale. The lake had a surface area of 118 square kilometres (forty-six square miles).[162] It was twenty-five miles long.[163]

The oldest yacht club in the world was established in Cork harbour in 1720 bearing the title the Water Club of the Harbour of Cork.[164] Records for the club do not exist from 1765 to 1806 but it was re-established in 1828 as the Cork Yacht Club.[165] A yacht club existed on Lough Derg in 1837 when a regatta was held on the lake, although it was claimed that the origins of the club were much earlier.[166] Regattas were held on an almost annual basis with little interruption, even for the Great Famine, except for the period 1863–1871 inclusive. No obvious evidence has come to light as to why this barren period occurred though it would appear that it was linked to an absence of patronage. The *Nenagh Guardian* carried several letters on the subject as yachtsmen lamented the absence of a regatta, mindful that regattas in other locations in Ireland continued.[167] Of these letters, two specifically referred to Captain Holmes as the man to whom the successful staging of a regatta could be entrusted. He was an active supporter of the regatta prior to its cessation, hosting post-regatta parties. He was also Commodore of the Lough Derg Yacht Club.[168] When the regatta resumed in 1872, he 'kindly gave free access through his handsome grounds to visitors'.[169] This suggests that, owing to a lack of support from Captain Holmes, the whole enterprise which was the Lough Derg Regatta was compromised and, as a result, it failed to appear on the calendar for nine years. It further demonstrated the fragile and fickle nature of the sporting environment.

As with other sports, notifications of upcoming events and regattas were circulated to members. Advertisements were also placed in the local press. Regatta articles were similar to those for horse racing. Full details of the races were given, inclusive of the name of the commodore, sailing committee, prizes, entry fees and contact details for the honorary secretary.[170] On occasions, there was an 'ordinary' at a local hotel. One stipulation, which was adhered to in all regattas, was that all members of the club would 'provide their yachts with the plain red "Burgee" which has been adopted by the club'.[171] At the outset the club was based in Portumna Bay, with Lord Avonmore, Belle Isle, Commodore in the club's formative years.[172] The majority of the vessels used were yachts owned by many of the landowners residing near the lake. Bassett Holmes had a cutter yacht, *Avenger*, which was built on the shores of Lough Derg in 1852, by George Marshall, Ringsend, Dublin.[173]

Though there was a yacht club in existence, the evidence suggests that it was not as stable or strong as some would have desired. In June 1865, in a letter to the local press, 'A lover of aquatics' queried the discontinuation of regattas on Lough Derg 'for the past couple of years'.[174] The writer continued that the regattas 'were the source of recreation and amusement of so innocent and harmless a character, and yet so health-giving, that no one could, I imagine, for a moment object to them.' In reply, the editor of the *Nenagh Guardian* concurred with the views of the letter writer, noting that the regatta was 'eminently calculated to enlarge and refine those socialising and civilising tendencies of our nature, that ennoble and distinguish enlightened humanity' while also apportioning blame to the 'apathy of the inhabitants of our town and its neighbourhood'.[175] Thus the editor was inclined to look for an explanation for the absence of a regatta in the attitude of the population at large rather than focusing on the members of the yacht club. In 1866, a similar letter of discontent from 'Alpha' urged 'some active and influential resident' to promote the regatta. This plea was once again to fall on deaf ears.[176] By 1871, matters had still not improved and another letter writer, 'A lover of sport', lamented the absence of a regatta on the lake.[177] The writer noted that 'we have horse races annually, which attract the scum of society from every part of Ireland', something, he hoped, which would not happen at a regatta. In a similar fashion to the writer of 1865, he too called on Captain Holmes to take the initiative, stating that Holmes would receive the support of every gentleman in the neighbourhood, and I promise him by every merchant and shopkeeper in Nenagh'. By July 1872, normal service was resumed. The regatta was re-established thanks to the exertions of the High Sheriff of Tipperary, Captain Bassett W. Holmes. Yachts varied in tonnage – Bassett Holmes' *Corsair* weighed fifteen tons, while W. Waller's *Fairy* weighed six tons.

In regattas, yachts were handicapped accordingly, with the smaller craft given a timed head start ahead of other entries. Holmes resided at St David's, which was close to the lake. When the regatta of 1878 ended, 'some two hundred of the upper ten thousand, who were at St. Davids', were entertained by the Holmes family.[178] This is one of the key elements of yachting in north Tipperary. It further facilitated the country house residents to meet on a regular basis.

An important element of yachting as a country house sport was that it was principally people who lived in these houses who participated in regattas on Lough Derg. Many resided close to the lake. But there were others, who lived away from its shoreline, such as the Bayly family of Debsborough, who were also active in the affairs of the yacht club. Such was the nature of the surrounding topography and geography that the regattas could also draw on participants from counties Clare and Galway. Yachts from further up the Shannon also participated.[179] When a list of names of those attending meetings of the Ormond Archers in 1859, the Lough Derg Regatta in 1872 and the Ormond Croquet Club in 1875 are cross-referenced, there are twenty instances of the same family surname appearing at two of the three meetings.[180] There are ten family names which are found in attendance at all three events. This was indicative of continuity and familial association over a sustained period. That these families maintained contact throughout the year indicated that considerable time and finances were directed towards sporting activities. This in turn led to local business benefiting from the economic spend involved in supporting these activities.

It also helped – and this was the case across all sports and recreations – that families were prepared to rotate meetings, thus sharing the burdens of organisation and expense. Granted, there was only one lake, yet the residences on its shores and in the surrounding countryside were used for tennis parties, post-regatta 'at home' parties, and other social occasions. It created a bond of fellowship and friendship which bound the Ormond country together. This bond continued through the winter hunting season where the same family names reappeared in a different sporting context, while following hounds with the Ormond and King's County Hunt. This was a form of social elitism and exclusivity – they were not associated, and neither did they want to be, with the mercantile class; it was all about creating a social milieu that was exclusive. There were many individuals whose links brought them into contact with more than one sporting sphere. Bassett Holmes, for example, was not only associated with yachting but also served on the committee of the Ormond Tennis Club and hosted meetings at his home.[181]

Lough Derg Yacht Club played a valuable role in the lives of the landowners and communities of north Tipperary. It was a high-status sport, one which required much capital, both in the accruing and maintenance of yachts. Yachting also required time away from one's residence and land, especially when regattas were held. A regatta lasted for three consecutive days. Races lasted several hours, necessitating a level of fitness that was not required for croquet or archery, though lawn tennis did involve physical exertion. Yachting on Lough Derg was another example of the way in which the country house community manipulated and utilised the countryside to their advantage. It was another status symbol, one which has a long legacy in County Tipperary.

CONCLUSION

Sport within a country house setting was neither regular nor continuous. The number of estates where sporting activities took place under the patronage of a resident landlord was not as extensive as it may initially appear. The degree to which sports came and went in Tipperary is reflected in the way estate games were played. Archery, despite its initial success, its expensive social occasions and the attractions of its medieval connotations and insignia, was eclipsed as the lawn games of croquet and tennis became established. The sporting trends of fashionable London were replicated in rural Tipperary. Without regulatory bodies underpinning sport in Ireland, this state of flux continued. Whether certain sports became established and survived was to some extent determined by the presence or absence of a regulatory body, as with horse racing and cricket. But without the support of local organisational structures, fundamentally based on the country house and estate lands, many of these sports would never have become popular in Tipperary. There were no urban masses in the county to support the growth of sport. Much of the early sport in Tipperary took root among a group of people that were socially removed from the majority of the population. They were also predominantly rural. This was where sport flourished, waxed and, as in the case of archery and croquet, waned.

CHAPTER 3

THE HUNT COMMUNITY

INTRODUCTION

Hunting to hounds can be traced back to the eighteenth century in Tipperary when the Ormond Foxhounds were active in the field.[1] Marjorie Quarton has shown that fox hunting took place around Nenagh from 1738.[2] Elsewhere, in February 1771 a 'sporting doe' was released at Bouladuff where 'a good ordinary and other accommodations' were available near the hunt grounds.[3] In May 1772, Redmond Everard advertised for sale 'thirteen couple of foxhounds, well entered and hunted, with six couple of whelps fit to enter'.[4] Everard lived near Thurles but it is unclear if he hunted his pack in an organised fashion. A meet of the Tipperary Hunt which took place in 1823 was the subject of poetic verse fifty years later.[5]

Prior to this, fox hunting took place in neighbouring County Cork where the Duhallow Foxhounds were active. This pack dated from 1745, making it the oldest hunt in Ireland. This predated the 'new style of fox hunting' in the 1750s by Hugo Meynell of the Quorn Hunt which set the pattern for other hunts to follow. The Duhallow Hunt offers support for Iris Middleton's argument that structured fox hunting pre-dated the activities of Meynell at Quorn.[6] Indeed, much earlier than this is the example of Bishop Dopping of Meath, who maintained a private pack in 1697.[7] Around 1807 in south Tipperary, William Barton, of Grove, 'a descendant of an old Lancashire family from Barton, near Preston', kept a private pack of hounds. A family tradition maintained 'that the Barton pack was going strong even in the eighteenth century'.[8]

Hunting to hounds continued to grow in Tipperary in the nineteenth century. This chapter shows how, from 1840 to 1880, the rate of growth increased even more. There is no evidence to suggest that the hunting experience from 1840 was radically different from that which took place at the end of the eighteenth century. Hunting to hounds was not a necessity. It was something that the landed class and military officers liked to do during the winter months. As their passion for hunting increased so too did the number of hunt packs and the number of hunt meetings. Hunt packs met on a regular and formal basis throughout Tipperary in the same way as similar packs met throughout the rest of Ireland and Great Britain. Hunting, either after foxes, hares or deer, preoccupied many people over the winter months. Less frequently, in the summer months, otters were hunted. Formal county boundaries were not overly important in a sporting context and the patronage of hunt packs clearly illustrates this. A database of the dates and locations of the hunt meetings has been compiled. This allows for an understanding of how important the hunt was to those who followed it.[9] Financing the hunt was a regular concern for many huntsmen and in particular the master of each respective pack, especially those which were subscription packs. Where existing records have been identified, they are used to assess the financial demands which the office of Master of the Foxhounds (MFH) brought to the incumbent.

In the overall context of hunting in County Tipperary, Lord Waterford (with his estate at Curraghmore, County Waterford) and the 14th Earl of Huntingdon (Master of the Ormond and King's County Hounds) were influential in promoting and supporting their respective hunting country. The support and financial backing which the Marquis of Waterford gave to the Tipperary Foxhounds was very important to the hunt community in Victorian Tipperary. The degree to which he established hunting lodges in south Tipperary and the continued additions to his kennel of dogs was testament to his love of hunting. In a sense, he was the first superstar of Tipperary sport. His presence at a hunt gathering or race meeting ensured that large fields of spectators and supporters were there to see him. He was extremely popular with upper-class society. His supporters waved baby blue handkerchiefs when he appeared. This was his trademark colour.

There was never a season from 1840 to 1880 when hunting did not take place. From the middle of the 1860s there was an upsurge in hunting activity recorded in the local and national press, a trend that was also apparent with cricket. In fact, during the winter season of 1879–80, immediately prior to the onset of the Land War, the level of hunting peaked at 356 meetings. This was only the second time that this figure was recorded, the other occasion being the hunting season of 1876–77. However, it is unknown how many meetings were cancelled due to frost or bad weather.

The indiscriminate killing of foxes with poison, by hunt saboteurs or individuals protecting their fowl was very much frowned upon by the various masters. They needed to ensure that there were sufficient foxes available to complement the hard riding, the thrill of the chase and the camaraderie in the field which were important aspects of the hunt. The poisoning of hounds was also an issue that could severely impact on a hunt pack and one with which the MFH had to contend. While foxes were perceived as vermin, the loss of a hunt pack or several dogs, through poison laid on lands, impacted on the finances of the hunt community, irrespective of whether it was a private or a subscription pack.

There was a socio-economic benefit from hunting to hounds in Tipperary. Coverts required maintenance and upkeep. Earth-stoppers were required to prevent foxes from going to ground early in the morning. A whole range of equine trades were required to maintain horse stock, ranging from veterinary expertise to harness and saddle makers. Suppliers of riding apparel advertised in the local press, as they also sought to bring added value to their business. In essence, while the hunting experience provided a sporting and social outlet for many families and individuals in the long winter months, there were many people whose livelihoods were derived in part from the community of the hunt. They relied on the success and continuation of the various hunt packs to create sales and profits at a time of low agricultural output in the county.

THE HUNTING EXPERIENCE

Hunting to hounds in Tipperary took place under five categories: fox, hare, deer, otter and drag hunting. There is minimal evidence for the last three when compared to that of fox or hare hunting. Fox hunting was undertaken countywide in Tipperary from 1840 to 1880. Hare hunting with harriers was more pronounced in the south of the county, especially around Cahir, Cashel and Tipperary. Using quantitative data derived from the contemporary press, a yearly breakdown of hunt meets shows the progression and popularity of hunting during the 1860s and 1870s.

While hunt territory was jealously guarded, there is some evidence to suggest that there was an element of crossover in mid-Tipperary. This was possibly due to the nature of the quarry hunted – a hare as opposed to a fox – and also the demise of some packs. Sometimes the scheduled date for a specific hunt pack coincided with that of another pack. This suggests that there were different locations from which separate hunt packs would set out, though they still covered much of the same hunting country. It is likely that permission to hunt hares on the country of a fox-hunting pack was given. Evidence for deer hunting is limited, suggesting that this form of hunting was only rarely followed between 1840 and 1880. Fox hunting was much more widespread, while hare, otter and drag hunting had followers to lesser extents. In mid-Tipperary hunt packs were not as large as the Tipperary Foxhounds in south Tipperary. In the mid-Tipperary area there was a crossover of different hunts across the period as various packs rose and fell depending on support and longevity.

However, it was not unusual for some harrier packs to hunt deer at irregular intervals during the season. It was a common feature of the hunting season for those who followed with the Barne Hounds, which regularly hunted deer in 1841.[10] Mr Mansergh's hounds were also afforded the opportunity to hunt deer, as were the Clonmel Harriers, the Woodford Harriers and the Arravale Harriers.[11] The Ormond Hounds appeared, at times, unconcerned as to the type of quarry they hunted. In November 1856, they hunted a fox one day and when they met on the next occasion they hunted hares; while this would not have been a popular choice with the true followers of fox hunting, it was noted that the game was 'sufficiently plentiful'.[12]

Otters were principally hunted in and around Nenagh. Lieutenant Greene, one of the local military officers, took to the rivers around the town during the summer months of 1870 with his pack of otter hounds, as has been outlined earlier.[13] Another visitor, Mr Hill, brought his otter pack with him in the summer months of 1870 and 1871. His dogs were described as the best otter pack in Great Britain.[14] Not much is known about Mr Hill or indeed why he came to Tipperary with his otter hounds at this time. Contemporarily, in Wales, the Hon. Geoffrey Hill hunted his otter hounds from Maesllwch Castle, in Radnorshire. This was 'one of the most noted [otter] packs'.[15] The military at Fethard barracks were the only ones that followed a drag hunt. With drag hunting a pack of hounds followed a scent which was laid or dragged over a specific hunting country with a defined start and finish. This could take place during the summer months where the drag would not interfere with crops as the course had been previously defined. It was also a means of keeping hounds exercised.

Deer, fox and hare hunting took place over the winter months when lands were fallow and grass and crops were not under threat of damage from horses. Notices appeared regularly in the press for huntsmen to take heed of newly sown crops. Apart from the foxhound packs it is difficult to identify which packs were followed by mounted followers, by people on foot, or both. The likelihood is that there was a prevalence of both styles for all meets. A meet of the Tipperary Foxhounds in March 1873 attracted over sixty mounted followers 'and quite a cavalcade of fashionable equipages. Conspicuous amongst the four wheelers was the well-appointed drag of the Inniskilling Dragoons.'[16] When the Ormond Hunt met in December 1876, 'the crowd [was] so large on all sides that the foxes were headed by the people on foot, and did not break covert'.[17] This was in stark contrast to the Garrykennedy Harriers which had, in April 1877, an 'unusually small' attendance. The followers amounted to just 'five mounts with the two whips'.[18]

Table 3.1 Hunt packs in County Tipperary, 1840–1880

NAME	HUNT SEASON	TOTAL MEETS
Archerstown Hounds	1843/44; 1846 to 1848	10
Arravale Harriers	1867/68 to 1880/81	592
Ballintemple Blazers	1879/80	4
Ballyboy Harriers	1841/42 to 1842/43	69
Barne Hounds	1839/40 to 1856/57	157
Cahir Garrison Hounds	1846/47 to 1880/81	722
Cahir Hounds	1857/58	26
Cashel Rock Harriers	1850/51 to 1879/80	647
Castletown Harriers	1870/71	3
Clanwilliam Harriers	1841/42; 1861/62	48
Clonmel Hounds	1857/58 to 1880/81	1,144
Curraghmore Foxhounds	1859/60 to 1879/80	63
Earl of Huntingdon Hounds	1876/77 to 1879/80	13
Fethard Garrison Drag Hounds	1873/74	11
Garrykennedy Harriers	1876/77	34
Greenane Hounds	1856/57 to 1861/62	161
Grove Hunt	1839/40	47
Kilkenny Hunt	1839/40; 1878/79	2
King's County Harriers	1867/68	1
Lieut. Greene's Otter Hounds	1870	5
Mr Bennett's Hounds	1864/65; 1866/67	20
Mr Butler Lowe's Hounds	1843/44	1
Mr Thos. Connolly's Harriers	1868/69	1
Mr Gason's Hounds	1865/66	4
Mr Hill's Otter Hounds	1870	2
Mr Jackson's Hounds	1865/66	14
Mr Longworth's Hounds	1864/65	2
Mr Manning's Hounds	1864/65	1
Mr Mansergh's Hounds	1866/67 to 1873/74	352
Mr Parker's Beagles	1869/70	1

NAME	HUNT SEASON	TOTAL MEETS
Mr Parker's & Mr Waller's Beagles	1868/69	1
Nenagh Harriers	1841/42; 1848/49; 1855/56	61
Ormond Hunt	1839/40 to 1862/63; 1866/67 to 1880/81	1,304
Redmondstown Harriers	1839/40 to 1840/41	31
Redmondstown Otter Hounds	1868	1
Slieveardagh Harriers	1852/53 to 1859/60	15
Templemore Beagles	1870/71	1
Templemore Garrison Hounds	1839/40; 1863/64; 1864/65	16
Thurles Harriers	1859/60 to 1860/61	29
Tinvane Hunt	1844/45 to 1849/50	8
Tipperary Foxhounds	1839/40 to 1880/81	1,759
White Hill Harriers	1867/68	4
Woodford Hounds	1874/75 to 1877/78	119
Youghal Harriers	1877/78	143
TOTAL PACKS	**44** **TOTAL MEETS**	**7,649**

Sources: *CC, CG, NG, TA, TC, TE, TFP, TV, TWN* 1839–1881; *Hunting Journal of the 3rd Marquis of Waterford* (Dublin, 1901)

From the winter hunting season of 1839–40 to that of 1880–81, forty-four separate hunt packs active in some part of the county have been identified. They were scheduled to meet cumulatively on 7,649 occasions (Table 3.1).[19] However, it is unknown how many of these meets were lost due to frost, other adverse conditions, or cancellations for funerals.[20] Of the forty-four packs it is likely that twenty-seven were subscription packs, fourteen were maintained as private packs and three were maintained by the military.[21] Subscription packs were those that had an MFH responsible for maintaining the hunt country and the hounds and paying compensation for loss of fowl or property damage during the course of a hunting season. Members were required to pay subscription fees to the MFH to ensure that he would not be personally out of pocket due to the activities of the hunt club. Meet advertisements in the press gave members ample notice not to cross over newly laid fields, young wheat, or clover.[22] Furthermore, fowl money (compensation) was regularly paid out to those tenant farmers who claimed for losses to chicken flocks on account of foxes.[23]

Getting all members to pay their annual fees was easier said than done. Some packs were private and very ephemeral, with little regard to publicity. When Thomas Connolly, a doctor from Castletown House, County Kildare came to stay with the Parkers, at Kilcooley Abbey, he brought with him a stud of horses and his pack of harriers 'to hunt alternatively with them and with the Tipperary Foxhounds'.[24] There were eleven packs active in the 1870–71 and 1879–80 seasons. Ten packs operated in the county during the hunt seasons of 1868–69, 1876–77 and 1877–78. The five-year period prior to the onset of the Land War was the most active for hunting countywide. This is reinforced when the hunt dates are analysed, showing that one quarter of all scheduled meetings took place during this period. The total was 1,773 meets or 23.18 per cent.[25] What this evidence suggests is that opposition to the hunt in Tipperary was virtually non-existent in the years immediately preceding the Land War. This was to change once the land agitation commenced in 1881 and the followers of the hunt bore the brunt of it.[26] The Ormond Hunt 'continued to have trouble with the Land League' and from 1882 to 1896 they had only a few meetings.[27] However, in south Tipperary, by the autumn of 1882 calls were made to re-establish local hunts.[28]

During the Great Famine hunting to hounds continued throughout Tipperary, where there were seven active hunting packs out in the field. Their existence suggests a continuance of what had become a pattern from the eighteenth century, with hunting concentrated in the autumn and winter months. One thing which greatly assisted the growth of fox hunting in particular was that foxes were not subject to the game laws, as they were considered vermin as distinct from game. A prerequisite necessary to hold such a game licence was that one

Figure 3.1 Number of hunt meets in County Tipperary, 1839/40 to 1880/81

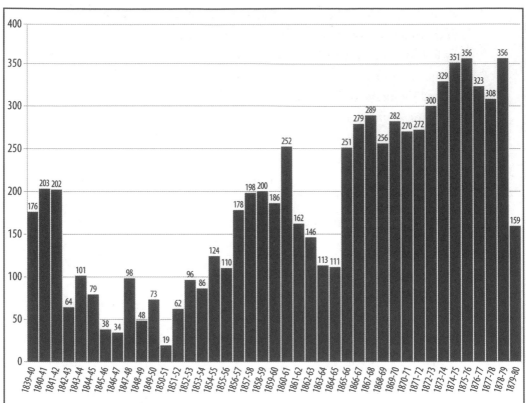

Sources: *CC, CG, NG, TA, TC, TE, TFP, TV, TWN* 1839–1881; *Hunting Journal of the 3rd Marquis of Waterford* (Dublin, 1901).

needed to have an estate of 1,000 acres or an income of £100 or more annually to qualify.[29] Clearly this excluded all but the wealthy from holding such a licence. Fox hunting was outside of game licensing laws and tenant farmers could, if they desired, follow a hunt provided that they were members. The list of hunt meets published in the local press suggests that the 1851–52 season had the least hunting activity (Figure 3.1). There were only two packs out in the field and they hunted for only nineteen days. The seasons of greatest activity were 1876–77 and 1878–79, when there were 356 hunt meetings. Based on the press schedules, this heightened activity in 1876 also coincided with the peak period for cricket playing in the county, which is dealt with in Chapter 6. In essence, this was all part of an annual sporting calendar of the landed gentry. When the hunting season ended the playing of cricket became one of their focal points for socialisation and entertainment.

During the 1870s reports of a sporting nature appeared with greater frequency in the local press. This can be seen when statistics for specific sports are compared against each other. A decline in hunting in the mid-1860s is explained by the non-appearance of the Ormond Hunt for three years owing to issues with local land agitation.[30]

Out of a total of 7,649 hunt meets recorded, the day of the week on which hunt packs were out can be positively established for 7,647 days. This was indicative of the whole organisational structure surrounding the hunt. It also demonstrates that there were many men and women, mainly landowners, who had sufficient time on their hands that they could afford to give to hunting. The results show that the most popular hunting day was Monday. Wednesday was the least favoured day, as is shown in Table 3.2. No definitive reason is offered as to why Wednesday was not a good day for hunting. What is suggested here, based on the evidence of the other weekday totals, was that Wednesday was taken as a rest day to allow horses and hounds recover after a day in the field, especially when pack numbers were small and dogs were used two or three times a week. Hunt meetings never took place on a Sunday.

Table 3.2 Day of week for hunt meets in County Tipperary, 1840–1880

Monday	1,695	Thursday	1,397
Tuesday	1,575	Friday	1,559
Wednesday	371	Saturday	1,050
		TOTAL	7,647

Sources: *CC, CG, NG, TA, TC, TE, TFP, TV, TWN* 1839–1881; *Hunting Journal of the 3rd Marquis of Waterford* (Dublin, 1901)

The three most prolific hunt packs in Tipperary were the Tipperary Foxhounds (1,759), the Ormond Hunt, which was also joined with the King's County Hunt at various periods (1,304) and the Clonmel Hounds/Harriers (1,144). These were the only hunt packs which met more than 1,000 times during the period of this analysis. Three packs met more than 500 times, five met on more than 100 occasions, sixteen met ten times or more and nine met on less than ten occasions. Of the packs identified, eight appeared in the press listings on a single occasion, though in all likelihood they were out in the field much more than this.

Apart from the poisoning of Lord Waterford's hounds in 1842 (see below), the various hunt packs for the next thirty years suffered no interference or unrest. Even the construction and development of the railway network in the country from the mid-1840s was never a cause of friction between the railway companies or the various hunt bodies. The range of hunting experiences varied and newspaper accounts of the various meets over the years told of 'brilliant runs', 'the run of the season' or a 'sporting day' as self-styled hunt reporters 'Larky Grigg' and 'Tally Ho' wrote bi-weekly accounts of hunt meets. Indeed, a claim could be made that 'Larky Grigg' was the first dedicated sports reporter in Tipperary, such was the volume and regularity of his columns 'from our special correspondent' in the *Clonmel Chronicle*.[31]

The evidence from the press also suggests that hunting to hounds meant different things to different people and that the various classes derived their own benefits from hunting. For the labouring class they got a spectacle, a form of spectator sport which added colour and excitement to what was often a humdrum and difficult existence. The participants had the thrill of the chase, a social occasion and an opportunity to meet their contemporaries during the long winter months. In an account of a run by the Ormond Hunt, on 23 February 1872, it was remarked that 'the countrymen who witnessed the run were highly delighted, and gave every assistance ... several rushed up to the master begging him to come to Old Court soon again, as there were two more foxes to be had there, and declaring they never saw such a hunt in their lives before'.[32] But this was to change. In March

Figure 3.2 Meet dates of the Tipperary Hunt, 1871

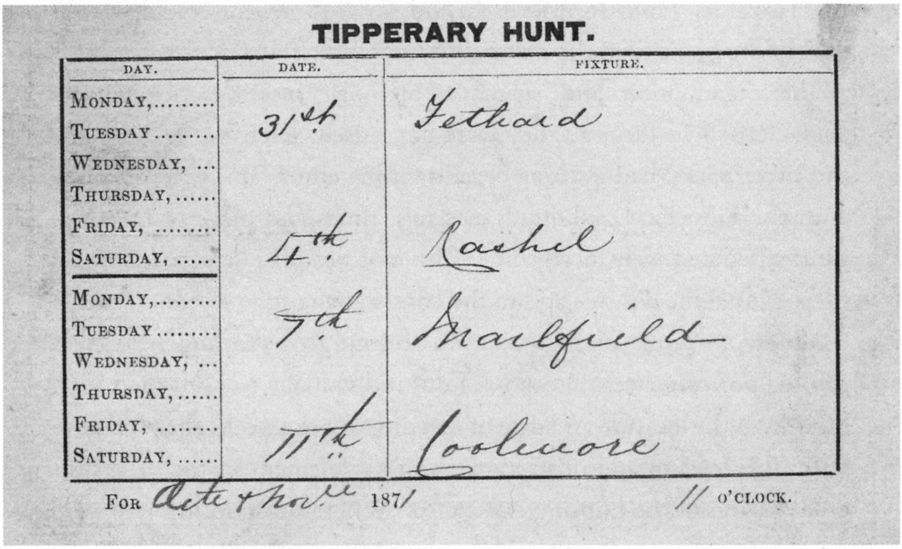

TIPPERARY HUNT.

DAY.	DATE.	FIXTURE.
Monday, ... Tuesday .... Wednesday, ... Thursday, ...	31ˢᵗ	Fethard
Friday, ... Saturday, ...	4ᵗʰ	Cashel
Monday, ... Tuesday .... Wednesday, ...	7ᵗʰ	Marlfield
Thursday, ... Friday, ... Saturday, ...	11ᵗʰ	Coolmore

For *Octr & Novr* 1871   11 O'CLOCK.

Source: Murphy Archive, Tipperary Studies, Tipperary County Council Library Service, Thurles

---

Figure 3.3 Subscription fees due to the Rock Harriers, 1878

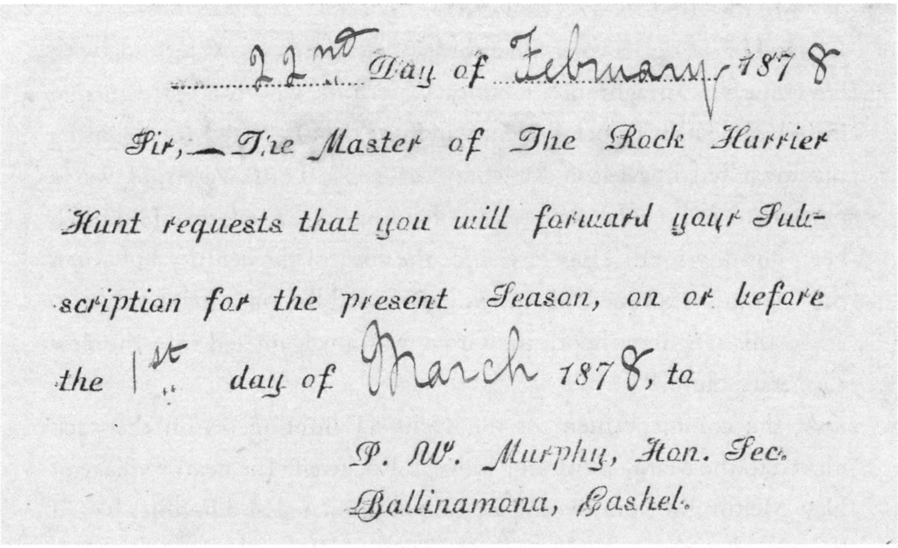

22ⁿᵈ Day of February 1878

Sir,—The Master of The Rock Harrier Hunt requests that you will forward your Subscription for the present Season, on or before the 1ˢᵗ day of March 1878, to

P. W. Murphy, Hon. Sec.
Ballinamona, Cashel.

Source: Murphy Archive, Tipperary Studies, Tipperary County Council Library Service, Thurles

1874 the burning of a covert at Dangan prompted some members of the Tipperary Hunt to offer a reward for information which would lead to the identity of the culprits.[33]

The organisation and structure of hunt meetings was clearly characterised in the way they were advertised. Each hunt, especially the larger packs, had a strong organisational ethos. This was very clear with the Tipperary Foxhounds as dates, times and place of meetings were scheduled well in advance, with notifications sent to the local press. Not alone did this add to the consistency of the season, it added reliability in terms of the successful running of the hunt. Pre-paid printed postcards were also posted out individually to hunt members, indicating the location and date of meetings for the weeks ahead (Figure 3.2). This level of administration was a key element in the successful organisation of the hunting experience. Where subscription fees were due, a similar means of informing members was also used, as is shown in Figure 3.3.

HENRY DE LA POER BERESFORD, 3RD MARQUIS OF WATERFORD

It was Henry de La Poer Beresford, 3rd Marquis of Waterford, with his estate at Curraghmore, County Waterford, who was instrumental in enlarging the Tipperary Hunt in June 1840. Noted for 'painting the town red in Melton Mowbray' in 1837, Lord Waterford was a passionate and regular supporter of fox hunting. The Grove Hunt had been hunting south Tipperary since the start of the century but when the Marquis 'expressed his intention of establishing a kennel or two … in this neighbourhood' the Grove was amalgamated into the new Tipperary Hunt.[34]

At the commencement of the 1840–41 hunting season the pack moved to the Marquis' hunting lodge at Rockwell. The nearby village of New Melton Mowbray was 'splendidly illuminated and bonfires blazed in every direction to welcome the "Tips"'.[35] The logistics of running, resting and moving foxhounds around south Tipperary was a feat in itself, but Lord Waterford ensured its success by having in place separate hunt packs which were alternated around the county. In April 1841, the Marquis travelled to England to enhance his hunting interests, where he purchased a further twenty-five couples of foxhounds. This raised the complement of hounds in his possession to three packs.[36] This new stock, from 'Mr. Villebois' Hampshire kennels and Lord Lonsdale's "Border Hounds"', added to the strength of the Marquis' pack and his ability to hunt at even greater regularity.[37]

In 1842, he married Louisa Stuart, daughter of the 1st Baron Stuart de Rothsay, and they settled in Curraghmore House, County Waterford.[38] At the outset, the Tipperary Hunt met three days a week, but by February 1842 this had increased to four days a week, and was further aided by the purchase of an additional pack of hounds in August of that year, kennelled in Rockwell.[39] Altogether, there were seventy-five couple of hounds kennelled and ninety horses stabled at Rockwell. The hounds were taken back to Curraghmore at the end of each hunting season.[40] Yet despite the resources and money spent on supporting and building up the Tipperary Hunt in its formative years, the largesse of the Marquis was not without its detractors. Committed as he was to hunting in Tipperary, his beloved hounds received a serious setback when several of them were poisoned at Dangan covert on 29 December 1842.[41] This act provoked widespread indignation and revulsion among the hunting community and landowners at large. An address in the name of over 300 gentlemen, military officers, farmers and Roman Catholic clergy in support of the sporting interests of the Marquis was published in the local press.[42] Lord Waterford subsequently moved his hunting establishment to Lakefield, Fethard, but apparent malicious intent was to follow him there also. In October 1843 his stable block was subjected to an arson attack. The nationalist *Tipperary Free Press* openly stated that Waterford 'oppressed no one – expelled no one – insulted no one. Wherefore then should he be molested?'[43] But the paper did infer that there was some local hostility to his employment of Carrick-on-Suir or Curraghmore tradesmen at Lakefield in preference to Fethard tradesmen. It did not, however, elaborate if this was the reason behind the fire. In any case, Lord Waterford had had enough. In an open letter 'to the gentlemen of County Tipperary' he outlined his reasons for abandoning fox hunting in the county, 'feeling that such a system of annoyance more than counterbalanced the pleasures of fox hunting for which I alone proposed to reside at Lakefield'.[44] His tenure in Tipperary was brief but his legacy was lengthy. The Mastership of the hunt was transferred to James Millet. The Marquis placed one pack of his own hounds at the hunt's disposal when he departed the Tipperary hunting scene.

In the 1843–44 season, a subscription of £600 was entered into for the management of the Tipperary Hunt for the first time in its history.[45] This was a large sum of money for the Hunt to raise, mindful that thirty years later the subscription fee was £700.[46] It was an indication of the level of support the hunt community enjoyed in the pre-Famine period. Subscription packs were a feature of fox hunting in England from the late eighteenth century. In 1798, George Baker, of Elmore Hall, took on the duties of MFH of the Durham County Hounds for 'an annual subscription of 800 guineas'.[47] David Itzkowitz has shown that by 1820, hunting countries had taken on some form of 'rudimentary organisation' which was then left to 'interested sportsmen to see what arrangements could be made' for the future success of the hunt.[48] The transfer of the hounds from Lord Waterford to Millet was an early example of a subscription pack in Tipperary, similar to those in existence in England where retiring masters were replaced by a committee. This happened with the Albrighton Hunt in 1830.[49]

Those who followed and subscribed to the hunt were men who could afford it; they had time and money to indulge their winter passion. 'Old Whip', a letter writer to the *Nenagh Guardian* in March 1844, summed it up quite simply. Taking offence at the contents of a prior letter published in that paper, 'Old Whip' noted that 'grocers, taylors [sic], etc' and other business people in Nenagh 'have more sense than to lose their time in such idle pursuits; all the persons I could see at the hunt that day ... have sufficient property to support them independently'.[50] Hunting to hounds was a socially elite pastime which the propertied class could indulge in principally because they wanted to and they could afford to. Hunting was more than simply paying a subscription fee, it was an entrée to a sporting and social life where gentlemen could socialise exclusively around the hunt.[51]

However, many people wished to hunt with the Marquis as it gave them celebrity association. It was noted when the Tipperary Hounds met near Cahir in November 1842 that there was 'seldom witnessed a more numerous field of sportsmen'.[52] Similarly in March 1863, when the 4th Marquis' Curraghmore Hounds hunted with the Tipperary Hounds in Fethard, 'all the fashion and beauty of the surrounding counties of Kildare, Limerick, Kilkenny, Waterford and Tipperary were well represented. There were a great number of ladies on horseback and from about 300 to 400 gentlemen in pink and other colours.'[53] The appearance of so many people was due in no small part to the participation of the Marquis. The presence of such a large gathering was one of emulation and it epitomised hunting as one of those 'socially representative events carried out within the landed class'.[54] His financial strength and willingness to provide hounds, horses and a kennel were key ingredients in establishing a hunt in Tipperary, which was strong in all of its essential components. But when he departed for Curraghmore a subscription hunt was established, one which would now rely on its members to keep it sustained.

HORSE STOCK FOR HUNTING

While not all hunt communities provided horses for each participant, some, such as the Ormond Hunt and the Tipperary Hunt, did keep stables for members. This was required when hunt meetings were frequent and horses needed rest. The role of the tenant farmer in providing horses and the financial rewards which he could make from the sale of a good horse was an important element in an emerging equine community. Central to this was good breeding. Stallion stations were in place around the county, indicative of the level of organisation that was in place as owners sought to generate income.

While the various hunts were self-regulated and subscribed, it was important that they maintained the support of local tenant farmers as hunts were alert to the need for good community relations. The committee of the Tipperary Hunt, for example, was ever vigilant in this respect and cognisant of the need to keep the tenant farmers onside. At a meeting in May 1864 it was observed that:

> ... keeping a pack of foxhounds was of great service to a county, in improving the breed of horses so greatly sought after, and in affording an inducement for the gentry to remain at home where sport can be had, and spend their money in this country instead of becoming *absentees* ... [and] give every encouragement to their tenantry to support the foxhounds as the best means of promoting an improved breed of horses.[55]

In England during most of the nineteenth century 'an average hunter cost around £75 to £150, and £300 to £400 was generally considered a high price'.[56] For the Marquis of Waterford much of his hunting expense was recouped at his annual stud sales, though prices varied considerably. In 1856 he sold seventy horses ranging in price from £400 at the top end down to £7 for a yearling. Geldings, fillies, yearlings and brood mares were knocked down at less than £30 each. The racing stock commanded better prices.[57] However, the Marquis was tragically killed while returning home after a successful day in the field in March 1859.[58] His 'extensive and celebrated stud' came under the hammer the following June with potential buyers from all parts of Ireland, England and France in attendance.[59] This was indicative of his status and the quality of the horses at his disposal. Once more prices varied greatly, especially for the racehorses. The most expensive prices paid on the day were for the hunting horses. Of this stock, fourteen hunters sold for £100 or more. The top price paid for any horse in the auction was £300. Fifteen horses were sold for less than £100. The cheapest horse sold for £30. The sale also saw twenty-nine couple of hounds sold. Fifteen couples realised £76 3s and fourteen couples were sold for £55.[60] Another example of the sort of money generated from horse sales was that made by John Going, MFH. He sold one of his horses at the Punchestown races where he received '£250 for a four-year-old horse untried, except to fox hunting'.[61]

Farmers also bred horses and these were often offered for sale to various members of the hunting community. One hunter which the Marquis of Waterford purchased for £35 from a tenant farmer was subsequently sold for £200.[62] The local press also noted that it was good business for farmers to breed horses and maintain the hunting stock as there would always be a market. In late 1869, P. Quinlan sold a 'weight-carrying hunter to Capt. Craige, of Edinburgh for £100'.[63] Horses were central to hunting and with a demand for hunters several people took the opportunity to make some money from their stallions. Newspapers regularly carried advertisements as to where celebrated stallions would stand during a particular year. It was not uncommon for stallions to stand at several different locations during any given week. John Bennett, Oldtown, Templemore ran his own pack of hounds from 1865 to 1867. His stallion Fingall stood for the 1871 season. The stallion was limited to covering sixty mares. His stallion served gentlemen's mares for £2 10s and farmers' mares for one pound less.[64] The fee for a thoroughbred mare was four guineas, with five shillings charged for the groom. Half-bred mares were serviced for half this price and the groom's fees were also halved. Working farmers' horses stood for one and a half guineas, with half a crown going to the groom. Similar fees and standing arrangements in many areas of Tipperary were widely advertised in the press.[65] This laid a sound foundation for the growth of horse racing. A demand for thoroughbreds and hunters gave many farmers and stallion owners an opportunity to expand their own income, by way of stud fees or the subsequent sale of a horse.

However, a difficulty with inferring too much about farmer involvement from these press advertisements is that no evidence has been identified to indicate who actually brought mares to these stallions. Neither is it known for what purposes were the foals used. The social status of the people who brought their mares to the stallions might have impacted on the desired use of the subsequent foals. Farmers bred horses for use on the farm as much as huntsmen bred them for hunting. What is clear is that there was a demand for stallion services and this need underpinned agricultural, hunting and racing needs to a degree which is, as of yet, undetermined. The sheer volume of hunt meetings ensured that there was always a demand for horses in Tipperary. There was also the chance that a horse well ridden in the field would catch the eye of likely purchasers. There were several means by which diligent men could prosper from the hunt community and those that did were regularly and handsomely rewarded.

FINANCING THE HUNT

When compared with contemporary hunt clubs in England, as with other aspects of sport and recreation in Tipperary, there was no new money or industrialists behind hunt committees. Reports of hunt club meetings in Tipperary which appeared in the press show that all the leading positions were filled by landowners. These were regularly deputy lieutenants, justices of the peace or in the case of Lord Waterford, a marquis. But financing a hunt did not come cheaply. Delmé Radcliffe, Master of the Hertfordshire Hounds, was advised that 'you will never have your hand out of your pocket, and must always have a guinea in it'.[66] For a calendar year in the late 1830s Delmé Radcliffe estimated that the costs for an establishment of twelve horses and fifty couples of hounds was £1,885 11s 0d.[67] For the various hunt clubs in Tipperary their expenditure never came to such a high figure.

A problem with insufficient finance was always to the fore when the Tipperary Hunt Club met for their end of season review. In May 1863 it was stated at a meeting of the club that an outlay of £700 was required to maintain the hunt in a normal year. However, rarely had income reached £400.[68] It left a shortfall and this fell to the master, John Going, to cover. John Going (1822–1873), based at Wilford, was the head of one branch of the extended Going family that had residences at various locations around County Tipperary.[69] The Going lineage descended from Robert Going of Cranagh, whose 'will was proved in 1732'.[70] The fact that the two county representatives in parliament were not on the list of subscribers to the Tipperary Hunt was deemed regrettable, on the basis that the members refused 'to support their county hounds'. It was further stated, that the neighbouring Master of Curraghmore Foxhounds in County Waterford received from 'his small constituency

£700 and is supplied with horses and every requirement necessary'. John Going, at times, did not have an easy tenure as Master of the Tipperary Foxhounds as there were constant financial concerns about the levels of subscriptions and the viability of the hunt.

A continued shortfall in subscription fees tested his patience. In October 1871, at another meeting of the Tipperary Hunt Club, Mr W. Burges acknowledged the important role of John Going, though it was at a 'great pecuniary loss to himself as master'.[71] This was a recurrent theme, as in 1872 Going himself commented that he had 'suffered considerable pecuniary loss from keeping up the hounds, especially through the famine years from 1848 to 1852, when I did not receive as much as actually paid the men's wages'.[72] Going had assumed the Mastership of the Tipperary Hunt in 1846.[73] Total outlay for the 1863–64 season was £487 17s 6d. This represented a saving of £162 on the previous year 'owing to the economical management of the hounds and the reduction in the price of fodder', mindful that there was not one blank day in the season.[74] It was no small coincidence that one of the members claimed that they had 'better sport for less money'. But the savings were not to last! At a subsequent meeting of the Tipperary Hunt in May 1872 the accounts, when presented, showed that by the end of the 1871–72 season the total expenditure was £796 13s 10d. This represented an increase of over £300 on the returns of 1863–64. Table 3.3 outlines the receipts for the season.

A shortfall in subscriptions for the 1871–72 season meant that, yet again, Going had to contribute from his own funds to meet the

Table 3.3 Income for Tipperary Foxhounds, 1871–1872

Subscriptions for 1871	£543 5s 0d
Field money	£164 19s 9d
Manure at kennel	£ 8 0s 0d
Total receipts	£716 4s 9d

Source: *Clonmel Chronicle*, 8 May 1872

Table 3.4 Members who increased subscriptions to Tipperary Hunt, June 1872

NAME	OCCUPATION	SUB. FOR 1871	SUB. FOR 1872
S.H. Barton	Estate owner (5,119a)	£25	£30
William Burges	Unknown	£20	£25
Lockyer Burges	Unknown	£20	£25
James Chadwick	Landowner (356a)	£10	£15
William Ryall	Landowner/farmer (87a)	£5	£15
Samuel Perry	Estate owner (2,768a)	£10	£15
Richard Grubb	Landowner (635a)	£5	£7

Source: *Clonmel Chronicle*, 8 June 1872.

expenses. Though subscriptions were up by £21 10*s* on the 1870–71 season, the expenditure was also up. This was primarily due to an increase in the prices for oats, and also wages. The club proposed to raise the subscription to £700 so that they could retain the services of Going as master or 'resign all hope of the future hunting of the country'.[75] The reality was that there was little onus on the members of the Tipperary Hunt to ensure that the hunt survived, apart from paying their subscriptions. This was something that did not go unnoticed. At that same meeting, Captain Moore commented that 'Tipperary ought to be ashamed of some of the subscriptions … they are so small. In England the least sum to constitute a person a member of a hunt is £10.'[76] At another meeting in June the increased subscription fees of seven members was outlined to the meeting. Those who increased their subscriptions in 1872 are represented in Table 3.4. Sixteen new subscribers for 1872 are represented in Table 3.5.[77]

The small sum of £182 1*s* was subscribed, with £700 eventually promised in subscriptions. Patrick Walshe, a new tenant farmer member, outlined his reasons for subscribing. He stated that what led him to

Table 3.5 New subscribers to Tipperary Hunt, June 1872

NAME	OCCUPATION	SUB. for 1872
Richard Smith, Cahir	Mill owner	£2
Edward Grubb	Milling	£5
John Cooney	Business	£5
R.W. White	Landowner (666a)	£3
Rickard Wall (for his servants)	Landowner (376a)	£5
John Shee	Landowner/farmer (29a)	£3
Benjamin Going	Business	£5
William Hunt	Unknown	£5
Charles Clibborn	Unknown	£5
Captain Milman	Military	£5
Patrick Guiry	Unknown	£5
John N. Langley	Estate owner (1,724a)	£5
James Quinlan	Unknown	£2
Patrick Walshe, Glenbower	Tenant farmer	£2
James O'Connell	Unknown	£2 2s.
A. Frend	Unknown	£1

Source: *Clonmel Chronicle*, 8 June 1872

contribute was a 'desire to keep up the fine old sport of fox-hunting as a means of keeping the country gentry around them. If they did not remain at home the farmers could not live.'[78] This sense of attachment reflected the ties which bound some landlords and tenant farmers. What is more intriguing here is that tenant farmers were not normally eligible to subscribe as members of a hunt. The fact that the Tipperary Hunt was prepared to open its subscription list to tenant farmers in 1872 is indicative of the financial pressures faced by the MFH and the hunt in general. This was not specific to the Tipperary Hunt. The Westmeath Hunt also permitted 'bona fide' farmers after 1875, with thirteen of them added to the membership profile of the hunt.[79]

Coupled with this development, though the land was owned by various landlords they also required the support of the tenant farmers to indulge their fox hunting passions. It required goodwill on both sides, in relation to access and the potential for crop damage. Accounts of the various meets, however biased in favour of the hunt, regularly reported that farmers and country people were supportive of the practice. The interaction between the tenant farmers and the lower classes with the hunting community mirrored that of England.[80] In Walshe's case, by subscribing to the hunt he raised his own social status. Though he would have had no choice about who hunted over his rented land, as the hunting rights belonged to his landlord, his support would not have gone unnoticed. Essentially, every member of the local community knew their place and accepted their status. But by supporting the hunt by whatever means, tenant farmers such as Walshe were giving tacit support for its continuation. But this support was not going to last. In Tipperary there was no threat from an emerging industry or large metropolitan area to undermine the rural nature of the county. Rather, what undermined the whole countryside alliance of the hunt was the Land War. This ripped apart the whole fabric which united landlord and tenant, master and servant. It ultimately led to the collapse of the hunt as the 'peculiar privilege' of hunting over a farmer's tenanted lands was for the most part denied to the hunt. The erection of wire fences, the burning of coverts or general disruption to the organisation of the hunt community all had a negative impact.[81]

Yet financial constraints were a constant threat to the Tipperary Foxhounds. At a meeting of the hunt in May 1873 several contentious issues arose.[82] The meeting was informed that the 7th Dragoon Guards, based at Cahir barracks, could hunt cheaper with the Waterford Foxhounds than with the Tipperary Hounds. The garrison regularly kept a pack of harriers which ran in the name of the regiment stationed there. Officers hunted with the foxhounds on days when the harriers were in the kennels. Having resigned from the Mastership of the hunt owing to ill-health, John Going offered the hounds to his successor on condition that he 'hunt this country as it has been hunted, and that he will keep up pure blood in the kennel ... should the hounds be given up now, or at any future time ... I claim them as my property'. The difficulty now lay in getting a new master.

At a meeting of the Tipperary Hunt Club in Clonmel no successor was willing to come forward and it was decided 'to have the pack advertised in the *Irish Sportsman, The Field, Bell's Life* and the local papers'.[83] The social cachet of being MFH was not enough to initially attract a prompt response to the vacancy. Promised subscription fees were expected to amount to £700. This left a shortfall of £40, of which £20 was a bad debt. The non-payment of subscription fees, it was felt, was the main reason why gentlemen would not offer their candidacy for the office of Master. The difference between the more affluent hunt clubs in England and those aspiring to that status was clearly outlined by Captain Moore, who informed the meeting 'that in England gentlemen of large means are anxious to come over to hunt the pack for the season in each year ... the hunting we have now would be very different from what it would be if £8,000 or £10,000 per year English money were spent ... carrying on the hunting on a scale that we could never attempt'.[84] In spite of this tantalising scenario Moore added that 'the general rumour is the farmers will not tolerate anyone in charge of the hounds save a local gentleman'.[85] This ultimately fell back on the Going family. It was stated that the farmers were anxious that the hounds remain in the hands of a member of the Going family, a resolution seconded by John Hanrahan, a tenant farmer from Ninemilehouse. Hanrahan commented that his family were 'well aware of our obligations to the Going family'.[86] After much discussion Benjamin Going offered to take the hounds for one year if no suitable gentleman could be found to take them after they were advertised for sale.

At a subsequent meeting on the matter a letter enquiring about the vacant position of Master, from William Sergar, Colchester, was read out to the members.[87] Sergar argued that £600 was inadequate to hunt the country as in England this would cost £12,000. To take up the position he required a guarantee of £1,000 'to do the business in a handsome, workmanlike manner'.[88] The influential opinion of Lord Donoughmore appeared to have swayed the day as he said 'he would not like to see Tipperary hunted by extraneous aid'.[89] It was to prove a critical intervention, one which may have ultimately saved the Tipperary Hunt from collapse. In England the increasing numbers of outsiders attracted to the various hunts, coupled with decreasing tenancies, meant that farmers were not supporting the hunt as they used to.[90] All indications were that the same would happen in Tipperary. Once more attentions turned towards Benjamin Going. He subsequently agreed to take over the pack for one year, provided that the coverts were attended to. The issue here was one of scale. If the Tipperary Hunt was going to attract the best master, then a basic requirement was that all members should pay their subscriptions on time and honour a commitment made to him. Clearly, this was not happening with some members. Sergar was not too demanding in seeking basic requirements to finance the hunt.[91] It was something which the members failed to grasp completely, irrespective of their desire to have the pack remain in the hands of the Going family. The fact that no member was willing to come forward as Master demonstrated that the financial strength was not there for the hunt to exist long-term if the issue surrounding the Mastership was not resolved.

Subsequently, true to his promise, Benjamin Going gave up the hunt in April 1875. A new Master was once again sought, one who would hunt the country two days per week.[92] This new Master, Mr Bellamy, Blackheath, Kent was duly appointed in June 1877 with a guarantee of £700 in subscription fees. For this figure he would 'supply horse, saddles, etc., pay for the kennel and afford good sport'.[93] His tenure was brief, however, as in March 1878 Captain MacNaughten was elected the new Master. His term of office commenced on 1 May.[94]

Problems with payment of annual subscription fees to the Tipperary Hunt were also replicated with the Ormond Hunt. In 1868 James N. Atkinson paid £5 subscription to Captain Saunders. Atkinson hoped for good hunting as the country was 'well stocked with foxes this summer by Welsh, getting about forty from [the] Kerry mountains'.[95]

Welsh, who was the Master in 1867, made a present of them to the club, not wishing to keep them any longer. No-one would accept the Mastership and a committee of management was formed. A nominal master, secretary and treasurer were appointed to carry on the business. Captain Saunders was appointed the interim Master. Captain Stoney gave a kennel at Kyle Park and accommodation for horses, huntsman and helpers near his house. Denis Crane was retained as huntsman for £50 for the six months ending 1 May 1868. A groom appointed to mind his horses received ten shillings per week, the kennel man received seven shillings per week, and the earth warner (M. Kennedy) received five shillings per week.[96]

Though there was a prestige associated with the position of Master, the recurring theme of 'pecuniary loss' was also heard in Ormond country. In February 1872 a meeting of the Ormond Hunt was held to discuss the appointment of a new Master. George Jackson had resigned from the position. Jackson explained that it was his opinion that 'the Mastership involved pecuniary loss to every gentleman who had ever filled the post'.[97] It was a problem in Tipperary that was not easily resolved, irrespective of the amount of guaranteed subscriptions the respective hunts received. Lord Hastings, King's County Hunt, was appointed Master and he stated that all he required from the members were foxes. He would supply horses, hounds and men and hunt two days per week, provided he was guaranteed £200 in May and £200 in January. This guarantee he received from three unnamed members.[98] But to achieve this fee an increase in subscription rates to the Hunt was necessary. When initially informed of Hastings' demands, Andrew Crawford stated that 'the Ormonds never subscribed £400 a year'; the sum, after hard struggling, came to £250.[99] However, Hastings was guaranteed his money and the Hunt was able to continue.

But all was not well with some members of the Ormond Hunt. In February 1873 a letter was forwarded to the *Nenagh Guardian* complaining of a loss to subscribers because the hounds were not hunting. The newspaper noted that the concluding part of the letter was 'altogether unwarranted' and the editor neglected to publish it.[100] It sparked a wave of responses to the paper in support of Lord

Hastings, highlighting the indignation which the members felt towards the letter-writer. James N. Atkinson had initially set the ball rolling by questioning the title of the pack as it appeared on 'the cards of meets'.[101] He argued that the pack should be called the 'Ormond Hounds' and not 'Lord Hastings' Hounds'. Hastings replied and he referred to the arrangements which had been made at hunt meetings in the previous year. At these meetings he said that he would supply the hounds. He further added that it was not a problem if his hounds were advertised as the 'Ormond and King's County Hunt'.[102] Then the issue surrounding the paucity of hunting days arose. There was some concern expressed that the Hunt did not meet regularly enough. It prompted the Hunt committee to call a meeting whereby the solidarity of the members conveyed to Hastings their full support. 'Thirty-four sporting gentlemen' attended and resolved that their 'best thanks' were due to Hastings 'for the satisfactory manner in which he has hunted the country during one of the most trying seasons on record'.[103]

At a review of the 1873–74 hunting season a feeling was expressed by W.T. Trench (Treasurer) that Lord Hastings would not continue as Master as he was out of pocket by £82 11s 4d on the season. It was further stated that it would be impossible for Hastings to continue for 'the ensuing season unless the £82 were paid and £400 guaranteed for the forthcoming season'.[104] To a man in his position it appeared that he was being difficult in trying to extract the outstanding contribution from other hunt members. But, historically, the sum of £400 had not been attained in any of the seasons for which it had been guaranteed to Hastings. The total subscriptions for 1872–73 amounted to £344, while up to 18 April 1874 only £372 13s had been subscribed. This shortfall plus fowl money, fines and other expenses only exacerbated Hastings' losses. The stand taken by Hastings also gave him the opportunity to omit the Ormond country from his hunting territory. All told, W.T. Trench informed the meeting that he had heard Lord Hastings say that hunting the two countries, Ormond and King's County, 'cost him £800, [and] that the entire hunting of the country costs him over £1,200'.[105] Before the end of the 1875–76 hunting season Hastings announced that he was giving up the Ormond country. The distance was too far for him and 'the expenses so great for two days a week'.[106] The financial demand on Hastings was too great for him to indulge his passion and support his friends in their desire to chase foxes. But indulge them he did. For three seasons he hunted the Ormond country with 'great satisfaction to lovers of sport in this part of north Tipperary, and won great popularity for himself among all classes'.[107] His absence left a void in the Ormond country, one which was not easily resolved. The Hunt Club resolved to raise the subscription income to £500 and if this was achieved representations would be made to Lord Huntingdon to remain on as Master of the Ormond Hounds.[108] It left the community of the hunt in a quandary. Hastings did not have a change of heart. He left the Ormond Hunt country, but in doing so gave them the pack which he had used for the previous three seasons.[109]

The primary difficulty with both the Tipperary Hunt and the Ormond Hunt was internal and stemmed from an inability to sufficiently recompense the Master for losses endured during the hunting season. There were also problems associated with the almost perennial shortfall in subscription fees. There was nothing unique in the financial difficulties experienced by both hunt bodies. The Westmeath Hunt Club had similar difficulties, where officials and committee members also had the unenviable task of getting members to honour their financial commitments, as well as subscribing 'funds to maintain infrastructure'.[110] When compared with the leading fox hunting packs in England one could infer that there were delusions of grandeur in Tipperary in terms of what the members aimed for as opposed to what they actually got for their money. That these two hunt packs were regularly on the brink of financial embarrassment in the 1870s did not make them unique. In Australia, the Adelaide Hunt was also a victim of financial uncertainty in its early years. The pack was advertised for sale several times during the 1850s.[111]

Moreover, the malicious burning of the coverts of the Tipperary Hunt in 1879 resulted in the offer of £100 reward for information leading to the identity of those involved.[112] It added an extra expense to a club that could ill-afford it. This was the start of land agitation and unrest aimed at the Tipperary Hunt. Ongoing threats to the survival of hunt packs in Ireland and England were the order of the day as the agricultural depression of the late 1870s set in. The impending impact of the Land War was yet to be felt. That the hunt packs survived the impact of the Land War and were able to re-establish themselves and return to the field demonstrated that there was a great will and desire for the sport to continue.

THE MILITARY

Surprisingly, given the proliferation of military barracks in Tipperary, there was little comment in the local press about military involvement with hunting. This was in stark contrast to Westmeath, where 'hunting was central to the lifestyle of many members of the Mullingar-based military regiments'.[113] From 1846–47 officers at Cahir garrison were active hunt enthusiasts. From the 1861–62 season to the end of 1880 a pack of harriers hunted from the garrison each year. These took to the field under the name of seventeen different cavalry regiments, testament to the turnover of regiments in the barracks. To maintain horses in peak condition regular hunting was a key feature of this barracks. Not content to sit around, officers sought opportunities to hunt with neighbouring packs. The officers of the 3rd Dragoon Guards hunted with the Tipperary Foxhounds on days when their own pack of harriers was not in the field.[114] Not alone did this expose them to a different type of hunt, it brought them into closer social contact with the elite members of south Tipperary society. That the military could afford to devote so much time to hunting illustrated the relative calm which existed in south Tipperary at that time.

When a regiment received word to depart for its next posting it was common that the harriers were advertised for sale in the local press.[115] Mr. J. Goodden, 4th Dragoon Guards, offered for sale fifteen and a half couple prior to his departure from Cahir.[116] When the 7th Dragoon Guards were moved to Cork in April 1875 the harriers were immediately put up for sale in couples.[117] It is unclear who the purchasers were. The 7th Dragoons were replaced in the barracks by the 5th Dragoon Guards who, on their departure twelve months later, also advertised their pack for sale.[118] By continuing a tradition of hare hunting in the district the garrison pack was filling a void, though it was observed that 'while one regiment may delight in this class of hunting, another may not be quite as enthusiastic'.[119] These fears were unfounded.

At Templemore barracks, a hunt pack was maintained for two seasons by Mr Poynter in 1864 and 1865.[120] Officers from Clonmel and Tipperary barracks hunted with local packs, but their names appeared infrequently in the accounts reported in the press.[121] There is no evidence that either garrison had a specific hunt pack. Contrary to the promotion of hunting to hounds by various regiments at Cahir garrison, the remaining evidence for Tipperary suggests that hunting was not a primary concern for other regiments. Cahir and its sister barracks at Fethard were primarily cavalry barracks where a plentiful supply of horses were available. It made sense to keep the horses active. An issue which likely impacted on the barracks at Clonmel was that there were already established hunt packs in existence, the Tipperary Hunt and the Clonmel Hounds.

THE ROLE OF WOMEN IN THE HUNT

Women were keen and active followers of the various hunt communities. In England, the presence of women as enthusiasts in the hunting field increased in the middle of the nineteenth century.[122] On 23 February 1849 a meeting of the Ormond and King's County Hounds was described by 'Foxhunter' in the *Nenagh Guardian* with some regret as he lamented the decline of 'The Noble Science'.[123] His mood lightened as he recalled the exertions of several followers depending on whether they were light weight or heavy weight. Either way it mattered little, as they were not 'allowed to gain many lengths on a fair visitor, Miss Goold'. Miss Goold was presented with the brush,[124] on account that 'no person of the field so well deserved it'. However, the appearance of Miss Goold did not open the floodgates to female participation.

Reports of hunt meetings at this time typically mirrored those throughout Ireland and England. They were brief and perfunctory.[125] The appearance of ladies in the field, however, helped to alter the way reports were written, which now included the names of those who participated. This was a new departure for the local Tipperary press and it did not find immediate favour with everyone. The Master of the Ormond Hunt felt obliged to ask the *Nenagh Guardian* to include the names of twenty more men who were omitted from a contributed report in the previous issue. He disliked mentioning names, which he felt 'should be always avoided', but he had to correct a wrong and include those whom he felt had been 'well up' at the finish of the meet in question.[126] It was not until the early 1860s that female names appeared regularly in hunt reports.[127] The participation and acceptance of women at hunt meetings demonstrated the ability of the hunt community to embrace those who could afford to be participants, whether they were lords, ladies, gentlemen or tenant farmers. The hunting field allowed for greater interaction between the gentlemen and ladies, with single gentlemen likely to ride hard wishing to impress the ladies. This added to the social aspect which the chase allowed – be it a fox or a prospective marriage partner.

The documentary evidence also suggests that female followers of the hunt were as enthusiastic as their male counterparts. When the Remondstown Otter Hounds met at 4.50 a.m. in June 1868 there were 'several women' in attendance to follow the chase of nine miles up and down river.[128] The correspondent, who sent in reports of the activities of the 7th Dragoon Guards Harriers at Cahir barracks, had a keen eye for the ladies and wrote lovingly about them. In one account he wrote of a Miss Quin, whom he described as 'certainly the *belle ideal* of a horsewoman'.[129] Three months later, after the pack met on the estate of Lady Margaret Charteris at Cahir, he commented on the hunt conditions and how 'those Irish banks, so novel to English huntsmen, were *made easy* to them by the *forward riding* of a lady on a highly-bred horse, who went from field to field, as if on *wings*'.[130] The important point here is that though men could admire the good hunting and horsemanship shown by a woman, the last thing any man wanted was for a woman to beat him to the kill! This indeed is what happened when the Tipperary Hounds came to the end of a run on the last meet of 1877.[131] 'The highly accomplished *equestrienne* – Miss Massy, of

Kingswell House, Tipperary' was close to the hounds at the finish and witnessed the kill. Her exploits in the field resulted in the Master, Mr Bellamy, presenting her with the brush. The fact that these ladies could ride well demonstrated that, in all likelihood, they had taken riding lessons, something which most men probably did not.[132]

One location where women were especially welcome was at the hunt ball. In rural Tipperary the opportunities for social engagement were rare, especially for women. The hunt ball gave ladies an opportunity to dress lavishly, dance and meet their social equals in mid-winter. The Tinvane Hunt ball held in Carrick-on-Suir in January 1845 had 'upwards of one hundred and twenty of the elite of the surrounding counties' present and 'no further room for flirtation' was possible once the dancing commenced.[133] Attendance did not come cheaply. At the end of 1845 tickets for another hunt ball cost 10*s* for gentlemen and 7*s* 6*d* for ladies.[134] The Tinvane Hunt was the trendsetter. The hunt ball was the highlight of the social calendar. In 1846, the attendance of 'all the *elite*, sporting and fashionable' was all the more noticeable, especially when the Lord Lieutenant, a patron on the hunt, was in attendance.[135] This great social occasion in south Tipperary came to an end when the Tinvane Hunt gave up its country to Lord Waterford in March 1847.[136] It was not until twenty years later that hunt balls were a feature of the hunting season once more. A note in the *Nenagh Guardian* suggesting that the Ormond Hunt organise a hunt ball encouraged 'Mary' to communicate with the newspaper. She suggested that officers of the nearest garrisons should be invited. Above all, she wished that this should include 'some cavalry officers, and that they of course attend in uniform. Oh! The pleasure of waltzing with an officer in full uniform is beyond conception; the thought of it almost enchants me.'[137]

From 1867 to 1880 the active participation of women in the hunt field continued to grow. Not only did women hunt with foxhounds, they also participated in hare and otter hunt gatherings. Women were also found at the racecourse. The hunt club races were, in many instances, the perfect way to end the hunting season. From 1840 the Ormond Hunt held annual hunt races which were the precursor to more fashionable national hunt meetings in subsequent years.[138] Hunt race meetings at Cahir (1857) and Fethard (1863), the latter under the auspices of the Tipperary Hunt, also gave women another avenue for social intercourse.[139]

Some huntswomen were as adept at horsemanship as many of their male contemporaries. That some of them were presented with the brush was indicative of their riding ability and that they were not as squeamish as some of their male counterparts may have assumed. With the sports of archery, croquet and lawn tennis, female participation was reserved for those from a landed background. What differentiated the huntswoman was that following the hunt was a more robust and vigorous activity, one which required several hours in the field, perhaps experiencing inclement weather. As the nineteenth century progressed, the sight of huntswomen was common among the hunt community of England.[140] That their contemporaries in rural Tipperary took to the field demonstrated that the hunt communities in the county were in tune with what was happening elsewhere. Improvements to female hunting apparel were also made with the introduction of a shorter safety skirt.[141] While designed to enhance the safety of the huntswoman, it was also a horse-riding innovation which was part of a growing commercialisation of sport in late nineteenth-century Great Britain and Ireland.

ANIMAL WELFARE

Concern for animal welfare was something which the hunt community displayed during this period. This related to the animals hunted and to the hounds or the horses involved in the chase. An account of the Ormond Hunt season 1874–75 showed that only twelve foxes, from fifty-two finds, were killed. During this season the hounds were out twice a week, or forty days in total.[142] With two fox hunting packs in the county more or less consistently throughout the period under review, one could extrapolate that if each killed twelve foxes in a season it would amount to the death of just under 1,000 foxes over a forty-year period.[143]

Hunting hounds were cared for very well by all Masters and hunt committees. An isolated incident was reported that a hound was killed by a train when the Remondstown Otter Hounds were out in June 1868.[144] But the greatest threat to hounds was poison. While poison was laid to protect game on preserves where shooting took place, persons with sinister intent also laid poison to kill hounds. In one such instance in November 1876 the Earl of Huntingdon lost five hounds to poison near Birr, County Offaly. One of them was a stud-dog valued at £100. This was the first such instance recorded in that county and it led to outrage locally. The Tipperary view was somewhat different as the fact that it happened in Offaly was seen as 'a matter of congratulation that such did not happen in the hunting country of the Ormonds'.[145] The onset of the Land War saw poison used as a weapon of choice by hunt saboteurs. In March 1883 Captain Langley, Master of the Tipperary Hunt, lost five hounds to poison at Rathkenny covert. He lost a further eleven, also to poison, at the kennels in early February 1884.[146]

Farming was a business and rabbits were a constant problem for farmers. Consequently, of great concern to foxhunters was the indiscriminate use of rabbit traps. In the spring of 1872 a great difficulty arose over the destruction of foxes due to the increased use of such traps around the county. It caused Mr Tennant of Mobarnane to write to the hunt on the matter, noting that 'it had become a question whether he or the rabbits were to enjoy his property at Mobarnane'.[147] A discussion arose as to the use of ferrets to kill rabbits. Major Kellett commented that 700 rabbits were killed by ferrets in 1869. Some argued that ferrets had not as much impact as traps or snares. Mr J. Langley employed two Englishmen and they took 1,014 rabbits at a sandpit where, under supervision, no harm was done to foxes.[148] The difficulty here was that foxes were also getting trapped and this went very much against the grain with those associated with fox hunting.

Though fox hunting led to the death of foxes – though not at all meets, as has been shown – fox welfare was also important to the hunt community. When five foxes were found killed and dumped in a field John Going was outraged. The killing and dumping of the animal carcasses was anathema to the Tipperary Master. Conversely, when a fox went to ground when the King's County Hunt was out in January 1879, it was dug out. Some expected it to be set free and hunted again but Mr Biddulph grabbed the fox and threw it into the middle of the pack.[149] This led the landowner, Mr W.P.H.L. Vaughan, who was also a member of the hunt, to describe the act as 'unsportsmanlike'. Masters from four separate hunt clubs wrote in support of Biddulph's actions. Lord Waterford deemed it necessary on the grounds that if hounds go out day after day and do not get blood 'a fox should be killed in any way possible on the first opportunity, or else the work of the hounds must deteriorate'.[150]

Apart from the untimely death of Lord Waterford, fatalities to men and women were uncommon in the hunting field. The death of horses was a different matter. In the course of a fifteen-mile run in February 1851 'forty horsemen' set out with the Ormond hounds. Two horses were killed during the chase, which was described as a testament to 'the severity of the day's sport'.[151] But this type of hard riding epitomised fox hunting in Tipperary in the 1840s. Both Lord Waterford and Valentine Maher, Turtulla, were well known for their hard riding in Melton Mowbray, something which they brought back with them to Ireland.[152]

While there is no denying that many animals were killed, foxes, while seen as vermin, were worthy enough for huntsmen to pursue with hounds. As Griffin has shown, there was a great danger that but for preservation initiatives offered by some hunters the fox would have followed the wild boar and wolf into extinction.[153] The management of preserves and coverts was duly adhered to by the hunt followers of Tipperary and its surrounding counties. External malevolent forces also sought to undermine the hunt as hunt packs were poisoned. This led to the death of many hounds. The indiscriminate killing of foxes was something the hunt community did not wish to see either.[154] Horses were ridden hard in the field but injuries here resulted from accidents. In assessing animal welfare in the context of the hunt community, it was somewhat ironic that it was the poster boy of the hunt and racing fraternity of Tipperary and Waterford, the 3rd Marquis of Waterford, who paid the biggest price of all with his untimely death on his return home after a day in the field.

CONCLUSION

What the growth and development of hunting in its various forms in County Tipperary demonstrated was that a pre-Famine preference for fox hunting countywide had continued. Two of the packs, the Tipperary Hunt and the Ormond Hounds, were subscription packs and this tradition continued after the Famine, even though the Ormond Hounds had periodic difficulties in keeping their part of the county active. A third pack, Mr Langley's Foxhounds, was a private pack and though not as active as the former two, his withdrawal from hunting left a fox hunting void in mid-Tipperary which was largely filled by harrier packs. In the 1860s an increase in the number of harrier packs accelerated the degree to which hunting embraced the whole county. When the hunt locations are analysed it can be seen that some areas did not see any hunt activity. This was the hill community on the west, around Kilcommon, and in the south of the county, where the Galtee Mountains covered large tracts of land. However, the Galtee Mountains was a popular area for shooting parties.

A common difficulty with all hunt packs was one of finance, especially with subscription packs. Financial difficulties experienced by the hunt clubs were reported in the local press. This demonstrated a move towards informing hunt supporters of the internal mechanisms of the hunt club. It also served as a way of highlighting the difficulties which each club faced. Hunting to hounds was also important to the growth and development of the horse racing community in Tipperary and Ireland. While thoroughbred horses were prized for their horse racing ability, horse owners, many of them farmers, enhanced their yearly income with the provision of a stallion standing at stud near where they resided. This gave employment to groomsmen and provided the hunt with horses as necessary. Though the hunt may trample over young corn, it was pointed out that those who bought the oats were none other than the horse owners. Those who had the means of disposing of dead farm animals were the hunt pack and those who purchased hunters from the farmers were regularly the hunt horsemen. The community of the land was bound up by connections which ran much deeper than just rent payments. The hunt community had connections which spread far and wide, ranging from farrier to saddler, and hotelier to farmer. Valuable employment was provided to many people whose livelihoods depended on horses. The hunt community in Tipperary from 1840 to 1880 was an integral part of this growth.

CHAPTER 4

THE TURF
HORSE RACING DEVELOPMENT
AND COMMERCIALISATION

INTRODUCTION

As has been shown, the community of the hunt was extensive throughout County Tipperary. This was further enhanced with the continued development and growth of horse racing throughout the nineteenth century. Sporting activities relating to horses were such that a whole range of ancillary trades and goods were necessary to underpin what became an important employment sector. Horse racing and hunting to hounds overlapped. Hunt races were a feature of both the racing and hunting seasons. Hunt races were very common as the hunt season drew to a close in March or early April. They were also a feature of both sports in County Westmeath.[1] While the hunt races attracted many established members of the hunt community to the racecourse, their appeal was much broader and hunt races established themselves as an integral part of horse racing in Tipperary. This chapter looks at the spread of race meetings around the county in this period. It shows how there was a move towards regulated meetings, where the involvement of Turf Club personnel assisted in the management of courses, facilities and race organisation. Due to an enlarged race programme countrywide, some local meetings lapsed due to too few horses racing for diminishing prize money. The races at Cashel are looked at in detail to demonstrate how racing was organised and supported during this time.

Prior to 1840 horse racing had an established tradition in the county. A three-day meeting was held in Thurles in 1732.[2] Also in 1732, there was a week of racing on the course near Cashel which was sponsored by the Green Cloth Club.[3] Nothing more is known about this club. Some years later, in 1775, there was a five-day race meeting in Nenagh.[4] Cashel and Nenagh also held meetings in 1777.[5] All three locations featured in the nineteenth century as horse racing became regularised. However, the degree to which these locations featured was not uniform. As James Kelly has shown for the eighteenth century, 'in certain instances the organisational task was undertaken by local bodies, which provide the first tantalising evidence of an embryonic associational culture in horse-racing'.[6] The scant evidence for Tipperary supports this view. Like-minded gentlemen came together to arrange race meetings which, though they may have been run over three, four or five days, in essence amounted to a small number of races. In the case of Nenagh, in 1775, there were five races run over five days, with each race run off over a series of heats to determine the winner. This race format carried on into the middle of the nineteenth century and while showing continuity, it also demonstrated that there was little change to the overall race structure, however limited it was.

There are nine townlands recorded in Ireland which bear the name Racecourse.[7] Three of these are found in Tipperary. Apart from the racecourse at Thurles, the other two, near Cashel and Clonmel, have historically held race meetings. However, the undefined courses there have left no mark on the landscape and survive only as a place-name location. A village community which bears the name 'Horse and Jockey' is also testament to the heritage of horse racing in the county.[8] Horse racing differed from other sports in Tipperary in that it was nationally federated before any other sporting body in Ireland. This is of great importance as the federating body, the Turf Club, based at the Curragh, County Kildare became ever more influential in the regulation of horse racing in Ireland as the nineteenth century progressed. The managerial roles which Turf Club personnel took on in Tipperary extended the reach of sport to include individuals who did not normally have any association with the county. This was a gradual process. Meetings continued to be arranged locally, with local sponsorship. But as the century progressed and the racing calendar filled up with meetings there was a need to regulate the scheduling of race days. Typically they became annual events across Tipperary. But with that also emerged a pattern of deference to the Turf Club. This helped to give meetings status.

An imbalance in sporting publications on certain aspects of sports history in Ireland is reflected in the dearth of research into the growth and development of horse racing and the various trades and services associated with it.[9] The classic study is Fergus D'Arcy's history of the Turf Club, the Irish equivalent of the Jockey Club in England. Aside from this there are a few narrative studies specific to various aspects of horse racing in Ireland, from both a national and local perspective, which also offer insight into how steeplechase and flat racing developed in the nineteenth century.[10] From a Tipperary perspective, the sole contribution to this field is a contributed article to a local historical journal which discusses the re-development of Cashel races and its stand house at the latter end of the 1890s.[11]

In essence, the model of racing which developed in Tipperary, and especially that of racing over fences, mirrored that which took place in Great Britain. The Turf Club, general patronage, railway companies and horse owners came together and turned what was a largely unstructured eighteenth-century associational activity into an important sport within the county.

DEVELOPMENT OF HORSE RACING

To understand the development of horse racing in Tipperary it is necessary to show how the sport was organised in the mid-nineteenth century. By quantifying the dates and schedules of meetings, patterns are identified from which the development of racing countywide can be shown. The results show that pre-Famine horse racing in Tipperary was relatively unstructured in terms of its organisational framework. Race meetings took place when dates on the calendar became available and were not already booked by a neighbouring town or prominent meeting in other parts of Ireland, notably at the Curragh, Punchestown or Baldoyle. The attraction of these prestigious meetings impacted on the ability of local meetings to attract sufficient horses to fill some races. Spring, summer and autumn meetings in the Curragh were well established and standardised from the eighteenth century.

At a meeting of members of the Jockey Club, the precursor to the Turf Club, in 1777, the 'office of Keeper of the Match Book' was instituted.[12] This was a very early date for organisational structure in sport in an Irish context. A match book was used to record 'details of agreed matches', while other rules deemed that 'details of stakes, conditions and entries' were to be notified to the club well in advance.[13] This was the beginning of a defined structure which eventually led to the codification of how racing was organised in Ireland in the nineteenth century. D'Arcy noted 'that the Curragh Jockey Club had faltered around 1782–83, only to be revived as the Turf Club in 1784'.[14] Members of the Turf Club officiated at races around the country acting as stewards to ensure that rules and regulations were adhered to.

As far as horse racing in Ireland was concerned it was the Curragh which was the most important venue. In 1775, it had four meetings, in April, June, September and October.[15] In 1786, it was still the principal event, though having only three meetings, in April, June and September.[16] Dublin's growing population had ready access to the Curragh. The schedule of meetings indicated that the allocation of dates was governed by the Turf Club. This demonstrated that horse racing as a sport was federated, institutionalised and centrally controlled from very early on.

The initial race format in Tipperary was one of steeplechasing, with relatively few flat races included on the card. The quality of horse stock was not one which depended on thoroughbreds, but rather hunters and chasers which could clear the fences and walls that were typically a feature of local courses. Several early horse races were 'matches' arranged by local gentlemen or military officers, often for a set wager. The outcome of a 'pounding match' at Clonmel was referred to the 'Jockey Club' so that a resolution to a disputed result was found.[17] This was evidence of central control, with an appeals process in place to assist in resolving disputes. This was an isolated case. Everything was local at this time. Still, this type of event attracted great interest and it was a common feature of steeplechase meetings. Steeplechase courses were laid out on open country, inclusive of whatever obstacle or fence was in the way. Races of this type were unpredictable and, as such, chance played as much a part in the outcome as did the skill of the jockey or the stamina of the horse. Examples of these are the steeplechase races which took place in 1840 from Rathronan demesne to Prior Park, and similarly from Knockelly Castle to Mortlestown Castle, both in the south of the county.[18] At this time there was no requirement to enclose courses as these were only occasional meetings that were essentially point-to-point races. These required no fixed infrastructure. Courses were enclosed once there was an opportunity for profit, with regular meetings and income for the landowners.

Figure 4.1 Number of horse race meetings in Tipperary, 1840–1880 (Total = 283)

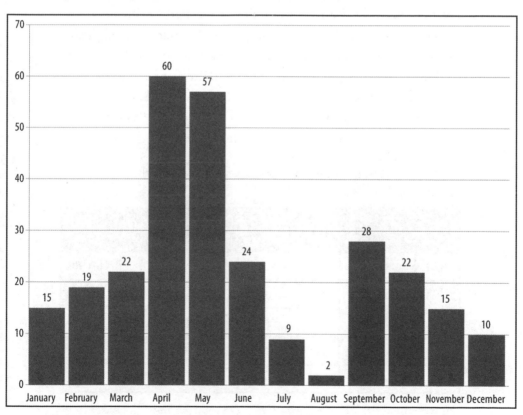

Sources: *CC, CG, NG, TA, TC, TE, TFP, TV, TWN*

In total, inclusive of single race events, 283 race meetings have been identified from the start of 1840 to the end of 1880. Fifty-five race meetings, inclusive of those that had two days' or more racing, have been identified for the period from 1840 to the end of 1845 at the commencement of the Great Famine. Ten meetings have been identified during the main Famine years 1846–48 inclusive. The remaining 218 meetings took place during the years 1849–1880. The months when all races took place are shown in Figure 4.1.

Figure 4.1 shows that April and May were the favoured months for holding race meetings, sixty and fifty-six respectively. These coincided with the end of the hunting season.[19] Most meetings took place over the first half of the year, with 197 in this period compared to eighty-six in the latter six months. These meetings were spread countywide, though once more the hill district of north-west Tipperary was an area devoid of any involvement. As has been shown in the introductory chapter, evidence for sport, apart from hurling, in this part of the county was negligible in the local press. There is a possibility that some local meetings were held there, however unstructured, but the relative absence of evidence for any sport infers that it was one area where racing did not take place. When some farmers' races took place at Latteragh in 1844, the local press described the area as a 'wild mountain district'.[20]

Table 4.1 Races meetings in Tipperary and Westmeath, per head of population

Year	Pop. of Tipperary	No. of races	Per Capita	Pop. of Westmeath	No. of Races	Per Capita
1841	435,553	11	39,596	141,300	1	141,300
1851	331,567	7	47,368	111,407	2	55,705
1861	249,106	7	35,587	90,870	2	45,435
1871	216,713	7	30,959	78,423	2	39,212
1881	199,612	6	33,269	71,798	5	14,360

Sources: *CC, FJ, IT, NG, TC, TFP; Hunter, Racing Calendar, 1871* (Dublin, 1872); Tom Hunt (Pers. comm.)

Five-year aggregate totals for race meetings are shown of Figure 4.2. When compared with those of Westmeath, from 1850, the data indicates that the popularity of racing increased in Tipperary in the 1860s whereas it had remained stable in Westmeath from 1855 to 1879.[21] When the numbers of race meetings in the two counties are looked at in conjunction with the census returns for each decade, the rate of race meeting as a per capita of each county shows that, apart from 1881, the appeal of racing was not that dissimilar in both counties. It had a universal appeal (Table 4.1)

Similar to Westmeath, Tipperary benefited from the role the various hunt packs played in the development of hunt racing and steeplechasing.

Figure 4.2 Frequency of race meetings organised in Tipperary and Westmeath, 1840–1880

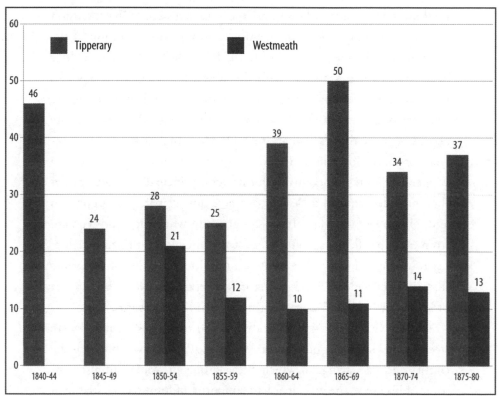

Sources: *CC, CG, NG, TA, TC, TE, TFP, TV, TWN*. Hunt, *Sport and Society*, p. 40 (Cork, 2007)

Though horse racing and hunting to hounds were evident in Ireland in the eighteenth century, it was not until the nineteenth century that their fortunes became more entwined in Tipperary. Hunt racing provided an end-of-season occasion for all parties associated with hunting to come together. Of the 283 meetings that took place, forty-one (14 per cent) were organised by hunt clubs. From 1840, the Ormond Hunt held race meetings at what was termed the 'Lismacrory course', which continued into the 1870s.[22] This was not a defined course which was enclosed and had race-day facilities; rather, it was a race track marked out on open countryside. The hunt races at Fethard, primarily associated with the Tipperary Foxhounds, were also a popular event on the racing calendar.[23]

The officials that organised the hunt races staged farmers' races at many meetings which, as the race articles dictated, were open only to those farmers over whose land the hunt crossed.[24] The inclusion of farmers' races on the cards of hunt races was in recognition of the support given by them to the hunt. The horses had to be 'at least three months in their possession', with the stewards reserving the right to define who was a 'tenant farmer'.[25] For the Ormond Hunt races the holdings of farmers in the district were not to 'exceed £100 annually according to Griffith's valuation.[26] Of this total, twenty meetings were organised by the Ormond Hunt and twelve by the County Tipperary Hunt. By organising hunt races, principally in late spring, they provided an end-of-season occasion for all patrons, supporters and followers of the hunt. It was an occasion when men and women, from each specific class, could meet at the same location and socialise, discuss, plan and flirt.[27] The hunt communities were one of the prime instigators of national hunt racing in Tipperary, enjoying the support of Lord Waterford and Lord Hastings as principal stewards.[28]

As is shown in Table 4.2, 934 of the 1,154 race types identified were steeplechase, hurdle or hunt races. While the Curragh was home to the classics and flat racing, to which the Marquis of Waterford also sent some of his horses, he was an ardent supporter of hunt racing. National hunt racing was the next evolutionary step in the fortunes of horse racing, and the establishment of the Irish National Hunt Steeplechase

Committee in 1869 reflected this. The first secretary of this committee was Robert J. Hunter, who was at that time Keeper of the Match Book at the Turf Club.

Table 4.2 Horse race types identified in County Tipperary, 1840–1880

Steeplechase	798	Match	27
Flat	126	Hack	6
Hurdle	30	Uncertain type	61
Hunt	106	TOTAL	1,154

Sources: CC, CG, IT, NG, TA, TE, TFP, TV. *Hunter, Racing Calendar 1845* (Dublin, 1846). *Hunter, Racing Calendar 1871* (Dublin, 1872)

From the 283 meetings recorded, 1,154 races have been identified. Table 4.2 gives a return of the race types. As may be seen in the data, steeplechase racing was the preferred type, with the returns for flat races and hurdle/hunt races evenly matched. Some meetings concluded with a match race. This was a popular event among gentlemen and military officers and it was typically run for an agreed amount of money.[29] Match races were popular up to 1851 because of the local nature of the meeting.

Race meeting reports identified in the local press were cross-referenced with results in the *Racing Calendar*. This calendar was compiled by the Hunter family, and was the Irish equivalent of the Weatherby *Racing Calendar*. In the official *Calendar*, 165 Tipperary meetings (58 per cent) were matched with newspaper reports. Prior to the Famine only fourteen meetings out of forty-six identified (30 per cent) were reported in the *Racing Calendar*. This suggests a race pattern that was localised and had nothing to do with race organisation elsewhere in the country. As Figure 4.3 demonstrates, the cross-matching between newspapers and the *Racing Calendar* attained higher proportions in the 1870s.

Figure 4.3 Frequency of race meetings organised in County Tipperary, 1840–1880 as identified in R.J. Hunter's *Racing Calendar* and compared with the Tipperary press data

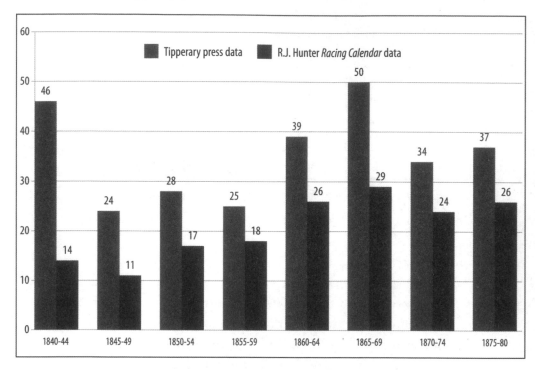

Sources: *CC, CG, NG, TA, TC, TE, TFP, TV, TWN*; R.J. Hunter, *Racing Calendar* (Dublin, annually 1840–1880)

CHARACTERISTICS OF RACECOURSES

In late December 1841 the race articles for what was termed the 'grand national steeplechase' at Carrick-on-Suir were published.[30] Typically, these races took place over courses that were arranged to suit the nature of the races in question, with natural hedgerows and field boundary walls incorporated into the obstacles that were jumped. Most races were run over a series of heats to decide the winner.[31] If three different horses won the first three heats, then a fourth heat was run among these to find a winner. The advantage of such a system was that an afternoon's racing could be enjoyed by spectators with the organisers only having

Figure 4.4 Location of race meetings in County Tipperary, 1840–1880

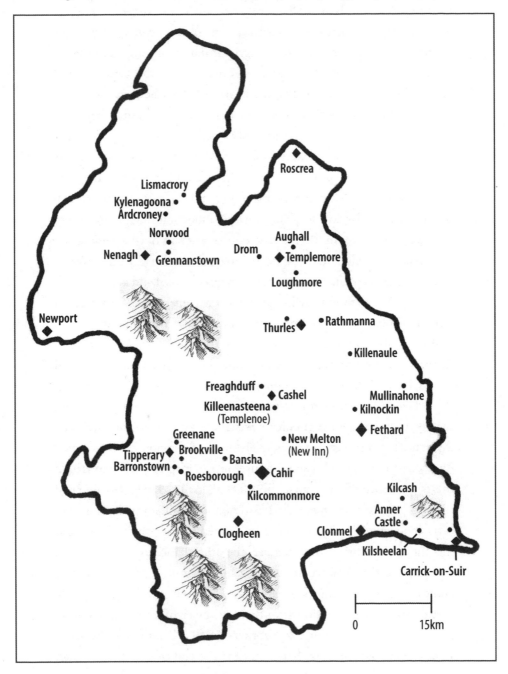

Sources: *CC, CG, NG, TA, TC, TE, TFP, TV, TWN*

to put up one prize. Though land was regularly used for race meetings, as at Lismacrory or Norwood, there is no evidence to suggest that there was any degree of permanence with the majority of courses. Once the racing was over the land reverted to agricultural use and any grandstands erected were dismantled. Races were organised by the Ormond and King's County Hunt annually from 1840 to 1846. These were run over a course laid out on the lands of Simpson Hackett at Lismacrory, near Borrisokane, in the north of the county (see Figure 4.4).[32]

Outside Tipperary town, the first recorded race meeting at the Roesborough course took place on 27 March 1848.[33] Over the next twenty-two years the fortunes of this course and also that of Barronstown fluctuated as the landowners had concerns about granting permission to the race committee. In 1872 a new course was laid out by Thomas G. Waters at Brookville and this appeared to have satisfied those involved in the organisation of the meeting.[34] Fences were erected and a stand house was built. Waters was a civil engineer from Kilpatrick, Monasterevin, County Kildare and was competent in racecourse management.

But in spite of the semi-permanent nature of these courses in Tipperary, their informal nature meant that only one, Thurles, featured in the 1840 Ordnance Survey maps.[35] That a racecourse appeared on these maps in a townland of the same name – Racecourse – shows that there was a defined circuit in existence;[36] it was not one whereby the route between the flags was solely at the discretion of the jockeys. The added inclusion of a stand house on the map further emphasised the permanence of the course. The fact that this course was mapped suggests that, at this time, it had assumed a club identity. This was an early innovation for horse racing in Tipperary and was sufficient for the Ordnance Survey to recognise the importance of sport on the landscape. Today, national hunt racing still continues at this racecourse, demonstrating a continuity of function.

A three-day meeting, similar to those in the eighteenth century, took place on the Thurles course in February 1840.[37] Thurles also hosted a second three-day meeting that year, near the end of October.[38] When the race articles for this meeting were published they stated that horses were to be entered 'with the keeper of the Match Book, Kildare'. This indicated that the course was taking some direction from the governing body of horse racing in Ireland, the Turf Club.[39] For towns that were fortunate enough to hold a second meeting in a calendar year, there was also a spin-off for the local business community – the Great Southern and Western Railway Company, the hotels and bars, and the blacksmiths and farriers all experienced the positive impact that another race meeting brought to their business.

However, these were the only three-day meetings in the county that year. The only other course which held a three-day race meeting was Cashel. Three-day meetings were held here in October 1845, October 1852 and October 1853.[40] In November 1843 support for the Thurles races was abruptly interrupted. P.B. Ryan refused the racecourse to the 'sporting gentry of Thurles' for race meetings.[41] It is unknown as to why he did this. As it was, for 1841 and 1842 he paid out rental fees of £236 2*s* 3*d* to Nicholas V. Maher, Turtulla, who owned the land.[42] Maher was a supporter of hunting to hounds, as has been seen, and also horse racing, so this adds further mystery as to why Ryan withdrew his support for the Thurles races. Racing was adjourned until a new course was obtained.[43] Despite the fact that there was a well-defined and mapped racecourse in 1840, racing only occurred on an intermittent basis in Thurles, and it was not always on the aforementioned racecourse ground. Racing took place in periods which can be defined in three phases – 1840–48, 1863–68 and 1877–1880. Racing during the middle period took place at Rathmanna, to the east of the town. This infrequency was not shared with the other courses in the county, even if the others did also have some years without racing. In October 1849 a four-day race meeting was held at the famed Cashel course.[44] But from 1854 onwards the most that Cashel races could offer to its patrons was a two-day meeting. From this date there were no more three-day race festivals in the county. In reality, like other sports, horse racing was transient until it had a fixed venue. Patronage, in the form of borrowing land for meetings, could only sustain it so far. This also accounts for the early proliferation of meetings. There were many meetings while racing moved around from home to home but there were fewer meetings once courses became fixed and regulated.

More evidence of the relationship between the overlapping horse racing and hunting communities was evident in and around Nenagh. Racing in the vicinity of Nenagh took place at several locations. The Ormond Hunt races were a popular event, with meetings from 1844 to 1849 held at Lismacrory, as previously noted.[45] Ardcroney, Dagg's Hill and Grennanstown were other locations which were used by both the hunt race organisers and the Nenagh race committee.[46] In the immediate aftermath of the Famine, military personnel from the 79th Cameron Highlanders, garrisoned in the local barracks, were instrumental in setting up the course, with Lieutenant Maitland acting as clerk.[47] But on the removal of this regiment from the town military involvement was non-existent from then on. The key thing here is that the military planted the idea of horse racing in the community. They established it and got it going. The post-military success in Nenagh was that the local community took charge of racing and continued to organise meetings. At Cahir, the military officers associated with the local garrison also actively promoted horse racing.[48] These were widely supported, with both the military and the local community prominent in the promotion of these meetings. Similarly, at Templemore, the military organised hunt race meetings, though not on such a large scale as in Cahir.[49]

However, at Nenagh, the lack of permanence around the whole issue of racing in the district only served to highlight the yearly uncertainty of organising a meeting. When Dagg's Hill was offered as a venue it was suggested that the establishment of a race for 'the Nenagh cup', to be run at three successive meetings, would ensure a race meeting 'for at least three years'.[50] But this appears not to have happened.[51] The issue of where the Nenagh races would take place was resolved in 1859 when the Roche lands at Norwood became available. Here the course was a firm favourite with the racing community, and the support of the Roche family as patrons was regularly praised. Race organisers depended on the goodwill of landowners to permit access. James Roche was treasurer of the Norwood races from 1859.[52] In 1872 he subscribed £10 to the race funds but he received £60 for the use of the course temporarily built on his land.[53] Once Roche had agreed to his land being used, the race committee organised the erection of a grandstand, fences and other ancillary services associated with race day. These were all removed once the racing was completed. Tenders were sought for the erection of stand houses, fences, and so on, almost as soon as the race articles were published.[54] Admission fees were charged to the stand, and this generated extra revenue for the race committee alongside profit from tenders and stalls.

Accounts for the races of 1873 showed that for two days at Norwood £106 19s 6d was taken from standhouse fees alone.[55] However, with an opening credit balance of £53 15s from the 1871 meeting, the treasurer closed the 1872 accounts with a credit balance of £37 0s 6d, which represented a loss on the 1872 meeting of £16 14s 6d. Though racing took place yearly, the timber used to construct the stands and the ropes used to define the enclosure areas were auctioned once the calendar of events was complete.[56] This suggests that there was an onus to recoup costs wherever possible and to meet the financial demands which the event incurred. It also suggests that there was no long-term vision in terms of goods, investment or storage. Saloons near or underneath the standhouse were also tendered out, with the highest tender accepted. Persons wishing to erect a tent for whatever purpose were also invited to tender at the Norwood races. Receipts for 'tents and roulette' brought in £47 for the races in 1872.[57] It was as if the overriding concern of the committee was to deal with each year as it came, without any long-term planning. To this end the business community and ratepayers of Nenagh were the ones to whom the committee turned when the race articles were published and financial support for the various events was canvassed in the town.[58] But things did not improve!

A deficiency of £52 remained after all costs had been met for the 1873 meeting, leaving the committee in a dilemma – would they publish a list of defaulters or try to get them to abide by their initial commitment?[59] But 'Subscriber' in a letter to the *Nenagh Guardian* took issue with this. He believed that the stewards and committee had already done enough by subscribing and giving their spare time in promoting the races. He felt that it was up to the 'merchants and traders' of Nenagh to subscribe the necessary funds to clear off the debts as they were the ones who profited most from the races.[60] James Roche died in September 1873. For a few years after his death race meetings were held infrequently; no-one was sure if they would take place or not. Efforts were made over the next seven years to revive the meeting but it was only successful in 1876 and 1879. On the whole, there was general indifference from the residents of Nenagh to the races.[61] This fact did not go unnoticed by the race committee who, on the evidence of the press reports, manfully endeavoured to maintain an annual meeting, but they were fighting a lost cause. It also demonstrated how fragile the whole enterprise was. Once the principal patron of Nenagh races died it signalled the beginning of the end for the meeting itself.

In the south of the county horse racing took place near Clonmel. While meetings were held on courses at Anner Castle, Kilsheelan and Gammonsfield in the 1840s, horse racing was not a common feature of the local sporting landscape.[62] Attempts were made to establish one-off meetings but they did not lead to continuity. In 1871, a race committee was formed with a view to establishing annual races at Clonmel 'in compliance with the expressed wishes of many of the gentry, merchants and others resident in Clonmel'.[63] However, one of those in attendance, Mr Phillips, was of the opinion that 'unless a really good stake was offered each day, it was useless to expect that good horses would come'.[64] He believed that such was the case at Cashel where a plate of £130 failed to attract 'more than six or eight horses'.[65] A tipping point had been reached. The race market had become crowded and the availability of quality horses to ensure a meeting's long-term success was not there.

Some committee meetings continued in Clonmel throughout the winter months of 1871–72, covering issues from the collection of subscriptions to securing land for the races themselves. Everything appeared to be straightforward until the local Roman Catholic parish priest, Dr Power, voiced his disapproval of the proposed race meeting. He had strong concerns about the whole atmosphere which accompanied race day. The race committee felt that 'those who promised subscriptions' refused to pay when Dr Power denounced the proposed events.[66] It was not the races as such which Dr Power was against but, rather, the hedonistic events associated with race day. In December 1871, at a race meeting at Kilmacomma, near Clonmel, there was 'a great amount of drunkenness throughout the evening, and a woman, on retiring home there from, was ill-used'.[67] It was an event such as this which bothered the priest. Forty-six members of the race committee were sent a circular to attend a meeting about these issues. Only nine attended and the race committee were short of support. It made a unanimous decision to dissolve the committee and hand back any subscriptions collected. On the whole, it was felt that there was apathy in the town towards the races and that 'the employers in the town were also complaining that their employees were absent from business on the following day'.

'S.R.' wrote to the *Clonmel Chronicle* highlighting the fact that this letter writer believed there were too many small races at too many meetings. These were to the detriment of horse breeding. 'S.R.' believed that these races were a source of 'idleness, intemperance and crime' and proposed that one centrally located meeting should be held on a large scale annually, which would attract the best horses and be of superior sport.[68] The problem, which 'S.R.' correctly pointed out, was one of sustainability, as opposed to the spectacle of racing itself. If there was poor-quality racing for too little money, the whole enterprise was doomed to failure. This letter drew a quick reply from 'an old turfite', who bemoaned the folly of 'splitting up a sum of money barely sufficient for one good plate, into some six or eight miserable stakes'.[69] 'Old turfite' supported the call of 'S.R.' for a large meeting, but one which would rotate around the towns of Clonmel, Fethard, Cashel and Tipperary and which the owners of the 'best racing blood in the country' would patronise. This plea fell on deaf ears. By 1877 another series of race meetings was proposed for Clonmel in the hope that 'the very rarity of the event would ensure a large attendance and a liberal patronage'.[70] Once again, it was a false dawn, and the most that Clonmel could hope for were the local harrier club races, which were held at nearby Clerihan.[71]

THE RAIL NETWORK AND HORSE RACING

Tipperary racecourse was the only course in the county where the rail network had a major bearing on the fortunes of racing. The opening of the Roesborough course coincided with the opening of the Waterford and Limerick rail line. The operating company had a station at Tipperary town, with a connection to Limerick Junction, both places close to the new racecourse. As the plans for the railway to Cork were enacted by law in 1845, the opening of a new race meeting at Tipperary was a commercial initiative to maximise the benefits that would accrue from the new rail link.[72] The very first train on the new line from Limerick station was to the races at Tipperary in 1848 when 'over 400 of the inhabitants including the rank, fashion and beauty of the city' travelled on this historic occasion.[73] The Waterford and Limerick line consistently offered return fares at single rates for race followers. This made good commercial sense.[74] Not only that, the rail company also sponsored races at the Tipperary track with the 'Railway Stakes' carrying a prize of twenty sovereigns when it was put on the race card in 1850.[75] In 1853, fifty sovereigns were added.[76] The symbiotic relationship between Tipperary races and the Waterford and Limerick Railway Company was great for racing but by 1870 there were growing concerns that 'trains from the four cardinal points ... brought full freights at not very moderate rates'.[77] There is no doubt that without the railway Tipperary races would not have remained a successful venture. It was located at the intersection of two primary rail networks, Dublin to Cork and Waterford to Limerick. It also benefited from the support of the Waterford and Limerick Railway Company, which offered return services at single rates despite concern in some quarters that the rates were not as moderate as they could have been. To the present day, Tipperary racecourse, at Limerick Junction, benefits from rail passenger traffic.

Central to the success of any meeting was the race committee and, unless strong and motivated, such a body was doomed to failure. The inability of the committee in Clonmel to maintain sufficient members to do the necessary work undermined any hope it had of ever securing subscriptions. This also hindered the drawing up of race articles and securing land for the races. Central to this was the involvement of the landowner on the race committee. James Roche, as treasurer of the Nenagh races, was key to the success of the Nenagh meeting. His death was a prime factor in the decline of the Norwood races as family instability likely affected the future of the meeting.[78] Similarly, uncertain land acquisition for the races impeded any hopes for continued racing at Thurles. While racing was an annual event in the town in the 1840s, long periods without racing were difficult to counter and consequently there was an ebb and flow in the regularity of racing at this location. Horse racing needed patronage, whether by an individual or a committee. Two examples are given which explore the different ways in which this was achieved. The first example relates to individual involvement, most especially that of Lord Waterford. The second example is that of a race committee at Cashel, where some of the principal players were also landowners and local businessmen who had an eye on commerce and profit.

HENRY, 3RD MARQUIS OF WATERFORD AND HORSE RACING IN TIPPERARY

Co-existent with his support of fox hunting, one of the principal supporters of horse racing in the county was Henry de la Poer Beresford, the 3rd Marquis of Waterford. As a steward of the Turf Club, he appeared in this capacity at meetings, not alone in Tipperary, but throughout Ireland. But it was as a benefactor to the racing community that he made an indelible imprint. As a purchaser of racehorses, both at auction and race meetings, he gave unparalleled support to the horse racing community of Tipperary. He contributed prizes to several meetings. In June 1840, at the New Melton (New Inn) races he donated a twenty-sovereign plate. He put up fifty sovereigns for the sweepstakes and ten sovereigns for a farmers' race at the same location in October 1840, following this up in November with an unsolicited ten-sovereign purse for the farmers' race at Carrick-on-Suir.[79] His support of farmers' races never waned. In 1853, in a sweepstakes race of one sovereign at Carrick-on-Suir races, he added ten sovereigns in a race 'for farmers' horses residing in his hunting district'.[80] At this time an unmarried farm servant receiving food and lodgings earned £4 per year. A landless labourer earned from eight pence to one shilling per day, or four pence to six pence if he also received food. When times were not so good, this rate was lower.[81]

The Marquis' support of horse racing demonstrates that he never forgot the important part the farming community played as guardians of the countryside, fox coverts, earths and the hunting country. These races gave farmers an opportunity to share the racecourse with the Marquis and other notables. It also gave them an opportunity to put on display a hunter which might attract the attention of a likely purchaser. Selling a horse which one had bred was another way farmers had of making money, especially if it was a good hunter. Though many races were selling races, whereby the winner was sold in the ring immediately after a race, the opportunity for farmers to make a handsome return on a horse was important. At the conclusion of the races at Tipperary in April 1849 Lord Waterford purchased Sir Arthur for 250 guineas and Bracelet for 100 guineas, adding to his already considerable stable.[82] At the Cashel races in October 1850 he purchased The Hermit after this horse won two heats of the last race on the card.[83]

Among the race meetings where the Marquis appeared as steward were the Cahir steeplechases in October 1843, the Ormond and King's County steeplechase and flat races in April 1844 at Lismacrory, and the Clonmel races at the Anner Castle course in May 1845.[84] With many horses in training, it was almost a certainty that he was going to have winners. Jockeys riding for the Marquis wore the baby blue silks associated with him and there was a great sense of occasion when they appeared on the course. While he had two winners at the Carrick-on-Suir races in May 1842, he lost a brown gelding, Manilla, at the New Melton steeplechase race in late October 1842.[85] Undeterred, the Marquis travelled to Naas, County Kildare, a few weeks later for the stud sale of the late Captain Madden, where he purchased five horses for 980 guineas.[86] The scale of his expenditure 'surprised everyone', with one of the horses, Navigator, bought for 300 guineas. He indulged his passion for horse racing and was without question the most influential figure in the racing community of Tipperary at that time. He was a steward of the Turf Club from 1841 until his death in 1859.[87] His attendance at a race meeting was sure to attract many visitors to the course just to see him and his entourage. When he attended the Thurles races in November 1841 he was 'accompanied by several distinguished and sporting visitors and was repeatedly cheered by the crowd'.[88]

An added source of wonderment was the presence of 'one of the Lord Waterford's vans for the conveyance of his stud, drawn by four horses … and [this] excited the curiosity of the people'. This type of van was popular in England in the late 1830s, reducing the need for horses to walk to meetings.[89] It was common for horses to compete only at local courses, whereby little walking was required. However, Lord Waterford's van gave him an extra dimension that allowed him extend the scope of his racing hinterland. This was an important moment where mechanical advances allowed sport to spread geographically. It was similar to transportation innovations evident in England, with jockeys moving between racecourses by means of the rail network. Horse transport vans were also employed to ferry horses from stable to racecourse.[90]

The untimely death of Lord Waterford in 1859 at the age of forty-seven, as a result of a fall from his horse Mayboy while returning home from a hunt meeting, was a great loss to the sporting community of Tipperary. There were many people who were in awe of him as he travelled from one race meeting to another. He had strong spending power, which ensured that many others aspired to move within his circle. But it was the quality of his horses and his stud that were his enduring assets. His horses won many races around Ireland and the Marquis purchased widely. His successor, while still a supporter of horse racing, was not as flamboyant as the 3rd Marquis, who was one of the main supporters of horse racing in Tipperary in the years 1840–1859.

THE RACES AT CASHEL

In terms of the importance of a particular course to the racing community, Cashel racecourse from 1840 to 1880 went from being a course of high esteem to one of low support during this period, the reason being an increased number of race meetings. As noted earlier, Cashel held a series of races in 1732. It is quite likely that at this date the races were held in the townland south of Cashel which bore the name Racecourse.[91] In September 1788 the meeting lasted for five days, though the number of races was small.[92] In the following year the meeting was spread out over six days, with fifty pounds on offer for the winner of each race, except for the last one, which was for £100.[93] The races of 1797 also took place over six days.[94] It was stated in 1844 that 'the last day of the old celebrated Cashel Races was the 15 October 1797'.[95] During the first half of the nineteenth century the races were held at various locations including Kilbreedy, near Camas, and Killeenasteena, immediately west of the townland named Racecourse.[96] But, unlike Thurles, there was no racecourse identified on the 1840 map for Cashel. The Cashel races in November of that year took place on a course 'lately chosen' at Templenoe, an area of land within the Killeenasteena townland.[97] The course was observed to be not as suitable as that at the Commons of Cashel.

Another course was laid out north-west of the town for the 1844 meeting. This course with 'artificial jumps arranged in sporting style', also attracted liberal patronage. The county MP, Nicholas Maher, contributed £20 and the Cashel commissioners gave a £50 plate.[98] Maher also owned the land on which the Thurles racecourse was sited.[99] In 1845 the borough MP, Timothy O'Brien, contributed to the race fund. This started a trend which continued until the borough constituency was disenfranchised in 1868 and subsequently abolished in 1870.[100] Cashel borough had a population of 6,971 in 1831, which had fallen to 5,458 in 1861.[101] The new course was laid out at Freaghduff and Eastlone. In 1850, William Ryall had ninety-one acres of rented land from the Earl of Normanton at Freaghduff and James Dunne had thirty-seven acres rented from the Ecclesiastical Commissioners in the adjoining townland of Eastlone.[102] The land, in both instances, was church land. The archbishop of Cashel made advantageous leases with the new occupiers; the Ryall and Dunne names were synonymous with Cashel races over the next thirty years.

The Ryall family were instrumental in establishing Cashel races at this site. James Ryall, a hotel proprietor in Cashel, was operating in a semi-professional capacity. In 1841 he took entries for the re-established meeting and in 1844 was named as clerk of the course for a three-day meeting which had a prize fund of £410 for a total of six races.[103] Entries were received by him at the hotel, where he also received a fee of five shillings for each horse entered.[104] His fees were on a par with those received by clerks in England.[105] Added income was earned with an 'ordinary' held each evening in the hotel at the conclusion of the races.[106] While it is unknown, it's unlikely that Ryall worked for a salary; mindful that the Cashel races took place yearly, he had enough vested interests from which to draw a substantial income: landowner, clerk of the course, and hotel owner.

There was also a social cachet associated with the role of race steward or race official. Among the ten stewards at the 1846 meeting in Cashel were the Marquis of Waterford, Lord Lismore, Viscount de Chabot, Hon. C. O'Callaghan and Nicholas V. Maher MP, all principal landowners in mid and south Tipperary, Cork and Waterford.[107] Not only that, but the prize money of £100 added to the Rock Stakes – a sweepstake of fifteen sovereigns each – appeared on the face of it to be a very large sum to assign to a horse race, mindful of the distress which many people were then experiencing. The support of Cashel commissioners and politicians was instrumental in attracting entries as well as giving support to the races themselves. Essentially the town commissioners were acting as financial backers for the races. By hosting a big sporting event they attracted additional revenue into the town and added to the prestige of the day. The Cashel commissioners also contributed fifty sovereigns to the 1846 meeting, all in the interest of promoting the town.[108] This was not something unique to Cashel. Clonmel Corporation also held a series of races in late 1844.[109] With large visitor numbers attracted to the town on account of the races, the outlay was paid back in kind with consumer spending raising extra revenue in the locality.[110] Advertisements were taken out in the local press by hotel owners. One such owner noted that he was 'grateful for the kind patronage bestowed on his establishment'.[111]

Races were typically held over two days, with two races each day. There was a mixture of flat races and jump races. The county and borough members of parliament felt the need to be present at the meeting. It did them no harm to be seen at sporting occasions, such as the races. Both county members, Nicholas Maher and Francis Scully, were in attendance at the 1846 meeting. From 1852 to 1855, the two county members and the two borough members were among those listed as stewards.[112] Sir Timothy O'Brien, the Cashel borough member, contributed twenty-five sovereigns yearly to one of the races. As races were run in heats at that time it was not unusual that three races were required to get an eventual winner. To this end, the race articles at several meetings typically noted that the winners of the first and second heats would contest the third and final heat.[113] But when a horse was entered for a few races it was then required to do a lot of racing. At the Cashel October meeting in 1852, Lord Waterford's Augustine raced in six heats over two successive days, though it won 'cleverly' both races in which it was entered.[114] Though artificial fences were part of the initial layout at Cashel, the course owners also incorporated walls into the jumps, one of which regularly caused falls, some of which were fatal. One such fatality was that of the jockey Colgan who was killed when his horse Crutches rolled over him in October 1852.[115] Several reports noted the severity of this obstacle and the course owners at various stages attempted to remedy the difficulty.[116] This new course, at Freaghduff, from the outset had a stand house, which was 'a substantial stone building' near which were 'the vehicles of many of our gentry … the Rock – glorious memorial of other days – towered proudly in the distance and the crowds of our fair countrywomen' thronged the hills adjacent to it.[117] The best viewing areas of the course were reserved for carriages, all facing the landmark icon which was the Rock of Cashel cathedral.

From 1853, Robert J. Hunter, Turf Club judge, officiated at various meetings around Tipperary. In 1859, when Paul Cusack became clerk at Cashel, Hunter was a regular official at the meeting. The fortunes of Cashel races waned in the mid-1850s however. No meeting took place in 1857, and James Ryall made his last appearance as clerk of the course in 1858. At that meeting he was assisted by Cusack in his capacity as superintendent of the on-course arrangements.[118] Cusack succeeded Ryall as clerk.[119] A race committee was subsequently established in the town and with the able assistance of John M. Bushe, Rockwell, subscriptions were obtained and the races were widely promoted.[120] For the races of 1865, James Dunne subscribed £50 towards the race funds.[121]

These efforts paid handsome dividends locally as the 1859 meeting drew 'lovers of the turf from all parts of the country', with the attendance 'immense'.[122] And yet the committee refused to sit still, and for the 1860 meeting the stand house was improved, with accommodation for one thousand people. To meet the demands for accommodation external to the racecourse 'the chief business [in the town] was the letting of almost every spare room in private houses and public place of resort, at enormous prices'.[123] The races were commercial in every sense of the word though there is no evidence to suggest that businessmen, such as hackney owners, contributed to the race funds, as happened in England.[124] James Dunne, a hotel proprietor in the town, and Paul Cusack were, by 1861, the new course owners and they made great strides in improving the course, fences and standhouse.

In spite of these advances it would have been difficult to obtain sponsorship for a second meeting. The September 1862 meeting at the 'Downs of Cashel', with still more improvements made by Cusack and Dunne to the course design and layout, were looked forward to eagerly. On race day 'the ring' was never 'more crowded or fashionably filled', while 'if the sporting men were numerous the horses were also numerous'.[125] All boded well for a great day's racing, or so it seemed. The first event on the card failed to fill, though the articles noted that four horses were to start or there would be no race. Nine entries had been received but only four came to the start line. Then one of them unexpectedly withdrew. So as not to disappoint those attending, the stewards waived the conditions of the articles and dictated that three horses could run, thus not leaving a blank on the card. The race then turned into a farce when two more horses withdrew, thus leaving Frailty to walk over the course.[126] The *Clonmel Chronicle* in its report noted that 'we could well see the *drift* of all this. We have but to *chronicle* that things could not be made "comfortable" for the four gentlemen who held back.' Clearly the whole episode revolved around gambling, and those in the know, under the principle of play or pay, were going to get their money's worth, largely at the expense of an unsuspecting public. This sharp practice, while unsportsmanlike, happened regularly.[127] Racing was not merely a sport to be administered but was, unlike some other sports, an occasion for gambling. While several races had only a few horses entered, anyone who gambled had a chance of winning something. The attractiveness of a gamble further enhanced the appeal of racing.

The carnival atmosphere of the Cashel races was another of its key attractions. Over the years the lower classes attended in large numbers, especially in 1863 when an estimated 40,000 people turned up for the meeting. The early harvest gave many people an opportunity to attend.[128] Inclement weather caused the second day of the meeting to be postponed for one day, not that Cashel business people were overly concerned as they 'reaped a golden harvest' with the shops and streets overcrowded with racegoers who had nowhere else to go. On the course the '*canvas quarter* looked bleak and drear'.[129] Tents erected for the sale of alcohol, food or other consumables were part of the race day experience and added to the gaiety and excitement. The stall holders provided increased revenue for the course owners. A woman from Charleville, County Cork, who sold ginger bread at the 1861 races, came before the magistrates, as she tried to make light of the purse of another seller in her vicinity. After getting 'unceremoniously ejected' she accused Patrick Maunsell of assault, only to have the case dismissed due to a lack of evidence.[130] What this case showed, however, was that people were prepared to travel considerable distances to sell their wares at the races. The course owners and race organisers made a handsome income from pitches allocated to tent holders, and a large amount of alcohol was consumed on the grounds.

Alcohol-induced disorder resulted in the appearance of many individuals before the local court.[131] Rioting was a more serious matter and after the 1865 meeting, seven men appeared before the magistrates. They received sentences ranging from twelve months to nine months with hard labour with their attempt to revive faction fighting.[132] Horse racing differed from other sports in the county and indeed Ireland and

Great Britain in that apart from the sporting aspect, it brought with it drunkenness, gambling, debauchery and sometimes violence. Victorian society was predisposed to law and order, rules and regularity, whether in the workplace, the market place or the sports ground. However, racing, by the nature of the travelling circus which followed it often deviated from these ideals. While the racing people who owned, trained and maintained horses, whether for sport or commercial interests, supported racing for what it was, there was another large body of race day patrons for whom a day out at the races was the primary appeal. There were tents available for alcohol and food, sideshow amusements and confidence tricksters. Stallholders were anxious to take as much money from race day patrons as they could get away with. An over-indulgence in alcohol was one of the principal causes of unrest and, as has been shown, led to many instances of drunkenness and custodial sentences for individuals prosecuted before the courts.[133]

More worryingly, though, was the reduction of the yearly grant from the commissioners to the Cashel race fund. They cut their subscription from £40 to £25.[134] While meetings were generally well supported by all classes in society, a decline in the attendance of the labouring class was likely due to emigration. Furthermore, a lack of support for the 1868 meeting was put down to 'the present number of "small" events' which the *Clonmel Chronicle* stated was 'calculated to promote the interests of steeplechase racing'.[135] Things improved considerably in 1869 with 'an enormous and fashionable attendance of the aristocracy and true lovers of the turf' present, with the seventy-six acres well filled with people.[136] An added revenue source that year was the charge of 2*s* 6*d* admission at the gate for mounted horsemen. But in 1870 matters reverted to farce once more. The writing was on the wall as far as Cashel races were concerned. It was felt that, indeed, the days of small events in the racing calendar were numbered. Organisers stated that 'we cannot afford to bid "farewell" to the Old Rock'.[137] There was £370 added to various races, but even the celebrated Rock Stakes failed to attract the required number of horses for the race to go ahead.

Aside from emigration, the want of a railway line was also given as a factor which impacted on the ability of this local meeting to survive.

The race committee agreed that something radical had to be done and into the breach stepped Thomas G. Waters. Waters altered the course and made changes to the paddock area. He also made improvements to the stand house. These improvements did cost money and as a result admission fees to the stand house were increased, as was the fee for carriages.[138] Efforts were made to keep the races an annual affair, with Waters still engaged as course manager, which is another example of the economic impact of a racecourse. A job had now been created and someone was required to fill the position. However, by 1874 the Cashel race meeting was abandoned due to a lack of funds. Long-time clerk of the course James Dunne was indisposed, which did not help matters. He was assaulted on his return from the Williamstown races; he received a fracture to his skull when he was struck on the head with a stone while looking out the window of the train.[139] As the borough was disenfranchised there was no local MP to contribute to the race funds. Furthermore, the auditor disallowed the granting of '£25 yearly by the Town Commissioners' to the race funds.[140] The Cashel races were now a hard sell and, try as they might, the race committee could not get the meeting back to the glory of former years. Local hunt races were commenced in 1873 and up to 1880 these were the staple events which Cashel offered to a largely uninterested racing public.[141]

The duties of the clerk of the course meant that this man operated on a semi-professional basis. Recording entries, receiving fees, laying out the course, among other duties necessary at race time, were attended to with due diligence. The development of racing drew on local meetings already established, if only on an ad hoc basis, prior to the emergence of a rail network throughout Tipperary. The course at Tipperary town was the only one to consistently benefit from the railway development. The developing pattern in Tipperary shows that there was a move towards central control of horse racing in Ireland in the 1870s.[142] Mediocre racing at this time at Cashel, Tipperary and Nenagh was a consequence of lesser-quality horses racing for diminishing prize money. If this continued, the quality of racing would suffer, and this was not something the Turf Club or Irish National Hunt Steeplechase Committee were going to allow happen.

The days of the Rock Stakes at Cashel, with 100 sovereigns in added money, were gone. The most on offer was a handicap race of forty sovereigns and other races carrying even less prize money. The scheduling of races also changed; they now took place in spring to coincide with the end of the hunting season. Though the quality of the racehorses had declined, the continued presence of a large number of tents and bookmakers showed that there were still people willing to support the Cashel races.[143] But the meeting was in an untenable position. With falling attendances and not enough horses taking part, the appeal of the Cashel races was gone. The local press lamented the decline of Cashel races from its glory days half a century earlier.

But why did Cashel fail? The development of the rail network throughout Tipperary coincided with the emergence of a new racecourse outside the town, which was initially signalled as an intermediary stop on the new Great Southern and Western Railway line connecting Dublin to Cork. Shares for this new venture were referred to as 'Cashels' owing to the name of the proposed end station in the initial 1844 Act.[144] In the end, however, the line did not even come close to Cashel, though the town was on the main Dublin to Cork roadway. Economically, it was felt that the town 'suffered in prosperity from the competition of other towns' due to the lack of railway communication.[145] The new GS&WR line went close to Tipperary town, which was on the Waterford and Limerick railway line. Tipperary town and its environs were doubly serviced by the rail network. It was the Waterford and Limerick Railway which from the start, and regularly thereafter, supported the races at Tipperary. While it is true that the Nenagh races at Norwood, and the Ormond and King's County hunt races at Lismacrory, were also remote from a rail network, the race committee at Nenagh worked with the rail company to facilitate racegoers. Horses were transported on the Great Southern rail line to Nenagh, with returns at single fare rates. Clonmel and Thurles, despite intermittent difficulties, were thus able to maintain a presence in the racing community aided in no small part by the assistance of the rail companies.[146]

The Fethard races, over the Kilnockin course, while sufficient for the Tipperary Hunt race meetings, failed to galvanise continued support like Cashel. Cashel races, with an invented nostalgia for the halcyon days of the late eighteenth century, were established by likeminded middle-class individuals who appreciated the commercial benefits that accrued from careful race management and upper-class support. That such support was willingly given by the Marquis of Waterford and others, allied to the attractive race money on offer, enhanced the reputation of the Cashel meeting. When patronage was withdrawn, especially financial support, the races lost their glamour. Cashel was not alone in this respect. Racing throughout Ireland was to enter a difficult period with the onset of land agitation and an 'economic depression [which] finished Londonderry in the early 1880s' being symptomatic of the distress felt nationwide.[147] But sport was about commercialisation and profit maximisation. With rail companies willing to offer attractive rates for other venues, Cashel was hindered before the race articles were even published. The main problem with Cashel was that it was in some ways a prime example of land speculation. A recommencement of racing coincided with the development of the rail network, which ultimately bypassed the town. The meeting was able to sustain itself until the racing market became saturated with poor-quality races and the money required to underpin the Cashel meeting was lost. The loss of the projected railway was a key element in the demise of the Cashel races. That it had the support of the local hunt community meant that the racecourse owners and supporters in Cashel had to re-invent themselves and amend their calendar and adjust profit forecasts accordingly. Evidently, local hunt racing was better than no racing at all.

In the north of the county there were no Ormond Hunt races in 1847 and 1848, with an apparent suspension of racing on account of the Great Famine. Racing resumed in 1849 with a meeting scheduled for Lismacrory.[148] Also at this time, the military departed Nenagh and the administration and organisational capabilities associated with the races went with them. Racing took place at Grennanstown in 1850. However, no more hunt races were held until 1854, when Lismacrory was once again the venue. Here they were under the watchful eye of Robert J. Hunter, judge and handicapper to the Turf Club. Though racing did not stop in the Famine years, it was very much curtailed in the county, especially in 1847. The only location which held meetings each year of this troubled period was Cashel.[149]

What this suggests is that there were two parallel worlds in Tipperary. There was the commercialisation of horse racing in Cashel and Tipperary on one side, but at the other end of the scale people were dying from hunger. While people in Tipperary did feel the effects of the Famine, the degree to which destitution and emigration followed was not as hard felt in this county as it was in counties on the western seaboard. The landed and business interests in Tipperary contributed to famine relief funds, in a sense fulfilling their moral obligation to subscribe. This task accomplished, life continued as normal.[150] The Famine did not have the same effect on everyone. People of means and regular income were largely unaffected. But many other people were not so fortunate. Cottiers died. Poorer tenants had the opportunity to emigrate or go to the workhouse. For many people, this decision was taken as a last resort. They had no other choice. The desire to live outweighed all other considerations. A visitor to Cashel in 1850 was 'painfully struck with the number of deserted shops [and] as he left ... he passed by a legion of cabins of every variety of mud architecture'.[151]

R.J. HUNTER AND T.G. WATERS

The economic implications of the Great Famine and the degree of unease and hardship which accompanied it were factors contributing to a decline in racing countywide. When the Famine ended racing resumed. Robert Hunter officiated at the Carrick-on-Suir races in March 1853.[152] Hunter, a member of a family long associated with horse racing in Ireland and the Curragh in particular, was the Keeper of the Match Book at the Turf Club from 1865 to 1885.[153] From 1853 to 1863 Hunter attended as a judge and/or handicapper at twenty-five race meetings throughout Tipperary. This rose to a minimum of thirty-seven attendances by the end of 1876. There was nothing philanthropic in his actions as his position as judge also paid financial dividends. The winner of each race where he officiated was dictated by the race articles to pay him one sovereign.[154] His appearance on the Tipperary racing scene, and other meetings countrywide, suggests that outside help, from the Curragh, was requested by course proprietors and race promoters. There was nothing in the race articles to suggest that locally arranged meetings were obliged to have Turf Club involvement, but the presence of a well-known official and judge added status to a meeting. Racing at this time became increasingly centralised and the Turf Club was the arbitration body for horse racing in Ireland. It was not that there was no local leadership but, as weight-for-age races were less of a feature of race-day, a knowledgeable handicapper and judge was beneficial. His attendance was necessary for meetings which aspired to attract better horses, owners and ultimately money. Furthermore, many steeplechase and hunt races were run under the rules of the Irish National Hunt Steeplechase Committee.[155]

Another man who was associated with the development of horse racing was Thomas G. Waters. Waters made his initial appearances in the county at Cashel racecourse for the 1871 meeting in his capacity as manager after the stewards had 'taken the ground into their own hands for the occasion'.[156] Waters was a 'well-known racecourse official and architect' who also redesigned Punchestown, County Kildare, and Ballybrit, County Galway racecourses in 1861 and 1869 respectively.[157] He attended to the development of yet another new racecourse near Tipperary town where he designed the layout at the Brookville course, as previously noted. He turned 'the sod where the different fences were to be made. He also gave directions as to the erection of the stand-house.'[158] Throughout the 1870s Waters made many appearances on the Tipperary racing circuit. He appeared as manager in the race articles for Cashel, Tipperary, Thurles and Newport.[159] In this respect, he 'combined his work as [a] racecourse designer with all sorts of official and semi-official appointments up and down the country'.[160] It is likely that Waters knew that his experience in racecourse design and management was desired and to this extent he was a full-time racing official. He was paid by the various race organisers around the country. At the Nenagh Norwood races in 1873 he redesigned the course by making it smaller, which meant that spectators saw more of the action. He also designed the standhouse on the 'Punchestown model'.[161] Six years later he was invited back to Nenagh as the race committee deemed that 'Mr. Waters is a necessity and in himself a great element in any races whose course is under his skilful management'.[162] It was further argued that racehorse owners have 'the fullest confidence in the safety of any course under his supervision'.[163] Waters for his part was more than happy to oblige, noting that 'should the committee trust the carrying out of the details to him and his son', he would endeavour to give complete satisfaction.

The Hunter and Waters names were synonymous with horse racing in Ireland; their names were regularly found on race articles or race reports from Tipperary during the 1870s. They were very relevant to the development of racing in Tipperary from the perspective of administration and racecourse organisation. In this sense they were quite different from Lord Waterford; whereas Hunter and Waters were paid for their services, Lord Waterford was an active participant and benefactor to horse racing in Tipperary and indeed throughout much of the country. The roles of R.G. Hunter and T.G. Waters in officiating at meetings throughout Tipperary were indicative of the professional approach undertaken by the Turf Club in relation to the management of the sport in Ireland. While it is true that some of the marquee meetings at the Curragh, Punchestown, Baldoyle and Cork Park racecourses attracted the leading owners and horses, it required local personnel for the sport to also have merit in a local context. Great credit was due to those who organised themselves into a committee to do the groundwork and establish subscription funds, mark out the land and provide a whole range of other ancillary services to make meetings successful. To ensure success, men of the calibre of Hunter and Waters brought with them knowledge and experience, as well as added value by their presence. This was something the Nenagh committee were all too aware of, though by then the halcyon days of racing at Norwood were fading fast into memory. The Hunter family was in an enviable position as racing administrators. From 1805, as 'proprietor and publisher of the Irish *Racing Calendar*', Robert Hunter continued a familial association with horse racing in Ireland, which became more evident with the involvement of his son, John Ryan Hunter, and grandson, Robert J. Hunter.[164]

THE FESTIVE NATURE OF THE RACING EXPERIENCE

The festival atmosphere which horse racing brought to a community brightened the lives of many people.[165] This atmosphere ranged from music, song and dance, to the beggars and cripples seeking alms. The races were also seen, however, as a great opportunity for thieving and violence. Coupled with this was the whole gambling experience associated with racing. Racing was the only occasion when entry was freely available to all the social classes. While the lords and ladies assembled in or near the standhouse, no matter how temporary the structure, the lower classes found their own merriment in the tented marquees that were erected at various areas on the course. Unlike the secluded games of country estates, race day provided a carnivalesque atmosphere, as work stopped and towns and communities more or less came to a standstill.

Race day, for many people, was a welcome change from the mundane way of life, each enjoying the festive nature of the day. There was alcohol-induced merriment, but the sense of occasion and the respite from work duties was reason enough to be part of such a rare event. To this end the press reports regularly carried accounts of the large numbers in attendance,[166] noting that 'the bold peasantry flocked in in hundreds', 'crowds of the peasantry "our country's pride" thronged to witness the sport', and 'thousands of the stalworth [*sic*] peasantry of the country also thronged to the scene of the sport'.[167] When the lower classes were notable by their absence, this also was recorded,[168] their absence put down to the fact that many of them had emigrated.

Reports of race meetings told of much merriment due to the nature of the race day experience. With large quantities of alcohol available, intemperance resulted and this frequently led to some form of violence. At the Ormond Hunt steeplechases in 1850 there were 'frequent scenes of drunken brawls, rioting and fighting' even though there were '150 police on the ground'.[169] The problem was that the police were frequently overwhelmed by the sheer mass of people present. Many of these were from the lower classes and with them came the begging and mendicant fraternity who lined the streets and roads leading to the racecourse. How genuine their claims for alms were was also a matter of some suspicion. At the Tipperary races in 1861, on the approach to the Barronstown course, it was noted that:

> ... there is nothing to mar the view except the *objects* that meet the gaze along the route, craving, with obsolete phraseology, the charity of by-passers. We have little sympathy with such representations of misshapen humanity. Revolting scenes like those speak not to the eye of pity. They are completely out of place, and awaken only a sickening sensation when suddenly obtruded upon the visitor to a race-course. We would be far from shortening the arm of charity, but when we know the thousand-and-one contrivance, to deprive the human form of its wonted shape and manly appearance, and when we hear the rapid flow of mendicant blessings, often terminated with as eloquent a delivery of impious curses, pity wings its flight and leaves behind but the traces of disgust.[170]

If these attempts at pity were one malign aspect of the race day experience, so too was the threat of violence, typically associated with factionalism in the 1840s. This was something the police and military were ready to counter. 'A pitched battle was talked of between the Black Hens and Magpies' during the Ormond Hunt races of 1843 as these two factional groups shaped up to each other.[171] Tipperary was plagued by factionalism in the 1840s and 1850s and the racecourse was an arena in which to pitch battle.[172] Consequently, there was regularly a large presence of police at the races to prevent such instances from occurring, though there is no indication as to how the police presence was financed.[173]

In 1856, one of the largest riots occurred at the Templemore races. Soldiers and peasants rioted and fought each other. Early reports indicated that some soldiers had been killed, though this was later disproved.[174] For their part, eleven men were sentenced to twelve months' hard labour when they came before the magistrates.[175] Another incident at Tipperary saw Daniel Ryan indicted for the manslaughter of John Ryan at Barronstown races. He was subsequently found not guilty by the magistrates.[176] Incidences of stabbings, skull fractures and broken teeth also came before the court.[177] Most of the cases revolved around drunken behaviour that eventually became aggressive. Theft was also common, with pickpockets making light of people's winnings on many occasions. Quite often the guilty party was apprehended on the course, where sentence was handed down by those assembled. In 1851 at the Clonmel garrison races 'two or three pickpockets got soundly thrashed' when caught red-handed.[178] Instances such as these presented a moral dilemma for the gentlemen who organised racing. While their class might frown on such illegal behaviour, they benefited financially from the race meeting itself. Stall holders and course owners needed patrons. With a large attendance likely, sufficient stall holders also attended and they paid course owners for their pitch areas. In essence, horse racing was an anomaly. It was not really part of the socially improving ethic of other sports. Whereas Victorian principles of sport leaned towards the muscular Christianity philosophy of a sound mind in a sound body, horse racing did not conform to this ethos.

One leading Turf historian, Mike Huggins, has argued that the *raison d'être* of horse racing was to facilitate gambling.[179] That horse racing and gambling went hand in hand was without question. While references to the odds for horses at races in County Tipperary were given in the local press from the eighteenth century, little evidence has been identified to suggest that gambling impacted greatly on the livelihoods of its residents. But one must assume that it did. If gambling affected family and work circumstances in Great Britain, then it surely had a similar impact in Ireland, including Tipperary. In race reports the odds quoted were more likely to be published than the name of the jockey.[180] Reports regularly noted that large sums of money changed hands in the ring. At the Cashel steeplechases in 1859, 'in the ring the betting ... was rather heavy and continuous. A considerable amount of cash changed pockets' on several occasions.[181] Not only that, the odds at Tattersalls commonly appeared in the local press in the same column as the list of forthcoming hunt meetings.[182] Newspaper editors were not slow in identifying what their readers wanted to see. When Chippendale won the Cesarewitch in 1879 it was reported that 'an assistant in one of the grocery establishments in this town [Nenagh]' placed a bet of £1 at 20/1 and won £20.[183] Shop assistants were as likely to place a bet as anyone else who took an interest in racing and gambling. It was only when a notable wager was made public that such an instance came to one's attention. Little is known about the bookmakers operating in the towns and villages of Tipperary, but one can assume that human nature was no different to that in the rest of Great Britain and Ireland. On-course bookies and the development of the on-course telegraph further enhanced the opportunity for gambling.[184]

Without doubt, gambling was very much part and parcel of race day. There were bookmakers, con-men and tricksters all ready and willing to extract as much money as they could, from whomever they could. The wealthy could gamble in the ring and the lower classes could gamble with the thimble-riggers and con-men. Whichever means it took it all added to the excitement of the day. That alcohol-induced violence occurred was a lamentable feature of many race days, something the organisers were keen to disown. But to stop it would have meant to refuse entry to alcohol traders which, in turn, meant a loss of revenue. Commercialism was the key to race day – the traders made money, the bookmakers and con-men made money, and the landowners made money.

However, the main concern of the landowners and race organisers was who controlled the profit generated from the various events and sideshows associated with race day. By roping off specific sections of the race venue to sideshows, vendors in tents and all other manner of food and beverage dealers, the course owners rented out specific sections and made money. At Cashel, James Dunne had a rule that all money due for tents was to be paid up front on the day before the races.[185] One 'itinerant seller of bottled ale', who took an action against the course owner, had his case heard before the magistrates in the aftermath of the 1863 Cashel races.[186] Having paid 7s 6d for admission he set up his tent 'inside the ropes' with 'about 150 dozen of porter and ale' bottles. He claimed to have lost about £4 when asked to move to another part of the course and sought to recover £8 in loss and damages. As a lone voice in a dispute with the course owner and race organisers the evidence against him led to a dismissal of his claims. This is but one example of the legal manoeuvres against the unregulated use of stall locations that was encouraged by the organisers to protect their reputation and also their profit margin. That said, some committees came under pressure to survive, largely due to an excessive number of races for small prize money rather than incidents on course which may have generated bad publicity.

CONCLUSION

Horseraces were the most widely supported sporting events in Tipperary between 1840 and 1880. No other sporting activity could match them in terms of spectator numbers or the money needed to ensure that meetings were financially viable, let alone successful. This required a great input from local business and private interests in terms of subscriptions and sponsorship. That money was generated from the races is without question. The races greatly added to the local town economy but were also such that an annual event was as much as any town could support. There was a symbiotic relationship between horse racing and hunting. The hunt community played a pivotal role in establishing race meetings county-wide. There was continued recognition of the value of farmers to the hunt community, this gratitude being demonstrated with the holding of farmers' races at various race meetings.

Though it was an influential body of men that was associated with horse racing in Tipperary, the organisation and structure put in place by them did not cross over to other sports. Neither did the lessons that they had learned about regulation, racing grounds, or profit maximisation. Rather, they used their experiences to support the racing circuit and meetings, not only locally but nationally. All of this took place under the aegis of the Turf Club and the National Hunt Steeplechase Committee. For the labouring and working classes, more than anything else, racing gave them a release from the daily routine of life. When they attended in large numbers at the various meetings their presence and lack of self-control often impacted on race results due to course incursions. Nevertheless, their presence made the occasion.

CHAPTER 5

THE ADVENT OF ORGANISED
ATHLETICS AND ROWING

INTRODUCTION

In an article entitled 'A word about Irish athletics', published in *United Ireland* in October 1884, the writer told of a decline in athletic sports in Ireland. He called on 'Irish people to take the management of their games into their own hands, to encourage and promote in every way every form of athletics which is peculiarly Irish, and to remove with one sweep everything foreign and iniquitous in the present system'.[1] The author of this article was widely believed to be Michael Cusack, a native of County Clare, who was resident in Dublin since 1874.[2] By 1884 he was repulsed by the route which organised athletics had taken in the capital city of Ireland.[3] Cusack objected to the fact that all athletics meetings were held 'under the rules of the Amateur Athletic Association of England, and that any person competing at any meeting not held under these rules should be ineligible to compete elsewhere'.[4] Since 1882 all athletic meetings in Ireland were held under these rules to the detriment of Irish athletes and athletics, he argued. In reply, Maurice Davin, a native of Carrick-on-Suir and one of the leading weight throwers of the 1870s, noted that while the 'English Handbooks of Athletics' were very good, they did not refer to many of the Irish games.[5] Cusack's claim primarily related to weight throwing and jumping events and their demise at athletic sports meetings.

Even though Tipperary is the focus here, nonetheless a brief overview of Cusack's attack on the administration of athletics in Ireland, as he observed them in 1884, is necessary to find out if there was any basis for extending his argument to the rest of Ireland. Tipperary is used as a template from which to assess this. His article in *United Ireland* was part of a movement then gathering pace which would ultimately lead to the foundation of the Gaelic Athletic Association in Thurles in November 1884. When the organisation was established and hurling and Gaelic football became codified 'the GAA had already reached its own rational compromise on amateurism for athletics'.[6]

Was there any basis for his attack on the athletic structure in Ireland prior to the foundation of the GAA? Essentially, were the men who took part in rural athletics meetings in Tipperary or rowing activities in Carrick-on-Suir and Clonmel similar to their contemporaries in the rest of Ireland and Great Britain? Both Cusack and Maurice Davin were from a farming background. They were representative of the type of athlete who competed at meetings around the country. In Tipperary there were two parallel sporting identities emerging in the 1870s, that of the amateur, such as Maurice Davin, and men who were good enough to compete in athletic events at various locations around the county, for monetary prizes. While they derived income from their winnings, they were neither amateur in the true sense of the word, nor full-time professionals. They had a natural talent and they used it to their financial advantage. The relevance of this is that there was a pay for play aspect associated with athletics in Tipperary. Some of these men earned, from their winnings, an income which ensured a high standard of living, not at all comparable with that of which farm labourers were accustomed. They competed in events with a disregard for the athletic principles of amateurism.

After the foundation of the GAA, Michael Cusack was open to athletes getting cash prizes rather than 'fish knives and butter coolers'.[7] He argued that with the money they received they would be able to go out and buy the fish, butter or whatever it was they needed.[8] In the true sense of amateur principles, the ideology of Cusack stood out as inconsistent. There were several examples where rural Tipperary athletes flouted the amateur principles. While 'the new world of amateur sport became exclusive and emphasised the strength of class discrimination', this discrimination did not deter Irish athletes from competing for money.[9] Athletic sports in Ireland were similar to those in England in that they were not class-neutral,[10] but in Tipperary, as in County Westmeath, there was a form of popular athletics in existence below the level of elite participation. This world of popular athletics had nothing to do with the concept of amateurism as it was known in elite social circles. This world was inhabited by the rural middle-class farmer and his sons who had the time and money to participate on weekdays or whatever day suited them.

At an athletic sports meeting at Carrick-on-Suir in September 1875 the Davins were conspicuous by their absence. All the prizes were listed as monetary. The big winner of the day was Richard St John. Of four events in which he competed, he won three and brought home £5 in prize money. This was at a time when male farm labourers engaged in the harvest in the Carrick-on-Suir district received twelve shillings per week 'and their support', with their female counterparts receiving thirteen shillings per week 'and their support'. It was noted that this was 'the first time in the history of local labour that the *other* sex received a higher rate of wages than their lords'.[11] In 1881, near Fethard, farm labourers earned ten pence per day, while other farm employees earned sums ranging from one shilling per day to six pounds per annum depending on their contract.[12] As is shown later on in this chapter, Richard St John was financially rewarded for his victories over the course of five years. This success bordered on professionalism, with the prize money from the sports in 1875 the equivalent of one year's wages for farm labourers (see Table 5.2). Yet he was allowed to participate in the four-mile race at the Irish Champion Athletic Club sports at Lansdowne Road in May 1877.[13] His previous record should have been sufficient to deem him ineligible. In Ireland, as in England, 'it is unlikely that the rule [relating to amateur status] was always strictly enforced'.[14] Hence there was no great fuss made about amateurism in athletics until Michael Cusack entered the fray. Cusack objected to 'pot hunters', claiming that abuses had crept into Irish athletics on foot of adopting events and styles then common in England. Cusack appears to have suffered from ignorance, or amnesia, in this respect as in Tipperary several athletes, such as St John, were very adept at pot-hunting at various sports meetings in the county throughout the 1870s. They were not alone in this respect as 'several promising men were turning up at every meeting, particularly in the South of Ireland'.[15]

This is the crux of the amateur debate in an Irish context. There were true amateur sportsmen who competed at Trinity College races, as well as at the Irish Champion Athletic Club meetings. However, in rural Ireland there were athletes who competed at a level below that of the true amateur, who neither cared for nor were interested in amateur principles. Rather, the debates and discussions that took place in England and elsewhere were largely academic and of interest only to a small number of men. For this body of competitive athletes in Ireland the amateur debate was totally irrelevant and this was the constituency which the GAA tapped into.

Athletics, similar to other sports, owed much of its initial structure and promotion to military officers as agents of diffusion. There was a sporting evolution taking place in mid-Victorian Great Britain and Ireland and in this respect, athletics and rowing were no different. As various sports became codified, their embryonic development had as much to do with invention as with tradition and continuity. A case in point here is Gaelic football, a game specifically engineered to be played on the same field as hurling. Gaelic football took elements of various forms of folk football, which gave it a unique identity, but it was essentially an invented sport. While athletic sports meetings were quite common within Ireland from the 1870s, this chapter also looks at the distribution pattern in relation to these meetings in Tipperary and the degree to which elements of amateurism were evident in their organisation.

Contemporaneous with the development of athletics was rowing, specifically in Clonmel and to a lesser extent in Carrick-on-Suir. Rowing is the second sport covered in this chapter, a sport which also had close associations with the spirit of amateurism. Like athletics, rowing too had events for amateurs and for men who competed for prize money. As is shown later, the engagement of professional trainers demonstrates the existence of a mindset that embraced elements of professionalism, especially when it came to competition.

THE GROWTH OF ATHLETICS

In the years preceding the Famine, a popular recreation for gentleman in south Tipperary was the novel amusement called 'pedestrianism'. Pedestrianism was a form of competitive walking, which was often professional. It was funded by both spectators and participants, who gambled on the outcome. It was the discipline from which the modern sport of race-walking developed.[16] Some of these events took place over cross-country courses, as many of these gentlemen were military officers and local professional men. For example, in Clonmel in 1842 some military personnel from the local barracks took part in a half-mile race 'across the country, embracing eight leaps'.[17] Typical of such events, 'some heavy bets' were laid on the outcome of the race.[18]

In his account of pedestrianism, Walter Thom argued that it was by 'exercise that the soldier is gradually inured to the hardships of the field'.[19] What the military officers brought to south Tipperary was a knowledge and experience of pedestrianism which was widespread in England and also in Scotland at that time, but not as well known in rural southern Ireland.[20] One writer noted that in early nineteenth-century England, sprinting and pedestrianism 'enjoyed aristocratic patronage'.[21] One of the principal reasons why such events occurred at this time was because the English officers were familiar with the sport prior to their posting in Ireland. These men had a lot of free time to take part in such activities and lay wagers on the outcome. It was an accident of military posting rather than design. It also gave some local gentlemen an opportunity to test their own abilities against the officers. Unlike in England, pedestrianism had a small number of participants in Tipperary, resulting in an equally small number of races. Essentially, pedestrianism in Tipperary was a frivolity and it soon gave way to athletic sports meetings. As these meetings became popular in the county it was no surprise to find the military leading their promotion. Yet the presence of the military contradicts Cusack's belief that when the 'so-called revival of athletics was inaugurated in Ireland ... labourers, tradesmen, artists, and even policemen and soldiers were excluded from the few competitions which constituted the lame and halting programme of the promoters'.[22] The 1860s was a watershed decade for the athletic movement in Tipperary as athletic meetings came to replace pedestrianism. What followed in its wake were athletic sports meetings.

The term 'athletics' is used as an all-embracing term which includes foot racing, racing against time, hurdling, leaping events and weight-throwing events. The 'first recorded athletic meeting' in Ireland was held at Trinity College, Dublin on 28 February 1857.[23] An athletics meeting was held in Drogheda in 1861.[24] One of the earliest athletics meetings in County Tipperary, with fifteen events up for decision, was organised by the non-commissioned officers of the 4th Hussars at Cahir barracks. This also took place in 1861. No breakdown of the event types was quoted in the press though reference was made to 'the spirit of the mounted [horse races] and foot racing'.[25] Military athletic sports had previously taken place in the Curragh.[26] The Cahir sports, ostensibly arranged to commemorate the 'memorable charge at Balaklava', had events that were solely competed for by men who fought in this famous battle. The holding of such a sports meeting was also contemporaneous with similar happenings in England.[27]

While the officers and soldiers had military tasks and duties to perform, their duties within the walls of the barracks also afforded them time for recreation.[28] In Templemore, the military were a key component in the growth of athletics in the town. Apart from supplying the parade field for athletics, there were also military and civilian races which attracted great interest. From 1869 military regiments, such as the 44th and 68th Light Infantry, held annual athletic events in the parade field, which was adjacent to the garrison.[29] An athletic club was then formed in the town. Mr Casey, a town commissioner and the club secretary, instituted an athletic sports meeting to take place in August 1871. While no records have been found for this club, it is likely that it was established on foot of the athletic interest generated in the town by the military. The exploits of the soldiers likely led to emulation locally, and a town club was then established.

There are no athletic sports meetings identified in County Tipperary organised by civilians prior to the military meetings. This is an important element in the popularisation of these sports in this part of rural Ireland. Anything that followed owed everything to the example shown by the military. In 1868, a largely civilian sports event took place at Fethard in a 'large field adjoining the barracks' and it was observed that 'such gatherings are fraught with many advantages: they tend to bind classes in kindliness of feeling, to develop manly vigour, and to create a wholesome rivalry for the attainment of an object, which benefits the competitors both mentally and physically'.[30] Events on the day included races such as the mile, 100 yards, 440 yards hurdle, running high jump, boys' races and the ever-popular 'throwing the cricket ball'. Infrequent school athletic meetings, usually no more than end-of-school-year outings, suggests that there was no developmental role undertaken by the county schools, such as Rockwell College or Tipperary Grammar School, to promote athletics. While schools in Dublin played a role in promoting athletics, this argument does not stand for Tipperary.[31] It is very likely that public schools, if not exactly disapproving of athletics, viewed such sports with suspicion because they promoted the cult of the individual and did nothing to enhance 'team spirit'.

Unlike other sports in which they were prominent, such as horse racing, hunting to hounds, cricket and archery, landlords and businessmen did not actively organise athletics during this period. There are instances, as at Cahir in 1870, where three of the landed elite had their names included in a list of ten patrons for the military sports, but there was no evidence that they were actively engaged in establishing athletic sports meetings.[32] The soldiers who competed at the latter end of the 1860s and at the start of the 1870s were not unlike those who took part in pedestrianism a generation earlier. The primary change was that gentlemen amateurs, the officers, were now replaced by competitors drawn from the lower ranks. Though the men drawn from the lower ranks were to the fore in the athletic events, it was the officer class which granted permission for the sports to take place, and it was the officers who led the committee which brought the athletic sports meeting to a successful conclusion.[33]

At the 'military and constabulary athletic games' in Nenagh it was commented that few would not 'ascert [*sic*] that the innocent recreation ... had any other than a sympathetic ennobling and exhilarating tendency both upon the crowd of spectators and the vigorous fellows who entered the lists'.[34] While the sports were the reason for the gathering of 'nearly all the respectable shopkeepers of the town, the town commissioners and their families, [and] a large contribution from the country around', the report commenced by highlighting the importance of the military to the community. It remarked that there was probably not a town in Ireland 'that would not also aspire to the *undefined status* [*sic*] imparted to every place where troops are quartered from January to December'.[35] This was a key element in the relationship of the military with the garrison town. The correspondent was well aware, as were the shopkeepers and town commissioners, of the economic advantages a military barracks brought to the town. This was not something that occurred occasionally – the military were present all year round. One cannot discount either that a commanding officer understood the economic importance of the barracks to the community. This was not specific to Tipperary.

From the start of the 1870s there was a sustained growth of the athletic sports phenomenon in Tipperary. From 1872 to 1880 the spread of athletic sports meetings in the county radiated from the south Tipperary hinterland of Carrick-on-Suir, home to the Davin family, to the rest of the county (see Figure 5.1 and Table 5.1).[36] Also making an appearance as a new agency of diffusion was the Catholic Young Men's Society (CYMS), Roscrea, which held a series of athletics meetings in the summer of 1873.[37] It was one of the rare occasions when sports were organised on a confessional basis in Tipperary. The CYMS was established in Roscrea, around 1863 or 1864.[38] A Young Men's Christian Association (YMCA) was previously established in the town, sometime around 1859.[39] This was a Protestant organisation, though no evidence has come to light to indicate if it was involved in any other sport in the town. The CYMS were also active on the cricket field from 1873 to 1877.[40] There was also a CYMS cricket team in Kilkenny.[41]

But unlike in England, and in particular Birmingham, while these cricket and athletic sports originated from a church organisation, they were unable to keep their activities going. In Birmingham, on the other hand, Aston Villa Football Club became an integral part of the life of many in the church organisation from which it drew its origins.[42] However, the origins of clubs in Roscrea and Birmingham are similar

Figure 5.1 Location of athletics meetings, 1868–80, key relates to map numbers in Table 5.1

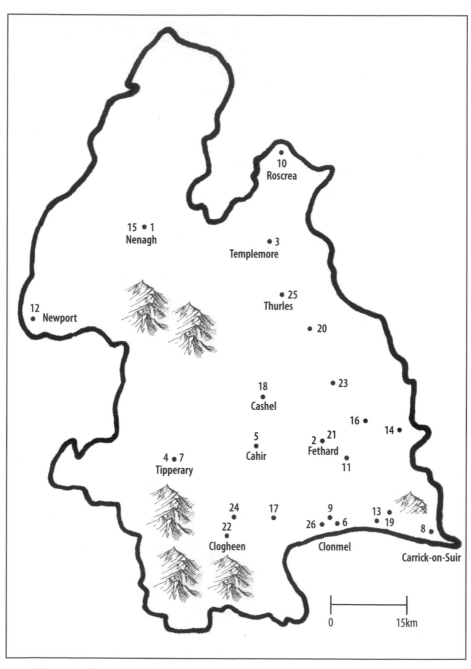

Sources: *CG, CC, NG, TFP* (1868–1880)

in one respect. The 'sporting initiative' came from the civilian members of clubs rather than from any direct involvement with the clergy.[43] During this time, the clergy, especially the Roman Catholic clergy, were noticeable by their absence from sporting matters throughout the county. In the context of the period, when the Catholic Church under Cardinal Cullen became increasingly Romanised and control over the flock was increasingly coordinated, this lack of interest in the recreation of parishioners is noteworthy. It was not until the GAA was founded that the Catholic clergy took an active interest in matters of Irish sport.

Table 5.1 Location of athletic sports meetings by inception date, 1868–1880

MAP NO.	LOCATION	YEAR	MAP NO.	LOCATION	YEAR
1	Nenagh Garrison	1868	14	Mullinahone	1873
2	Fethard Garrison	1868	15	Nenagh	1875
3	Templemore Garrison	1869	16	Drangan	1875
4	Tipperary Garrison	1869	17	Clogheen	1876
5	Cahir	1869	18	Rockwell College	1876
6	Clonmel Garrison	1870	19	Graigue	1876
7	Tipp. Grammar Sch.	1870	20	Littleton	1876
8	Carrick-on-Suir	1872	21	Fethard	1876
9	Clonmel	1872	22	Burntcourt	1877
10	Roscrea CYMS	1873	23	Noan	1877
11	Killusty	1873	24	Rehill	1877
12	St John's College, Newport	1873	25	Thurles	1878
13	Kilsheelan	1873	26	Clonmel Endowed School	1880

Sources: *CG, CC, NG, TFP* (1868-1880)

While Fethard held a sports meeting in 1868, the geography of athletic meetings suggests that the sport spread, year on year, around the central hub of Carrick-on-Suir and Clonmel. It was as if desire to emulate the Davins' success resulted in the athletics phenomenon spreading steadily outward from their south Tipperary base. Killusty, Mullinahone, Kilsheelan, Cahir, Drangan, Graigue and Littleton were rural towns and villages which, by 1876, had held an athletics meeting. These towns and villages were near to each other. This made for easier travel between home and the sports, mindful that several of these areas had no rail connection. Similar meetings in the north and west of the county may not have been reported in the local press. The absence of any reported events there is reflected in blank areas in Figure 5.1.

These sports had the potential to attract large numbers of spectators. At the sports in Carrick-on-Suir, in 1872, there were about 3,000 people present, while it was stated that 5,000 people were present at an athletic sports meeting in Mullinahone in 1873.[44] In Killusty, also in 1873, 'the muster of people on the ground could not have been far short of ten or twelve thousand persons'.[45] After two years the Littleton sports lapsed. The meeting was replaced by the nearby Thurles sports, which was eight kilometres away. An improbable '20,000 spectators' was estimated to have attended at these sports in 1878, their first year.[46] Not only were athletics meetings attracting regular competitors, they also attracted an interested public. The involvement of a local athlete brought with it reflected glory on his community. This adulation was a likely contributory factor in the development of athletic sports meetings in other towns and villages around Tipperary.

Apart from the Davin brothers, William Foley (Carrick-on-Suir),[47] Michael Tobin (Drangan),[48] Richard St John (Mullinahone),[49] Walter Duggan (Powerstown),[50] and T.K. Dwyer (Littleton)[51] featured regularly in athletics meetings during the period 1872–1876. Not alone did this happen at a meeting in their own town or village but at other events around Tipperary and Ireland. The nucleus of athletes who competed and won from south-east Tipperary soon spread to the middle of the county. This suggests a structured nature to the events. The entrance fee to each event was usually one shilling. Racing for a monetary prize was a feature of Irish athletics.[52]

The majority of athletics sports meetings were organised by committees formed for that specific purpose (see Table 5.1 for the inception date of meetings in Tipperary). Most meetings had a programme of sports which usually numbered fourteen events. Typically, first place in an event carried a prize of £1, with ten shillings awarded to the second-placed competitor. The irony of this was that most events rarely attracted enough competitors, who paid one shilling entry fee to match the prize money for the event. But not only that, it was not unusual for an athlete to enter and then not compete in an event. At the Littleton sports in September 1877, seventeen entries were received for the 220 yards race but only ten competitors ran. It seems likely that some withdrew when they saw the opposition, while others were entered and had their names published to boost interest in the event. Similarly, for the half-mile race, eighteen entries were received but only ten ran.[53]

This was not something that was specific to Tipperary.[54] Therefore, the organisers had to find some other way to meet the cost of the events, and one option was to erect a standhouse. While this incurred another cost, it was probable that the revenues of the day were balanced by the money generated from entry to the confined area. At the Powerstown sports in 1873 entry to the stand was two shillings. A press report noted that 'it was crowded throughout the day' and apart from the stand there were 'thousands on the course'.[55] Such was the festival nature of the meeting that many businesses and shops closed at 1.00 p.m. to allow employees to attend.

There are rare references in the press to an entry fee to a venue. In 1876, at the Nenagh Cricket Club sports, admission to the reserved entrance cost one shilling, and sixpence to the field. This is an example of fundraising by that club.[56] The programme of sports in 1879 noted that the entrance was sixpence to the sports and, for the grandstand, the fee was one shilling.[57] At a time when general admission fees were not levied at athletics meetings, let alone at horse race meetings, the entrance charge was a means of regulating those who actually entered the grounds. It was something which the Nenagh CC had put in place since the inception of its sports. Many people would not have been in a position to afford the sixpence admission fee so this worked as a filtering process, enforcing social exclusion without actually stating it was so.

Nenagh Cricket Club, from 1875, organised an annual series of athletic sports, which proved successful. These were widely supported by the inhabitants of the town, with 'at least two thousand spectators' present.[58] That a cricket club embarked on such a programme of events, given that it was active on the cricket field, suggests an organisational structure which was both committed and focused on embracing a wide variety of sporting activities and occasions. Over the next few years the club continued with its athletic sports programme. However, despite the self-congratulatory expressions conveyed in the press, the fact remained that the number of competitors was small. Though good prize money was on offer, the two shillings entry fee for some events was a deterrent to many people. Others attempted to force free admission to the sports by pushing on the gates.[59] Be that as it may, the sports brought valued custom to the town with 'cash receipts … possibly doubled' in the shops on account of the increased number of people coming into Nenagh.[60] So successful were the sports that, in 1880, a second series of events was organised for October.[61]

The accounts of the Carrick-on-Suir Amateur Athletic, Cricket and Football Club up to its first general meeting in March 1880 give some indication that the introduction of entrance fees was common. Accounts for the club sports in November 1879 show that entrance fees amounted to £1 8s but that 'money received at gate and cards of evening' came to £21.[62] This amount greatly assisted in covering the expenses incurred and, as such, one may infer that at some other meetings admission fees were charged to the general public.

There are some striking parallels between steeplechase racing and athletics meetings in terms of structure and organisation. Aspects of this cross-fertilisation included the list of patrons, reserved standhouse and enclosure, prize money events, and local organisation. A field was requisitioned by a local committee to hold an event that took place in an afternoon, to which, for the most part, general admission was free.

Those wishing to aspire to better facilities had to pay for the luxury of such goods or amenities.

Other agencies and individuals also sought ways of making money from the athletics phenomenon sweeping through south Tipperary. The committee which organised the Kilsheelan athletic sports, in September 1873, rented a field for the day only to discover 'almost at the last moment ... [that] their rule was transgressed by the owner of the land in permitting a publican to erect a tent in the field adjoining'.[63] At this juncture the selling of alcohol was prohibited at such meetings. Unlike horse racing, where beer tents were a common feature of the paraphernalia of the day, athletics were a different proposition. The organising committee of the Powerstown sports in 1873 were lauded in that they '*absolutely prohibited* the sale of intoxicating drinks on the grounds'.[64] The fact that any money accruing from such a tent was more likely to go back to the farmer rather than the committee was another point at issue. Consequently, all equipment associated with the sports was subsequently removed to another site, with 'the carpenter from Gurteen ... in very active requisition, for a stand-house was erected at a point commanding a full view of the enclosure'. In late 1874 a comment in the press advised that perhaps the Waterford and Limerick Rail Company might see fit to run a 'special' from Clonmel to Cahir for the forthcoming sports, on St Stephen's Day,[65] suggesting that it 'would be a paying speculation'.[66] This they did, carrying passengers to the town with return fares charged at a single fare rate. This greatly contributed to the attendance and it also gave this railway company another sporting connection. As mentioned previously, the Waterford and Limerick Railway Company regularly ran sporting specials to towns on its route.

Overall from 1868 to 1880 there were seventy-six separate athletic sports meetings. These included civilian, military and school sports. When compared with central Scotland the results are impressive. For the decade 1871 to 1880 there were sixty-eight separate meetings in Tipperary while for central Scotland the figure stands at just six[67] (see Figure 5.2). The population of Tipperary in 1871 was 216,713, while for central Scotland it was 2,047,000.[68]

Figure 5.2 Athletic sports meetings in County Tipperary, 1868–1880 (Total = 76)

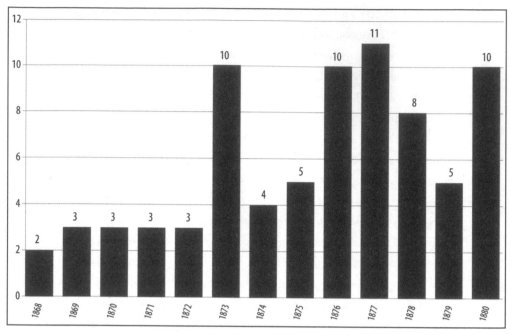

Source: *CG, CC, KM, NG, TFP* (1868–1880)

When locations are mapped and dates of meetings are analysed, the evidence shows that there was an expansion of such meetings on the back of similar ones at the various military garrisons countywide. The geographic spread was centred on the south-east of the county emanating from Carrick-on-Suir. Seamus Ó Riain has noted that these meetings were a 'spontaneous response to the demand for community recreation that was influenced by the track and field achievements of the Davin brothers'.[69] Local committees were quick to recognise the financial benefits which accrued from the holding of athletics meetings and hence these meetings sprang up in towns as easily as they did in the remotest rural villages. That there was an element of commercialisation with some of these meetings is without doubt. Insofar as athletes competed for money, so too did the committees. Their remit was one of business, as opposed to patronage, and this marked a change in emphasis in the sporting culture of Tipperary in the 1870s.

ATHLETICS IN THE 1870s

Though the Amateur Athletic Club, in 1866–67, 'specifically excluded mechanics, artisans and labourers' from participating in sports, there was no comparable body in Ireland to regulate athletics.[70] With the formation of the Irish Champion Athletic Club (ICAC) by Henry W.D. Dunlop, in Dublin, in 1872, which attracted many of the leading athletes as members, an impetus was given to other communities to emulate them and establish an athletics club of their own. From the outset, the ICAC attempted to 'impose some form of unified or central control on the management of Irish athletics'.[71] It sought to have All-Ireland championships on its grounds in Dublin which were open to all Irish gentleman amateurs. The Davin brothers competed at these meetings. The success of Maurice in the weight-throwing events resulted in his nomination to represent Ireland at international sports meetings in England.[72]

From an analysis of the results of the various athletic events in Tipperary between 1872 and 1878 it is clear that several men earned a handsome amount of prize money in the course of their athletic endeavours. It was not unusual for an athlete to enter and compete at several events on the same day. At the Powerstown sports in August 1872 William Foley of Carrick-on-Suir entered three events at a cost of one shilling each. However, he won the three events and took home £3 in prize money for his efforts.[73] But he did not always have such a successful day. Having entered five events, again at the Powerstown sports in June 1873, he spent five shillings, but won only one event, for which he received a prize of a 'silver sugar bowl'.[74] Similarly, in competing at ten separate meetings between 1873 and 1877, Richard St John of Mullinahone won £17 13s 6d, two cups (one valued at thirty shillings) and a 'flask' in the thirty-two events in which he competed. Data from the press reports suggests that for half of these meetings he paid one shilling entrance fee. One may assume that he made a handsome return on his investment for an outlay of thirty shillings (Table 5.2).[75] St John also brought with him a trait that was common among athletes – he competed as an individual. Most competitors chose 'to identify themselves by reference to their parish, village, or their townland of birth'.[76] Yet what St John

Table 5.2 Athletic career of Richard St John, Mullinahone, 1873–1877

EVENT	LOCATION	PLACE	ENTRANCE FEE	PRIZE	COMMENT
300 yards hurdle	Powerstown	2nd	1 shilling	10 shillings	
Hop, step & jump	Powerstown	2nd	1 shilling	10 shillings	
100 yards flat	Killusty	2nd	1 shilling	10 shillings	8 ran
300 yards hurdle	Killusty	2nd	1 shilling	10 shillings	
600 yards hurdle	Killusty	1st	1 shilling	£1	
Hop, step & jump	Killusty	2nd	1 shilling	£1	
100 yards flat	Mullinahone	1st	1 shilling	£1	
300 yards hurdle	Mullinahone	2nd	1 shilling	10 shillings	
600 yards hurdle	Mullinahone	1st	1 shilling	£1 10s	
100 yards flat	Kilsheelan	1st	1 shilling	£1 5s	
300 yards hurdle	Kilsheelan	2nd	1 shilling	10 shillings	6 ran
Hop, step & jump	Kilsheelan	1st	1 shilling	£1	
600 yards hurdle	Kilsheelan	1st	1 shilling	£1 1s	
100 yards open	Carrick-on-Suir	3rd	Unknown	Unknown	
440 yards	Carrick-on-Suir	1st	Unknown	£1 10s	
Half mile race	Carrick-on-Suir	1st	Unknown	£1	5 ran
Mile race	Carrick-on-Suir	1st	Unknown	£1 10s	4 ran
880 yards	Clonmel	1st	Unknown	30s or Cup	9 started
Mile race	Clonmel	1st	Unknown	Cup	10 started
100 yards	Kilsheelan	2nd	Unknown	£1	12 ran
120 yards hurdle	Kilsheelan	3rd	Unknown	Unknown	13 entered
440 yards	Kilsheelan	2nd	Unknown	Unknown	13 entered
4 mile race	Lansdowne Road	D.N.F.	Unknown	0	
Half mile race	Mullinahone	1st	Unknown	Unknown	
120 yards hurdle	Mullinahone	2nd	Unknown	Unknown	
440 yards hurdle	Mullinahone	2nd	Unknown	Unknown	
3 leg race, 440 yards	Mullinahone	1st	Unknown	Unknown	W. Pollard
220 yards flat	Littleton	2nd	Unknown	Unknown	
Half mile flat h-cap	Littleton	1st	Unknown	Unknown	2min 20sec
Hop, step & jump	Graigue	2nd	Unknown	Flask	
2 miles walking	Graigue	2nd	Unknown	7s. 6d.	
1 mile flat h-cap	Graigue	2nd	Unknown	10 shillings	

Sources: *CC, IT, KM, NG, TFP* (1873–1877)

did was no different to what many athletes did elsewhere. In the heart of Lancashire, Tom Marshall, a cotton loomer, supplemented his earnings of 'around £40 per annum' with prize money from athletics and football, suggesting 'that running and playing football for money were commonplace in the 1870s in Lancashire'.[77]

Central to many of the rural and largely agrarian-based meetings in Tipperary were weight-throwing competitions, which were always part of the programme of events. Throwing the 56 lb weight or hammer were very popular events.[78] At the Killusty sports in August 1873 the fifteen events on the card were contested 'by a superior class of young men, generally the sons of farmers'.[79] The participation of farmers' sons was as common for athletics as it was for hurling in Tipperary at the latter end of the century.[80] That it was so is of no great surprise as, of the sixty-eight meetings for which a day can be identified, nineteen took place on a Thursday (see Figure 5.3).[81] It would have been difficult for labourers to get time off work to compete in athletics, unless they were exceptionally good, as was the case of the paid cricket player. For the sons of tenant farmers it would not have been as problematic, as farming was amenable to leave-taking. After Saturday, Monday was the most popular day for athletic sports, a day which was also popular for playing cricket. What is remarkable about these sixty-eight meetings is that none of them took place on a Sunday. What this demonstrates is that it was necessary for the GAA to use Sunday for its games to make them accessible to as many men as possible.[82] As is shown later on, Sunday was a day for hurling in the 1850s, but this brought with it trouble of another nature – breach of the Sabbath. Yes, there was a law against it, but Sunday play, in essence, was a clear example of the different mindsets of officialdom in Ireland and the Roman Catholic population at large. The latter had no problem with games on a Sunday and this is reinforced with early hurling examples and 1870s' cricket in the county.

Competing on a weekday – mindful of the necessity of men turning up for work and the cost of keeping a family – was something that labourers could not do. Also, there was no tradition of 'St Monday' in Ireland, an excuse which was widely used in England when one was absent from work after over-indulging on the Sabbath.[83] Consequently, members of the professional class, military personnel, farmers and their sons were mainly the ones who competed. Maurice Davin was from a farming background, his brother Pat was a solicitor, William Foley was a farmer, as was T.K. Dwyer. To be a man of independent means, in a profession, or an officer in the armed forces made one worthy of inclusion as an amateur, provided one had never competed for money.

Figure 5.3 Athletic sports meeting in County Tipperary, 1868–1880, by week day (Total = 68)

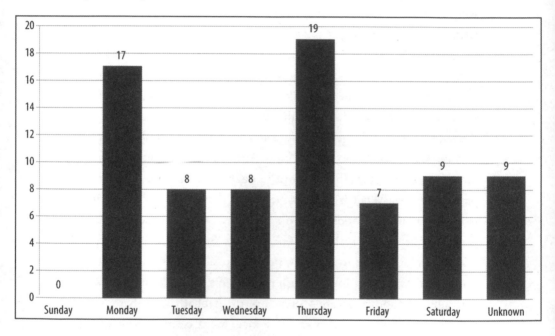

Sources: *CC, CG, KM, NG, TFP* (1868–1880)

Tipperary athletes, except for the Davin brothers and T.K. Dwyer, were not good enough to compete internationally. Evidence from the county showed that, at local events, athletes principally competed for money. The only major stumbling block was that of meeting the expense of the entrance fee. In England, class and social standing were important; 'for most of the social elite sport was an opportunity for differentiation not conciliation, and was used to restrict rather than expand contact with social inferiors'.[84] In essence 'the amateur rule [in England] was an instrument of class warfare'.[85] The same may be said of entrance fees and days when competitions were held in Tipperary irrespective of how the promotion of the sports was advertised. Financial and work impediments restricted many men from competing. The emphasis of the rural Tipperary athlete was not the same as that of the clichéd Victorian aspiring to a healthy mind in a healthy body. A romantic might perceive it as an athlete trying to be the best at his chosen discipline for the 'credit of the little village'.[86] But more likely, money was there to be won and if an athlete like Richard St John was good enough to win the money, he would.

The impetus for a growth in athletics manifested itself in south Tipperary. Carrick-on-Suir was the primary athletics hub, due initially to Maurice Davin's decision to opt for a career in athletics as opposed to rowing. It was one of the main factors, but so too was the influence of his brothers, Pat and Tom. The competitive edge they gave to Irish athletes in championship meetings against English representatives in both Dublin and London only served to enhance the reputation of Irish athletics. Weight- and hammer-throwing events were still part of the athletics programme and, if absent from some meetings, one of the primary reasons was that no-one wished to compete against Maurice Davin.[87] Davin, in reply to the mutterings of Cusack, was correct in noting 'many of the Irish games which, although much practised, are not included in the events on programmes of athletic sports'.[88] Davin felt that it was the absence of these events at athletic sports meetings around the country which had led to their decline, rather than abuses associated with athletics in general. True, there were some spectator incursions at athletics meetings in Nenagh; betting took place on some events, and monetary prizes were on offer at virtually all meetings. This was typical of a sporting environment still in its infancy; it had nothing to do with Unionist politics, as later argued by Cusack. The athletics meetings in Tipperary cannot be viewed as detrimental to hammer- and weight-throwing events principally because they still appeared on the programme and were, as Davin noted, 'much practised'.

ROWING

Contemporaneous with the emergence of athletic sports in Tipperary was the sport of rowing on the River Suir at Clonmel and Carrick-on-Suir, at the southern end of the county. Rowing is another sport that was closely linked to amateurism. By the time the River Suir reached Clonmel and then on to Carrick-on-Suir, its volume had significantly increased as it flowed south through the county. Clonmel is sited on the northern bank of the river and the morphology of the town developed parallel to it, in an east-west direction. Carrick-on-Suir developed in a similar fashion, with the principal area of the town also on the northern bank of the river.

The management of a rowing regatta was similar to that of horse racing. Local committees were to the fore in the promotion of regattas, with many races held over a series of heats. A committee was appointed by the 'local gentry' for the purpose of organising aquatic sports at Clonmel in June 1861.[89] The emergence of 'several prominent professional rowing families' in Carrick-on-Suir mirrored that which occurred among the rowing community on the Thames in England.[90] In Carrick-on-Suir, families specifically associated with rowing became prominent in boat-building and racing. Notable among them were the Davin brothers. For successful regattas, the committee needed financial support and into the breach, once more, came the landed and business classes from in and around the towns of Carrick-on-Suir and Clonmel. It is clear that some of the principal residents of the town were active in the promotion of the sports. Clonmel landlord John Bagwell regularly forwarded 'a handsome subscription' to the treasurer appointed by the committee.[91]

Regattas were held in both towns in 1871.[92] Though both were apparently successful, the regatta at Carrick-on-Suir was short-lived, coming to an end in 1872. An athletic sports meeting replaced the regatta.[93] There is no evidence to suggest that there was disharmony among the rowing community of Carrick-on-Suir, leading to the demise of the annual regatta. Rather, one of the primary reasons appeared to have been the switching of the Davin brothers from rowing to athletics. It has been shown with other sports that when some of the key personnel involved in the organisation of a club departed, the whole structure collapsed.[94] The same applied to the Carrick-on-Suir regatta. Maurice Davin specifically built boats for regattas and his departure from the sport was undoubtedly a key factor in its demise.[95] This is not to say that the Davin family stopped rowing completely, but the support they had given to the Carrick regatta was central to its survival. Another man who competed with the Davins in rowing competition, William Foley, also changed to athletics.[96] During their brief existence in Carrick-on-Suir, the regatta committee received support from leading landowners such as the Marquis of Waterford and Henry W. Briscoe, Tinvane, who was also Master of the Kilkenny Foxhounds.[97]

The Carrick-on-Suir regatta of 1871 attracted an attendance which 'could not have been less than some twenty thousand spectators gathered on the banks of the river'.[98] Though many could never hope to compete, the opportunity to attend as spectators was something that people were not going to miss. It did not matter whether it was on the Suir in Tipperary or the Thames in London, people came out in force to witness the sport.[99] What they also came out to witness was the spectacle associated with the regatta. At Clonmel in 1871, three bands played which 'greatly enlivened' the regatta experience, and such were the feelings of goodwill generated on the occasion, it was envisaged that the regatta 'be maintained as an annual event'.[100] That this was going to happen soon became evident. A meeting was called for the 'project of establishing a Rowing Club for Clonmel'.[101] At this meeting the reasons for establishing a rowing club were outlined. Almost immediately the new club set about developing plans to procure ground on which to build a boathouse.[102]

Those prominent in the town – the town mayor, town commissioners, solicitors, bankers, newspaper proprietors and landowners – were quickly associated with the club. Reports of club meetings, carrying their names, were widely published. The club president was Thomas Cambridge Grubb, a member of a long-established Quaker family. He was a corn merchant and had two mills operating at Richmond Place and Manor Mills.[103] As a river freight operator he also had business interests on the River Suir.[104] Winchester's Hotel in Clonmel was a location for club meetings when these were held away from the boathouse.[105] John Winchester, civil engineer, drew up plans for the new boathouse. Another club member, Thomas Horrigan, was appointed the contractor for the works.[106] That the boathouse was erected 'without any demand whatever upon public liberality' was deemed proof of what could be achieved 'by united and friendly co-operation'.[107]

Regattas organised by the Clonmel Rowing Club continued to be a feature of the sporting recreation in the town for the remainder of the 1870s. Such was the desire of the committee for the regattas to be successful, four specific areas of the town were apportioned to sub-committees. These sub-committees canvassed residents and businesses for subscriptions to support the regatta, which was a new departure for any sporting activity. A club now sought funds from the general public to support its activities. Heretofore hunt committees or race committees sought enhanced subscriptions from members but not from the general public. The success of the regatta in 1871 was said to be due to 'hearty support from the general public – a support which … will also place so creditable an institution as the Clonmel rowing club in a prosperous financial condition'.[108]

By early August 1872, £49 17s 6d had been collected, ensuring that funds were adequate to meet the costs of prizes on offer.[109] That the regatta was a commercial enterprise was further evidenced by the willingness, yet again, of the Waterford and Limerick Rail Company to run a 'special' train to Clonmel; it 'wisely determined to combine business with pleasure'.[110] The regatta took place on a Monday, with all businesses in town closed. It was noted that 'even the most staid of business men' felt compelled to observe the day as a general holiday and close their businesses at one o'clock as people made their way to the banks of the Suir.[111] For the regatta of 1875 the woollen and linen drapers issued a notice in the local press advising that their warehouses would close on the day of the meeting.[112] For rural shopkeepers to lose a day's business willingly was extraordinary.[113] Marquees and tents provided music, song and dance which enhanced the festival atmosphere in the town. One magistrate permitted the issuing of occasional licences for beer tents in the vicinity of the regatta, much to the dissatisfaction of the organising committee.[114] With the regatta attracting thousands to the town the commercial opportunities were exploited by many traders, some casual, but not by the shopkeepers, who had to close.

Though some of the races on the regatta programme were advertised as amateur events, the regatta itself was anything but amateur. In this respect it reflected the pattern of professional matches 'on the River Tyne where they signalled a general holiday with thousands attending'.[115] The advent of the regatta gave some retail businessmen an opportunity to increase the range of products they could offer to a discerning clientele. Andrew Milne offered 'blue serge boating suits' made to order, for thirty-five shillings. D.H. Higgins, the proprietor of a prominent sporting goods establishment, had among his range of stock 'two beautifully finished canoes, by a first class Dublin builder'.[116] This good business was also underpinned by ongoing subscriptions, some of which were used to pay off the debt on the club grounds.[117] A caretaker was employed to maintain the clubhouse and grounds.[118]

The club committee took a bold step forward in 1875 when they engaged the services of a trainer, Tom Hoare, 'under whose tuition the crews attained considerable proficiency'.[119] Hoare was an experienced oarsman, having spent much of his early career rowing on the River Thames where he was the National Champion in 1861.[120] From Hammersmith, London, Hoare trained the crews each evening. A communication to the local press noted that the club was to be 'congratulated on securing the services of a first-class trainer'.[121] Hoare also used some of the contacts which he had among the rowing community in England to obtain a firstclass four-oared out-rigger for the club from Messrs Robinson and Simms, Putney.[122]

The employment of Hoare marked a new approach to the sport by what was a relatively new rowing club. That it had the money to employ him for a brief period from August 1875 to May 1876 demonstrated the positive attitude of the committee towards competitive rowing. Hoare's employment as a professional to oversee what was, essentially, an amateur crew paid dividends for the club as, under his supervision, they won the Clonmel Cup at a very competitively fought regatta in August 1875.[123] Hoare, in accepting a gold ring as a mark of esteem for his 'generally eminent services in connection with the late regatta', added that 'it would always afford him pleasure to give his time on the selection of their boats and that he hoped in future to be associated with the victories of the Clonmel Rowing Club'.[124]

However, by 1876 Hoare had departed to take up a position as club professional with the Pengwern Boat Club in Shrewsbury when 'the committee decided to employ a professional'.[125] By this time a rule against engaging watermen as professionals was rescinded owing to the difficulty of colleges finding suitable amateur coaches.[126] A further drawback to the success of the Clonmel Rowing Club was that there was unwillingness among active members to turn up for training or participate in rowing competitions. The club captain, Gerald Fitzgerald, felt that while 'the club consisted of one hundred members and upwards, he could not say that there was really one crew fit to compete in an open race with another club'.[127]

After the departure of Hoare, matters did not improve. Another trainer, Mr James, was brought in 'at considerable expense' and was employed for some weeks during the 1876 season, only to find that 'more of the members did not avail of his services'.[128] James' tenure was not a lengthy one. Yet another trainer was brought in by the club, with Matt Taylor providing his services, achieving some success in 1879. Prior to his appointment with Clonmel, Taylor was trainer to the Dublin University Boat Club.[129] He was a native of Newcastle-upon-Tyne and, when engaged by the University club in the late 1860s, he earned £3 per week during the rowing season.[130] He was also a noted boat-builder. In an Oxford V. Cambridge boat race in 1872 the Oxford crew practised in their new 'Matt Taylor' boat.[131] At Clonmel, he successfully oversaw the local club as they won both the junior and senior wherry races during the local regatta.[132] He was still engaged with them as a trainer in 1880.[133] Taylor worked out of Ringsend in Dublin and had initially been contracted by Clonmel to supply them with 'two tub-pair oared boats'.[134] He supplied boats to many clubs, with some clubs advertising boats made by him for sale in the national press.[135] His time coaching the Clonmel crew added to his income, if, as one may infer, he was paid £3 per week when on duty with the club. This outsourcing of a professional trainer impacted on a club's finances, hence the need for Clonmel to canvass for funds. In 1865 and 1866 the Dublin University club allocated £20 each season for the hiring of a trainer. It is likely that a similar sum of money was required by the Clonmel club to engage the services of Hoare, James or Taylor.[136]

The Clonmel club progressed with the continued purchase of new boats and ongoing improvements to the boathouse and grounds surrounding it. Improvements to the clubhouse and land acquisition close by gave the club infrastructure and permanence. The committee was making a bold statement that the club was there to stay. These improvements required capital. Continued appeals for subscriptions, and the regatta itself, were highlighted as reasons why the 'traders and other inhabitants of Clonmel' should maintain their support.[137] In 1879, at the annual meeting of the club, it was pointed out that the club had liabilities of £33 10s 10d but the president noted 'they had now a large yearly income, and he was glad to find they had now no occasion to look for that extraneous aid which they were compelled to ask for in former years'.[138] What he failed to point out was that the subscription list for the regatta would remain. Money was still required and accordingly lists of receipts were published in the local press in July 1879.[139] John Bagwell, Arthur Moore MP and Viscount Lismore led the way, each subscribing £5. Each band which played at the regatta received £2 from the rowing club as the whole enterprise ensured a circulation of money in the local community. At the 1878 annual meeting it was stated that the boathouse and club grounds represented a 'property valued at about £350', while subscriptions, in the main, continued to increase year on year. These were good omens for the future of the club (see Table 5.3).[140]

Clonmel Rowing Club made a vital contribution to local sporting recreation. Cricket remained an important sport in the region, but rowing gave an extra dimension to the sporting experiences now on offer. Both sports came together when they held an athletic sports meeting in 1875, with seventeen different events making up the programme, though 'the majority of which [were] to be competed for by the members of the Clonmel Rowing Club and South Tipperary Cricket Club'.[141] While it was also noted that several of the events were 'open to all comers', in fact it was a closed shop. While many people attended as spectators and enjoyed the ancillary events, they could not compete. These events were largely commercial and designed to extract as much money from the public as possible.

Table 5.3 Clonmel Rowing Club subscriptions, 1872–1877

YEAR	SUBSCRIPTION RECEIVED		YEAR	SUBSCRIPTION RECEIVED
1872	£39 19s 6d		1875	£68 19s 6d
1873	£47 1s 10d		1876	£67 8s 6d
1874	£57 10s		1877	£81 19s

Source: *CC*, 13 April 1878

That the River Suir was navigable in Clonmel and Carrick-on-Suir greatly facilitated initiatives to have rowing as a sport in both communities. No evidence has come to light of rowing in the north of the county. Elsewhere, it was only at school sports days at Rockwell College that some regatta-type events were added to the amusements on offer for the schoolboys.

OVERVIEW OF ATHLETICS AND ROWING IN TIPPERARY

What was noticeable about athletics and rowing meetings in Victorian Tipperary was that social differentiation and exclusion were very much part of the whole experience. The small number of participants in events meant that some meetings were not held due to insufficient numbers of athletes turning up. With as few as three competitors in some athletics events, it was evident that there were just not enough men willing to participate. A lack of sufficient athletes ensured that the regular cycle of prize money fell into the hands of some talented local athletes who travelled the county to compete.

This was indicative of low competitor numbers. There was little point in an average athlete or weight thrower trying to compete against the likes of Maurice Davin, for example. The lack of numbers suggests that there was a kind of natural selection in operation, with only the fittest surviving to take on the big boys. Also, 'membership of a sporting institution' was a luxury the Tipperary labourer and working-class man could not afford.[142] In that respect they were on a par with their contemporaries in other parts of Great Britain and Ireland. Athletics events drew spectators, hence the large attendance figures at the various meetings. This did not ultimately promote a general sense of participation, however, so consequently the number of participants remained small. For the vast majority their only means of participation was as spectators. They had drinking opportunities, musical bands and sideshows to enjoy, all of which helped to relieve them of their money.

Mindful of the circumstances the country faced prior to the end of the 1860s with famine, social unrest and international wars, athletics events continued to spread northwards in the county. Whereas the ICAC attracted the leading athletes to its championship meetings in Dublin, the local meetings in Tipperary were initially established by a local community or club, which was often a cricket club such as the Roscrea CYMS CC or Nenagh CC. The role of the military in promoting athletic sports cannot be underestimated. While reports of 'pedestrianism' featured irregularly in the press, one can confidently assume that there were other instances that have gone unrecorded. Where the military were instrumental was in putting in place a programme of athletics events which, though typically confined to military personnel, were in essence the foundation of subsequent events for the wider community. At Fethard, this evidenced itself with both military and civilian events on the one programme, something that was later replicated at Nenagh and Templemore. However, unlike the military, the impact of schools was negligible in relation to the promotion of athletics and involvement with the wider community. While there were three principal schools which held a series of annual sports, this number is far too small to indicate an advocacy for athleticism in a rural context. As far as Tipperary was concerned, there was no athletics driving force which resulted from the school network.

Unlike Westmeath, admission fees were a feature of the athletics sporting environment in Tipperary.[143] The examples from Nenagh and Carrick-on-Suir are early in terms of how sporting bodies sought to regulate general admission to specific meetings. Reserved enclosures and grandstands had a history of charging for the privilege of being in the fashionable arena. A general admission fee charged by the Nenagh CC, in 1876, was the start of a movement towards regulated, commercial sporting events designed to maximise profit while also imposing a social barrier.

As for the athletes themselves, there is no doubt that the monetary prizes were incentive enough to travel and participate at meetings throughout Tipperary and elsewhere during the 1870s. The gamble of entering a number of events, for whatever it cost, was well worth it, as the leading men took home good prize money. The sport could not survive without men to compete and for a specific meeting to succeed it needed to attract the leading competitors. Simply put, neither could exist without the other. Patronage and subscriptions meant that, by and large, general admission fees were not levied. The foundation of a club in Templemore likely owed much of its impetus to the military in the town. The Carrick club was established in 1879, with moves made to establish new clubs in Clonmel and Tipperary town also in that year. However, the cornerstone of athletics in Tipperary had been laid with the advent of the athletics sports meeting in the 1870s.

Similarly with rowing in Clonmel, a central hub was established around which an influential body of men took control. The club committee was proactive in engaging the services of a professional trainer to assist the club in becoming successful. That this was not always the case does not reflect on the training regime but rather upon the willingness of the crews to train to the required standard. It suggests that some social status was conferred simply by being a member of the club as opposed to being an active participant. Similar to athletics, there were races for amateurs in the true sense of the word and for men who made their living from working on the river. Though one of the Clonmel rowers, C. Garner, competed for Dublin University, indicative of his amateur status, the club also catered for watermen's wherry races, the latter competing for monetary prizes.[144]

CONCLUSION

In relation to athletics and rowing regattas, while the specifics of these sports differed, the end result was the same. There were events on the programme to cater for amateurs and there were events that did not. Apart from valuable cups and medals, there were also monetary prizes. In small-town rural Ireland, the ability of many clubs to survive was dependent on their success in attracting as many members as possible to their ranks. This membership never presumed an association with any particular religion or political persuasion. Rather, all athletes and rowers existed side by side, with specific races for each class of competitor. This dual status process was not typical of the meetings Cusack alluded to in his tirade against the abuses in athletics, but they were typical of the meetings in Tipperary in the 1870s.

CHAPTER 6

BALL GAMES

INTRODUCTION

There were several types of ball games played in County Tipperary between 1840 and 1880. As croquet and lawn tennis were dealt with in a previous chapter, the attention here is on other ball games, some of which required the use of a stick or bat. These will form the first part of this chapter. Following on are ball games played with the foot or hand. Once more the roles of the landed and military officer classes were instrumental in the promotion of all forms of ball games with one notable exception, that of hurling. In relation to football, the landed class in south Tipperary played a style of football known to them, which they probably learned at school. This they played among themselves on an irregular basis. When military officers are added into the mix, the games take on elements of codification; features of the Association football code become apparent. Rugby, too, was directly introduced by the military officers, while similar claims may be made for the advancement of cricket countywide. Indeed, cricket was the leading team sport in the post-Famine era, especially in the 1860s and 1870s. The appeal of the game crossed the social divide and it was popular among all the classes. It is the first sport under review in this chapter.

Hurling took on a different character. Played by the tenant farmer and labouring class, it was shunned by the descendants of those families who patronised it in the eighteenth century. Hurling survived the vagaries of lawmakers who, in the legislative process, made sport in public spaces a restricted activity. It also survived the Great Famine, and hurling was a game that wasn't anywhere near extinction in the mid-nineteenth century, though famine and emigration were factors which greatly impacted on the amount of hurling played countrywide.[1] This chapter shows that the game was still played in Tipperary during this period.

Much of the written history of Tipperary sport commences in 1884, consistent with the foundation of the GAA.[2] Where comment is provided on pre-GAA hurling and football it is based on folklore and generalisation. 'The early days of football, athletics, handball and hurling' was outlined by Philip Fogarty in his GAA history of the county.[3] Unfortunately, his research fails to indicate where his information came from. Bob Stakelum noted that 'it is generally accepted that hurling was not widely played in Tipperary in the years between the famine and the foundation of the GAA'.[4] Similarly, Neal Garnham has given an outline of football-playing in Ireland from 1518 up to the mid-nineteenth century when it was 'if not completely extinct, something of a rarity'.[5] This chapter shows that football was widely played in Tipperary between 1840 and 1880. However, the way ball playing was described in official publications and press reports does leave the particular style of play open to question. Where ball playing is mentioned, it could as easily be a game played with the hands or the feet, or both. But its presence challenges the consensus view that ball games were a rarity in the country prior to 1884.

A generic term for the various types of football played, not only in Tipperary but throughout Ireland and Great Britain, is folk football. This type of football was as likely to occur in Tipperary as in other parts of the two islands. Large gatherings of adult males congregated on Shrove Tuesday to play in games of street football at various locations in England in the eighteenth century.[6] Concerned with the welfare of the town inhabitants and shopkeepers, the civic authorities sought to 'suppress the practice [due to] the great nuisance it caused'.[7] This is important when correlated with the evidence from Ireland. The government, civic and constabulary authorities in Ireland tried to prevent the playing of ball games on public roads or on town streets. It had nothing to do with the fact that these were Irish men and boys playing football or hurling, it was to do with civic order.[8] There was nowhere in Ireland, let alone England, in the eighteenth or nineteenth centuries where authorities took offence to ball sports in themselves. In common with England, 'it was the location of the sport that was contentious'.[9] There was little difference between a bellman crying down kite-flying in Wakefield, Yorkshire, in the 1780s and a young boy reprimanded at Clonmel Petty Sessions for flying a kite on the street in 1856.[10] Both were perceived as a nuisance to townspeople.

CRICKET

Definitive evidence of cricket in Ireland dates from 1792 when the Garrison of Dublin played against an All-Ireland team at the Phoenix Park, Dublin.[11] Accounts of other matches around the country, at irregular intervals during this period, prove that cricket was played in several counties. In the 1820s cricket emerged, but in the seemingly unlikely rural locations of Ballinasloe, County Galway in 1825, and at Norelands, County Kilkenny in 1829.[12] The game enjoyed the patronage of the local elite and, in the case of the Kilkenny team, it was William Bayly who provided it. These teams met again in June 1831, at Norelands. The Marquis of Ormonde, who resided at Kilkenny Castle, appeared in the home selection.[13]

From a Tipperary perspective, Samuel Barton, Grove, Fethard was on the cricket eleven at Harrow in 1835, the year he left the school.[14] One of the earliest cricket matches in which the participation of a Tipperary-based team was recorded took place in August 1836. A player named 'Barton' was on the team and though no forename or initial was given, one could tentatively infer that this was Samuel.[15] S. Barton and later Samuel Barton participated in cricket matches with teams carrying the name of Cahir CC in 1846 and Clonmel CC in 1849.[16] In 1851, when the Clonmel club challenged a military team selected from the officers and privates at the town garrison to a cricket match, there appeared on the Clonmel team Samuel Barton, as well as William Palliser and Wray Palliser. Both Pallisers had attended Rugby School in 1845 and 1847 respectively.[17] The evidence relating to these boys suggests that they had become aware of cricket while at school and were now playing on the cricket fields of Tipperary. At Rugby School 'the majority of its pupils came from the upper middle classes, especially the clergy and the rural gentry'.[18] That some families in Ireland sent their sons to public school in England should not come as any great surprise. The Palliser family had a tradition of sending boys to public school in England. Wray's father had attended Harrow School in 1801, leaving there in 1805.[19] Yet, while Rugby School became synonymous with the rugby code, there is no evidence to suggest that the Pallisers brought this game back with them, mindful that the game as played in the school in the 1840s was still somewhat in its infancy. Given the implied patronage which underpinned the growth of cricket, it was still a cross-class game in a way that other sports were not. This was a key element in the growth of country house cricket.

Sean Reid has observed that the 'Golden Age' of cricket in Ireland, based on his analysis of the John Lawrence *Handbook of Cricket in Ireland* annuals, peaked in the early 1870s, with the game going into decline during the latter half of that same decade.[20] From 1840 to 1880, 202 different combinations of cricket teams in Tipperary have been identified, though it must be emphasised that the majority of these were casual teams without club committee or constitution, let alone their own grounds.[21] It has also been possible, using the local and national press and the John Lawrence *Handbook of Cricket in Ireland* annuals, to establish that at least 921 cricket matches were played in this period which involved at least one Tipperary-based team (see Figure 6.1). This number is not wholly representative of the level of cricket-playing during this time. An analysis of matches recorded in the Lawrence handbooks, when cross-checked with the Irish press for the relevant dates, suggests that much cricket went unrecorded in local newspapers. It can thus be inferred that cricket in Ireland was under-recorded generally and, indeed, that many local games went unnoticed. It has been further pointed out that the inclusion of the word 'cricket' in nineteenth-century Irish-language dictionaries reflected the extent to which the game was a common feature of the Irish landscape at that time.[22]

Figure 6.1 Cricket matches in County Tipperary, 1840–1880 (Total = 921)

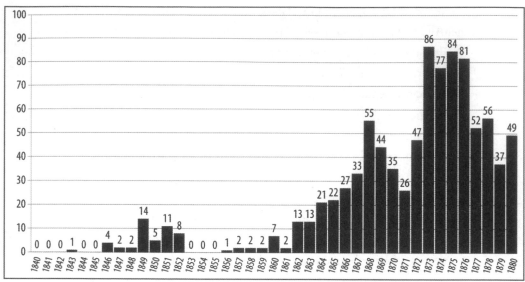

Sources: *CC, CG, IT, KM, NG, TA, TC, TE, TFP, TV, TWN* (1840–1880); Ashbrook Union Cricket Club scorebook, 1846–48; Lawrence, *Handbook of Cricket in Ireland* (Dublin, 1865 to 1881)

In the post-Famine era cricket developed around the larger towns. One thing most of these towns had in common was the presence of a military barracks, which were a key element in the growth and spread of cricket in Tipperary. Be it a cavalry barracks, as at Cahir, or infantry barracks as at Clonmel, Templemore or Nenagh, cricket soon became a key element in the sporting activities of the officers and privates. Indeed, in 1840 a note in the *Tipperary Free Press* indicated that the Board of Ordnance had directed that cricket pitches were to be laid down in Cahir, Fethard and Templemore for the use of troops.[23] An important element here is the point of origin. Any familiarity which local men had with the game through their schooling does not seem to have been a factor in the growth of the game. It appears that these men were unable to organise a team network. The garrisons were the key agents in making this happen. The ability to organise a team network then diffused into the local communities, especially those in close proximity to a military barracks.

The growth of the game in Tipperary was also greatly advanced by the development of the railway network. This helped to bring the game to those rural locations that were in close proximity to a railway station. New rail stations at Templemore, Thurles, Clonmel, Nenagh, Cahir and Dundrum greatly facilitated the movement of teams, with Dundrum a favoured location for many contests in the 1860s. The schools also advanced the game, none more so than three of the leading boarding schools in Tipperary. These were Rockwell College under the auspices of the Jesuit Fathers; Tipperary Grammar School, also known as The Abbey, primarily a Protestant boarding school, though aspiring middle-class Catholics also sent their sons there; and St John's College, Newport.

From 1840 to the end of 1880 cricket in Tipperary was unrivalled as a field sport (Figures 6.2 and 6.3). The geography of the game was such that, by the end of this forty-year period, it had spread countywide, though the contemporary press reports suggest that the upland area around Kilcommon, in west Tipperary, was somewhat immune to the game.

During the 1870s, military, school and gentlemen's teams actively played cricket. The prevalence of ephemeral rural clubs at this time suggests that, such was the level of exposure to cricket, the laws of the game were greatly understood by many and equipment and playing fields were readily available. The degree to which this occurred may be gauged from the number of people who were members of the Nenagh CC. In the records viewed, there was no reference to a third or fourth team at this club. Even mention of a second eleven was a rare occurrence. In 1876, Nenagh Cricket Club had 250 members, but only one team. The majority of the club were non-playing members.[24] Moreover, the model of the game in Tipperary mirrored that in England. It was essentially a rural game, one which fitted into pre-industrial working practices.

In Tipperary, between 1840 and 1880, inclusive of two-day matches, of which only fourteen in total were identified, it has been possible to establish that there were at least 932 days when cricket was played. Of these days, the specific day on which cricket was played can be identified for 811 of them (Figure 6.4). An analysis of the day of play demonstrates that certain restrictions applied to the military and school

Figure 6.2 Cricket teams, 1834–1869   (● = 1 team)

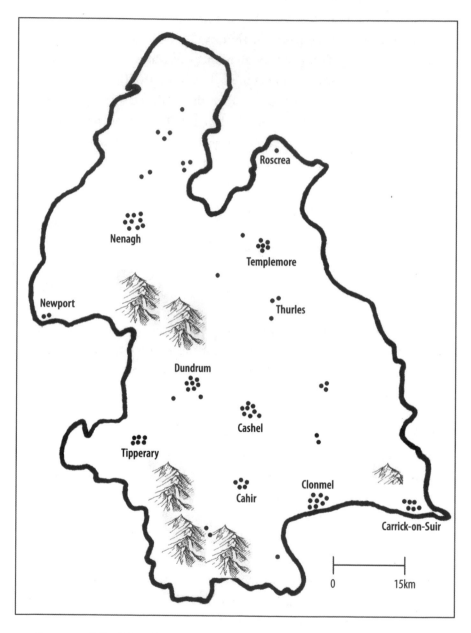

Sources: *CC, CG, IT, KM, NG, TA, TC, TE, TFP, TV, TWN* (1840–1869); Lawrence, *Handbook of Cricket in Ireland* (Dublin, 1865–1869)

Figure 6.3 Cricket teams, 1870–1880   (● = 1 team)

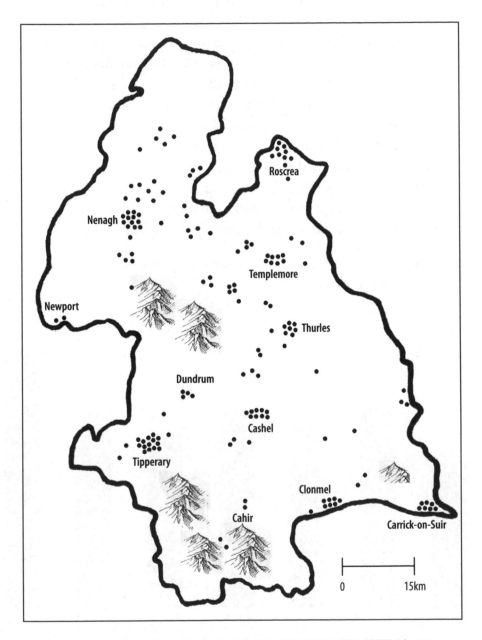

Sources: *CC, CG, IT, KM, NG, TA, TC, TE, TFP, TV, TWN* (1870–1880); Lawrence, *Handbook of Cricket in Ireland* (Dublin, 1870–1880)

teams but not to others. For instance, Rockwell College and Tipperary Grammar School never played on a Sunday and neither did any of the military teams, whereas many of the local townland and social teams did. For many of the rural and urban clubs the weekend was the most popular time for playing cricket, with Saturday the favoured day. From the middle of the 1870s onwards, Sunday was also quite popular. Of the eighty-six Sundays identified, seventy-eight of them were from the 1874–1880 period. The fact that Sunday playing was prominent demonstrated that many clubs were drawn from men of a Roman Catholic persuasion. It also suggests that Sabbath observance in regard to the playing of sport was less of an issue by the late 1860s and early 1870s than it had been in the 1850s, when many men and boys were brought before the magistrates for playing hurling and football. Early

Figure 6.4 Day of the week for cricket playing in County Tipperary, 1840–1880 (Total = 811)

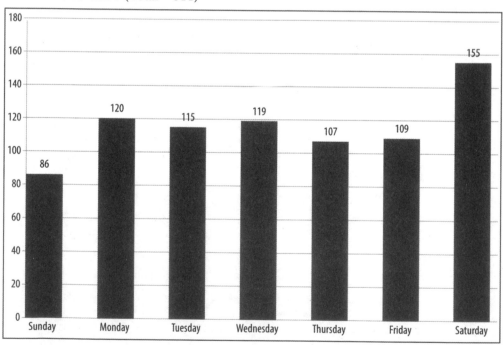

Sources: *CC, CG, IT, KM, NG, TA, TC, TE, TFP, TV, TWN* (1840–1880); Ashbrook Union Cricket Club scorebook, 1846–48; Lawrence, *Handbook of Cricket in Ireland* (Dublin, 1865 to 1881)

evidence of cricket played on a Sunday is seen in the south of the county with the Carrick-on-Suir and Clonmel Commercial clubs meeting in 1864.[25]

Evidence from the press reports suggests that there was no set time for matches to start – it could be at eleven o'clock in the morning, at noon or in the early afternoon. They finished at around seven o'clock in the evening, which allowed for travel home by horse-drawn carriage.[26] Further analysis of cricket match reports from Tipperary, in the post-Famine years, supports Neal Garnham's assessment that the 'aftermath of the Great Famine allowed cricket to supplant native pastimes that had fallen into decline'.[27] Throughout Tipperary every day of the week was popular for cricket, though some more so than others. Saturday, as noted, was the most favoured day, with 155 matches featuring. The months when it was most popular are shown in Figure 6.5.

Figure 6.5 Cricket playing by month in County Tipperary, 1840–1880 (Total = 850)

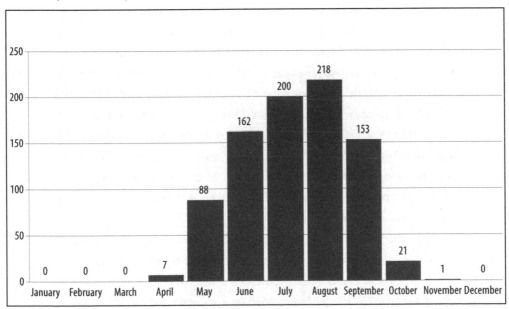

Sources: *CC, CG, IT, KM, NG, TA, TC, TE, TFP, TV, TWN* Ashbrook Union Cricket Club scorebook, 1846–48; Lawrence, *Handbook of Cricket in Ireland* (Dublin, 1865 to 1881)

Of those playing cricket, the military were involved in 223 (24.21 per cent) of the matches. These were military teams playing against each other on a home and away basis – for instance Templemore barracks against Nenagh barracks, and similarly Cahir barracks versus Clonmel barracks. At a larger barracks, such as Clonmel, two separate regiments or infantry units garrisoned there competed against each other. It was principally the military teams who were prepared to travel to fulfil fixtures; they were regularly on the road when it came to Saturday matches. Military members also supplemented the playing elevens of local town or gentlemen's teams. This was especially noticeable in the team selections, where a fixture against a stronger team deemed it necessary that the best players in the locality played.

It was not just grown men who played cricket. Some schools within Tipperary and in the neighbouring counties were prominent cricket locations. Grouped together, the school teams were represented in 179 (19.44 per cent) of all matches played. Tipperary Grammar School participated in 97 matches (10.53 per cent), while Rockwell College featured in 29 matches (3.14 per cent). The data compiled does suggest that neither Tuesday nor Friday were greatly favoured by either school. This is not wholly conclusive with regard to the grammar school owing to the large number of unknown match days – this data was derived from reports in the Lawrence handbooks which were not found in a subsequent re-examination of the local press. What was most interesting was that both school teams frequently played the same leading military and local club teams, yet, despite being only twenty-five miles apart, they never competed against each other. This suggests that there were local and probably religious factors at play. A specific reason, if one existed, has not been identified.

Gentlemen's teams were also a popular feature on the Tipperary cricket circuit. This type of team featured in seventy-two matches (7.81 per cent). These teams might represent a local estate, a local business or be selected by a local landowner or a military officer. The reports analysed do not give any indication as to whether gambling was associated with matches involving gentlemen's teams, though one could reasonably assume that at some stage it did arise. All days were popular for cricket but Sunday was frowned upon where a gentleman eleven was involved. Again, somewhat similar to the military, teams of gentlemen visited other clubs more often than they played at home, where there may not have been a cricket pitch available. Clubs that were established within close proximity to the rail network were more likely to travel further to play cricket. There are 222 matches recorded (24.1 per cent) that include the participation of a team from outside the county. Teams from all of the eight counties which border Tipperary as well as from Dublin took part. These included military barracks teams from Cork, Limerick and Offaly.

Gentlemen paid money to join clubs and they also paid a fee to play cricket, as can be seen in the scorebook of the Ashbrook Union CC, Durrow, County Laois. The Ashbrook Union team was centred on Viscount Ashbrook's estate. What this scorebook also shows is that some men, likely employees on the estate, were paid to play cricket.[28] Ashbrook Union CC competed against the Templemore garrison team on four occasions in 1847 and 1848. The rules and regulations for the season 1847 show that the club members were required to pay 'one shilling for every match they are on the losing side' and 'one shilling and sixpence, including a luncheon of cold meat, for each practice day'.[29] The members were also expected to pay five shillings for each match in which they played, in addition to their additional subscription. This stipulation indicated that cricket, at this time and at this club, was above the reach of many men and was a sport that was only open to those who could afford it. However, a further clause named five men who were 'chosen as players of the club' for the 1847 season. They were 'paid two shillings each for practice days, and the same per day for matches against other clubs and their expenses'.[30] It is unknown if these rates were in existence for the 1846 season. For the 1847 and 1848 seasons there were forty-four cricket matches played by the club, of which thirty-one were internal games and thirteen were against other clubs. One man, who was only ever referred to by his surname, Shawn, played in all forty-four matches. He was one of the five men named as 'players of the club', along with W. Moore (forty-two matches), James Moore (thirty-two matches), White (thirty-eight matches) and Dooling (twenty-two matches). With each man paid two shillings per match, the club over the two years paid out £17 16s in match fees, at a time of great national distress.[31] It is also probable that these men were employed on the estate in some capacity. One man, named only as Kearney, featured on the team in 1848. Living in Durrow at that time was a Miles Kearney who was a stucco plasterer, whom one may assume worked in Durrow Castle. In all likelihood, men who worked on the estate also played on the cricket team.

While it cannot be proved that similar payment arrangements existed with clubs in Tipperary, one can confidently assume that such occurrences did take place. It was paid employment and a means by which a man could remain in a locality if he displayed ability with the bat and ball, skills which might be of great use to his employer. As such, these men were among the first paid sportsmen in rural Ireland. This payment of players, coming as it did in the middle of the Famine years, does not appear to have been a burden on the Ashbrook estate. It followed eighteenth-century trends in England, where skilful cricket players were retained as employees on estates, whether as a gardener or a groom. In other instances, a local man might show some promise with a team, and then be recruited by a willing patron who was anxious to build a successful team of his own. Consequently, he was employed for various tasks, one of which was to play cricket.[32] Though cricket in the 1870s had become widespread, and even communal in nature, its formative years relied heavily on patronage. In this respect, it was no different from the patronage offered to it in England. It was this, more than anything, which underpinned the growth of cricket in Tipperary and the rest of rural Ireland.

Comparative analysis with cricket in Westmeath shows some divergent results. While there were seventeen matches recorded in Westmeath in the 1850s, and thirty-one in Tipperary for the same period, the returns for 1860–1879 are different.[33] In that period there were 315 matches recorded for Westmeath, while 818 were recorded for Tipperary, of which 581 took place in the 1870s.[34] A sharp decline in cricket playing had taken place in Westmeath due principally to the removal of key personnel from the county, ultimately leading to clubs collapsing in their absence (Figure 6.6). In Tipperary the game was played mainly by clerical officers and tenant farmers who regularly found opposition in the form of the military cricket team. A fundamental problem with cricket, as Sean Reid has demonstrated, was that the game 'had a broad base but shallow roots that depended on local generosity that was not sustainable in the long term'.[35]

Figure 6.6 Cricket matches recorded in Counties Tipperary and Westmeath, 1860–1879 (Tipperary total = 817; Westmeath total = 315)

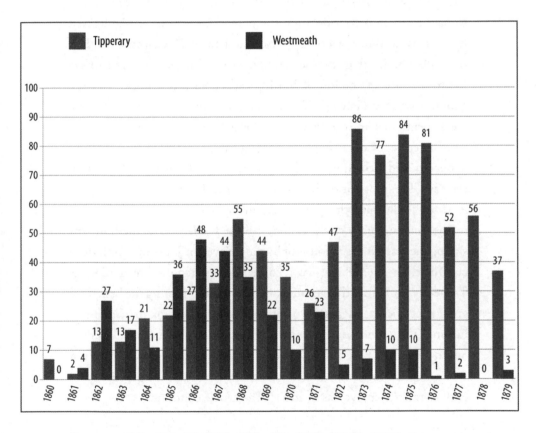

Sources: *CC, CG, IT, KM, NG, TA, TFP* (1860–1879); Lawrence, *Handbook of Cricket in Ireland* (Dublin, 1865 to 1881); Hunt, *Sport and Society*, p. 116 (Cork, 2007)

HURLING

There is no denying that there was a decline in hurling in the post-Famine era. That said, pre-1884 references to hurling in Ireland are not as easily found as those for cricket. Writing in the spring 1993 issue of *History Ireland*, Kevin Whelan noted that 'by the mid nineteenth century hurling had declined so steeply that it survived in three pockets, around Cork city, in south-east Galway and in the area north of Wexford town'.[36] In an important celebratory series of essays commemorating the 125th anniversary of the GAA, the closing lines of an essay on 'Football and hurling in early modern Ireland', on the face of it, appears not to have taken into consideration the potential evidence as highlighted by Marcus de Búrca, Pádraig Puirséal and Liam Ó Caithnia. Rather, the author states that 'the devastation of the famine appears to have led to the near extinction of hurling except for a few pockets of the country, notably Galway, Wexford and Dublin'.[37] Two of the three areas mentioned mirror those of Whelan, but in the third instance Dublin replaces Cork. However, hurling was more widespread, both in Tipperary and Ireland generally than previously believed to have been the case. The information here is also extended to pre-1884 hurling in Australia to illustrate this point even further.

The contemporary press cannot be used solely as a medium for stating the case for the amount of hurling played in Tipperary, or indeed elsewhere, in the 1870s. Two contemporary reports from County Tipperary, both from the summer of 1873, while outlining the beneficial growth of cricket, suggest two different interpretations in relation to hurling. The nationalist *Tipperary Free Press*, in a commentary about the South Tipperary Cricket Club, noted that 'in no other country – not even excepting England – are athletic sports so universally practised and enthusiastically enjoyed as in this'.[38] The article continues:

> ... no walk of life in this country – be it the most humble or most exalted – is without its games – where 'feats of skill and strength' call forth all the energetic vigor [*sic*] of the human frame – the lowly pleasant [*sic*] boy, after his week of weary toil, bounds with enthusiasm as he joins his party of a Sunday afternoon to play a

match of 'hurling' … In no county in Ireland is the love of athletic amusement so cherished as in Tipperary.

Though brief, the reference to the 'peasant boy' heading off on a Sunday to play hurling suggests that in south Tipperary the sport was still played even if the local press did not record any regular accounts of it. The likelihood is that hurling was, like cricket, a local sporting activity with nothing at stake but honour. In contrast, after reading an article from the Unionist *Nenagh Guardian*, based in north Tipperary, only three months later, one could be forgiven for thinking that hurling was actually well and truly buried. Entitled 'Hurling *versus* Cricket', the *Nenagh Guardian* looked to what hurling had meant to people in the past and set this against the contemporary appeal of cricket. The article commenced:

> The English game of cricket is now very much in vogue in Ireland. It has completely displaced the old Athletic exercise of Hurling, so prevalent some years ago. Hurling is almost unknown to the rising generation … But Hurling is now numbered among the amusements of the past …[39]

As Mike Huggins has demonstrated, 'it is worth exploring the interaction between the proliferation of sports journalism and its readers'. Huggins further noted that 'most sports journalists were themselves middle class and their role in constructing, disseminating and mediating in ideological discourse related to the construction of sporting identity'.[40] One can clearly see in these two contemporary accounts that, even within the geographical area of Tipperary, there were issues around how sport was reported. From the documentary evidence there is no doubt that cricket was the most popular team sport in Tipperary in the 1870s. Both contemporary press accounts shown above highlight the popularity of cricket, but they are clearly at odds in relation to the state of hurling.

However, the impulses that had driven both sports in the eighteenth century – hurling in Ireland and cricket in England – were similar. Both relied on patronage, both were closely linked with gambling, and both were rural-based. In the mid-1870s the patronage link was absent from hurling, while by that time cricket was so well established, it did not require patronage. Based on these two press reports, one could argue that hurling was still played in south Tipperary but that it had died out in the north of the county.

The issue of space and the places where hurling was played are important in understanding its alleged decline in the nineteenth century and the extent to which regulation impeded its growth. One reason for this was nineteenth-century legislation, which restricted space and the areas available for play or recreation, especially among the lower classes.[41] Hurling, involving whatever number of participants, required a lot of space to play the game. Certain restrictions applied to sport played on private land, commonage or the public highway. Where private land or commonage was not available, stopping men and boys from playing sports or games on the roads or streets had a detrimental effect on games. This was especially hard on young boys. The constabulary were vigilant and where offences occurred, it was customary that the offenders appeared before the local Petty Sessions court. Such was the fate of William Cormack, Templemore, who appeared before the local court on 12 May 1852, having received a summons from Head Constable George Patterson for playing hurling on the street. If the restrictions on play were not specifically saying so, the way they were enforced demonstrated that the authorities were determined to undermine the ability of the lower classes to meet for recreation, especially in public places. Local constables maintained a watchful eye on what went on in their own area.

In the aftermath of the Famine years, the various Tipperary newspapers do refer to hurling from time to time, though these mostly relate to Petty Sessions appearances for trespass or hurling on a Sunday. It is in the Petty Sessions records that new evidence for hurling in this period is found. Forty-three men from the communities around Fethard appeared before the local Petty Sessions court in 1854 charged with playing hurling on a Sunday or committing trespass while playing the game.[42] It will never be known how many more instances such as these took place. It is likely that some groups of men and boys may have been hunted away and told not to come back, that others absconded when they saw the constabulary arrive, while some may have been allowed to play. Similarly, near Bansha, in 1856, fourteen men were arrested for playing hurling, once again on a Sunday and, unusually, their occupations were given on the Petty Sessions records. Two farmers and twelve labourers were each fined sixpence.[43] The evidence also shows that from 1842 to 1880 Sunday play was a feature of hurling at a time when sport on this day in Great Britain was still prohibited.[44] Hurling on other days did not come under this law and so it went unnoticed unless there was an unsavoury incident which resulted in an appearance of someone before the courts. It also demonstrated that long before the GAA was founded, Sunday play was popular, primarily because it was the one day that was free from work. A similar trend had also emerged with cricket matches from the mid-1870s.

Figure 6.7 Hurling frequency by month in County Tipperary, 1840–1880 (Total = 63)

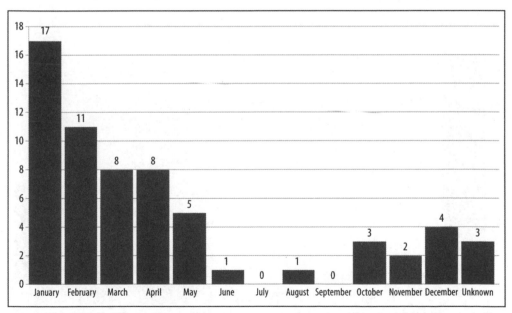

Sources: *CC, NG, TA, TC, TE, TFP, TV, TWN* (1840–1880); Ten volumes of Petty Sessions records from 1854 to 1860

The time of year when hurling took place in Tipperary, between 1840 and 1880, shows that January featured strongly, with play in all months except for July and September, though based on a small numerical sample of just sixty-three days (Figure 6.7). It appears that a shift had taken place in relation to the hurling calendar when compared to the eighteenth century.

Between 1740 and 1793 'hurling was essentially a later summer game' with 67 per cent of matches recorded taking place in July, August and September. This represented thirty-three games out of a sample number of forty-nine.[45] When compared with the analysis of James Kelly for the eighteenth century, Sunday clearly remained the favoured day for hurling, though Kelly did find that Monday and Thursday were also popular (see Figure 6.8).[46] However, the data suggests that a switch to winter play had taken place, which was indicative of the absence of the elite as patrons of hurling in the

Figure 6.8 Day of the week for playing hurling in County Tipperary, 1840–1880 (Total = 63)

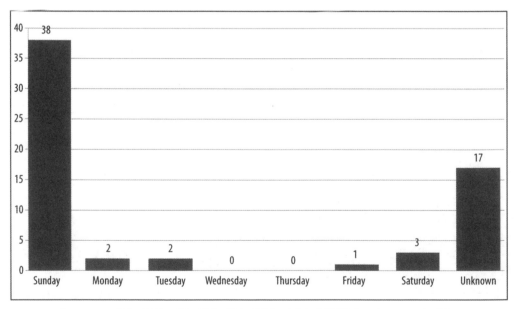

Sources: *CC, NG, TA, TC, TE, TFP, TV, TWN* (1840–1880); Ten volumes of Petty Sessions records from 1854 to 1860

Victorian period. Hurling matches on private land were progressively denied to the players and the game was pushed out onto the streets and roadways where it was played in a very informal and unscheduled manner. Quite often it was children who were prosecuted for playing hurling on the roads and streets. In Clonmel, in 1852, at the Mayor's Court the practice of hurling in the streets was described as 'an intolerable nuisance and must be checked'.[47] Children playing on the streets were easy targets for the constabulary.

By the third quarter of the nineteenth century hurling was often unruly and prone to violence. Disagreements, for one reason or another, whether it was a dispute between factions, a comment passed during play or even over a girl, often led to a row on the field which frequently resulted in serious injury or death. The evidence from the press and official reports were in stark contrast to the writings of the correspondent to the *Nenagh Guardian*, in 1873, as previously documented. He had noted that although 'scrimmages' brought some of these hurling matches to an abrupt and unpleasant close, on the whole 'they were, considering the circumstances, wonderfully free from anything seriously unpleasant'. This, unfortunately, was often far from true. There are sixteen instances recorded from seven counties in Ireland where a player died as a result of injuries received while hurling, principally on account of getting hit on the head. Tipperary featured at the top of the list with eight deaths, two each for Cork and Galway and one each in Clare, Down, Dublin and Offaly. While four of the deaths were noted as accidental, there were seven that were of malicious intent and five that are inconclusive as to whether the injury sustained was accidental or malicious. These deaths represented 16.5 per cent of the total hurling references identified countrywide. When other issues such as rioting and assault, at thirty-seven instances countrywide, are added to this number the figure rises to fifty-three, which is 55 per cent of the total. This figure is more than double that of eighteenth-century hurling, where, over a period of almost fifty years, 'approximately twenty-five per cent ... gave rise to some riotous or violent activity'.[48] This demonstrates that hurling was a sport that retained an element of aggression, something the Victorian sense of morality did not countenance.

Indeed, there is some evidence to suggest that personal animosity or family feuds were frequently behind some of these disputes, with retribution for past slights or offence taken out on someone during play. In 1862, a man, allegedly heading for America, was arrested in Cobh, County Cork after fatally injuring another man at a match in Two-Mile-Borris.[49] In another instance in south Tipperary, in late January 1871, a dispute between two families owing to 'a case of trespass about a quarry' and a subsequent tender for the repair of a road, ultimately led to the death of Edmond St John. He was a son of one of the parties involved and while at a match he received a blow of a hurley to his head.

A writer on the GAA in Tipperary has argued that 'Irish history from "the famine" [*sic*] to the start of the Gaelic Athletic Association is bitter in the extreme and it is little surprise to find that in this its darkest period, the native sport practically collapsed altogether'.[50] The perceived absence of hurling was a revisionist view by the early promoters of the GAA, which put them into a heightened position. They used the imagined absence of ball games in the post-Famine period to promote the role of the organisation in preserving, cultivating and reviving Irish games and pastimes. It has been argued that the Famine years were a watershed period in Irish sport, specifically relating to games perceived to be of Irish origin.[51]

Contrary to the belief among some GAA historians, this discussion has proved that there was much more hurling played in the nineteenth century in Tipperary than has previously been portrayed.[52] The evidence highlights the county as being prominent in terms of the number of pre-1884 hurling references identified. But as some observers and contemporary writers indicate, there is an acceptance that many of those who played hurling actually emigrated in the post-Famine era. As Seamus King has noted, 'it is most likely that the Irish who arrived in such numbers into England in the post-Famine period brought the game of hurling with them. However, it is unlikely that the game was organised in any meaningful way until after the foundation of the GAA.'[53] Using evidence from Ireland and Australia, it can be shown that there was widespread playing of hurling prior to the foundation of the GAA. Irish emigrants took hurling to Australia, where the game was very much alive in the late 1870s. Between 1876 and 1884 there were at least twenty-three teams in Australia, mostly in Victoria.[54] This led to the formation of the Victorian Hurling Club Association in April 1878.[55] If hurling was alive and well in Australia, one can assume it was alive and well in Ireland.

FOOTBALL

Football at this time was unstructured, largely undefined and under-reported in the local press. Due to the uncertainty as to the precise nature of what was deemed football in the years preceding codification, the nature of this play is commonly referred to as 'folk football'.[56] This type of football was local in nature. Rules were largely arbitrary and likely agreed prior to the commencement of the game. These games were played on feast days and holidays that were part of local traditions, marking the passage of seasons. In southern Ireland, one such form of the game was called *cad*. A letter-writer to the *Irish Times* in 1968 gave an overview of *cad* as played in the nineteenth century. It also contained the Webb Ellis myth, noting that 'an English boy, William Webb Ellis, learned the game from his cousins in Tipperary and by running with the ball restarted it at Rugby School in 1823'.[57] Instances of public order offences, typically due to ball playing on the street or a breach of the laws relating to the Sabbath, resulted in the appearance of men and boys before the courts, if caught.[58]

Apart from rugby, patronage was not afforded to the other football codes in the same way that it was given to horse racing, athletics, or cricket. In 1869, at Marlfield, Clonmel, on the Bagwell estate, such were the social and economic backgrounds of those participating in a football match, that the evidence suggests a game originating with the landowning class. This game took place 'between a scratch team of gentlemen' representative of Marlfield and Gurteen estates. The Marlfield team emerged 'victors by two bases to none'.[59] Elements of the game, as recorded in the local press, notably the scoring system, led a leading English football historian, Tony Collins, to conclude that they were playing football according to Harrow School rules. It was the 'the first report of a Harrow rules match that [he had] seen outside of the school itself'.[60] Eight of the players identified in the report were confirmed as Old Harrovians, while a couple of others mentioned were not positively verified.[61] For instance, two of the participants, Richard and William Bagwell, Marlfield, had left Harrow in 1859 and 1864 respectively.[62] This report demonstrates that a cross-fertilisation of cultural and sporting influence took place.

However, the limited incidence of this type of football was a reflection of the elite nature of the game rather than an indication that it was popular in south Tipperary. While this report indicates that Harrow rules football took place in the south of the county, one has to be careful not to 'interpret grandly from a short supply of material' and, in this instance, the evidence is very slight.[63] In essence, there was no further diffusion of this type of football. If it could not gain wider acceptance in London outside of Harrow School, it was even less likely that it would gain a foothold in south Tipperary where a few old boys got together for a match, a report of which one of them or their party submitted to the local press.

While sons of prosperous Tipperary residents attended public schools in England, there is no definitive evidence to suggest that they promoted the games cult in Ireland. While 'much of the rhetoric around sport had its origins in the English public school system',[64] the fact was that the number of boys from Tipperary who attended such schools on the British mainland was small. There was insufficient critical mass to suggest the transfer of the games ethic to this part of the country. Apart from the isolated Harrow rules football match in Clonmel, the only other evidence one may draw from the school records was that some of the young men played cricket upon their return to Tipperary. Both E. Waller and Fitzgibbon Trant attended Eton, in 1859 and 1865 respectively. Both featured on local cricket teams on their return to Tipperary but there is no evidence that they had played cricket at school.[65] John Bayly, from Debsborough in the north of the county, played in the Eton eleven in 1874.[66] He subsequently made two appearances for the Ireland team in 1884.[67] The family connection with cricket remained local when his father,

John Bayly, was elected president of the Ormond CC in 1884.[68] That sport was promoted in Tipperary Grammar School is without question. It is likely that there were elements of muscular Christianity involved here, balanced with a desire to promote athleticism in the school. But the cult of athleticism did not happen in rural Tipperary, irrespective of how many boys received public school education in England or within Tipperary. There were neither sufficient sportsmen to support it nor an active promotion of athleticism either inside or outside the school system within the county.

There were also issues of patronage underpinning the diffusion of sport, especially in relation to rugby football. The role of the officer class in some of the military garrisons was critical to the growth of rugby, something the foundation of the GAA did not break. For those lower down the social ladder, while opportunities for football playing did exist, their endeavours, by and large, were never recorded in the press. Consequently, which form of folk football was played is hard to determine. Where records do exist, primarily for Sabbath offences, these resulted in the appearance of participants, regularly children, before the local magistrates. On 19 February 1849, a bill for 'the more speedy trial and punishment of offences in Ireland' was passed. Critical to play and sport was Section III, where it was enacted 'that every person shall be liable to a penalty not exceeding forty shillings who shall, in any street, road, thoroughfare, or public place, commit any of the following offences … play at football or bowling or hurling, or any other game'.[69] Due to a lack of patronage and lands on which to play various games, men and boys took the only alternative left open to them, which was to take the games out onto the public roadway. Playing games on the street became an offence. If apprehended, prosecution followed, as the legislators sought to stop the nuisance caused by these men and boys on the 'public thoroughfare'. It was not that there was a ban on playing games but rather it was where these games took place which was the issue. With no access to land on which to play sport it was little wonder that some games went into decline. Games that did not meet with the approval of those who had land at their disposal were most likely to suffer.

Similarly, in the Highways (Ireland) Bill 1853, one of the clauses related to penalties incurred by persons playing 'at football or any other game on any part of the said highways'.[70] At Clonmel, when some boys appeared before the Mayor's Court, the mayor noted that 'the system of ball playing in the streets and public thoroughfares [had] become a most tolerable nuisance'.[71] In this instance, the extent to which patronage existed was demonstrated when a man intervened on behalf of the boys and 'promised to be security for their future good conduct'. As a consequence of his intervention, the mayor refused to send the boys to jail. However, subsequent mayors of Clonmel also had to deal with complaints of ball playing in the streets and churchyards of the town. Several of those prosecuted were children. Other instances related to trespass while playing football.[72] These attempts to rid the streets of activities which created a nuisance for townsfolk, shopkeepers and other business interests were reflective of what was also happening in Great Britain, with concerns about public order and the security of property used to provide a rationale for the clampdown.[73]

Where prosecutions were recorded in the contemporary Tipperary press the majority of the incidences reported show that there were only a small number of participants involved in each offence. Typically, two or three boys appeared before the courts, but there is no way of telling how many were actually playing before the police intervened. But there is some evidence to suggest that football of a more structured nature, in terms of large numbers of men coming together to play, also took place. In February 1866 outside Templemore, in the north of the county, seven men were prosecuted for playing football at College Hill on the Sabbath.[74] Also near Templemore, on the Longorchard estate at Templetuohy, there was an opportunity for tenants on the estate to play 'a match of football' during harvest home celebrations.[75] This was not only a feature of harvest celebrations in Ireland, it was also an aspect of harvest festivals in England.[76] This suggests that there was a cultural continuation of football in existence, rather than that the game was passed down by those who had learned it at public school.[77] This is a critical point in the development of football in Tipperary.

It is evidence of folk football in its purest historical setting local versions based around the religious and agricultural calendar.

OTHER FORMS OF FOOTBALL

There did not exist in Ireland, let alone Tipperary, a public school structure which was as widespread, or as influential, as the public school model that existed in Great Britain.[78] Tipperary Grammar School and Clonmel School were active in the promotion of the rugby code. No evidence has come to light of Association football at these schools. Other schools also promoted football but the way in which it was reported in the local press makes it difficult to determine the exact form played. These instances are interpreted as variations of folk football. Football playing in the post-Famine period appears to have been a continuation of the games which took place in the 1830s and early 1840s. Casual football took place on open spaces, irrespective of the consequences of falling foul of the local constabulary and magistrates. It was a feature of football in Ireland and Great Britain.[79]

The type of football played in Tipperary in the years prior to the foundation of the GAA is difficult to ascertain with any degree of certainty; it is unclear whether some of these games were a version of football which was of specific Irish origin. One Gaelic games historian noted that all the non-Gaelic football codes, with the possible exception of Australian Rules, 'had their origin in the different types of football played in English public schools'.[80] During the early 1860s 'football was played regularly in south Tipperary'.[81] At this time the various football codes had more features in common than they had differences.[82] This makes differentiation of the codes all the more difficult, unless specific comments are made from which one can conclusively demonstrate which code was actually played. It was something that was not unique to Tipperary.

In Ireland a football match between teams from Cork and Waterford was recorded in the spring of 1878, while another match, between two parishes in north Cork, took place a couple of weeks later.[83] Once more, one cannot be specific as to which code was played. In 1880, four years prior to the foundation of the GAA, football matches were played in mid-Tipperary. Each side had twenty-one players a-side and each was representative of four distinct local parish units.[84] When the GAA was founded in 1884 these same parish units were the basis on which clubs were formed. Evidence of these matches suggests that there was an embryonic parochial structure already in place prior to the GAA, albeit that early GAA teams also had twenty-one players a-side.[85] But whether these games were still a version of folk football or a style of football played according to Irish rules is not clear. The parochial nature of the teams and the regularity of playing numbers in each match suggests that there was a style of football generic to mid-Tipperary which had taken on elements of codification. This local variation was played by teams representing Templemore, Thurles, Moycarkey and Two-Mile-Borris.[86]

RUGBY FOOTBALL

In 1854, a football club was formed in Trinity College Dublin 'by a number of former pupils of Rugby and Cheltenham schools in England'.[87] On the basis of the evidence so far identified, this club was the first one to be associated with rugby football in Ireland. With the establishment of the Irish Football Union in 1874 and its later amalgamation with the Northern Football Union to form the Irish Rugby Football Union (IRFU) in 1879, a national structure was in place to oversee the development of rugby football in the country.[88] By that stage Ireland had played its first international fixture against England at the Kennington Oval, in 1875.[89] The presence of a national body assisted the growth of rugby football as it oversaw the development of the branch unions in Munster, Leinster and Ulster in 1877. Connacht was represented for the first time at an IRFU meeting in 1886.[90] The IRFU was then representative of rugby in all of Ireland and its central authority was pivotal to the development of the game.

In the north of the county there is evidence which points to another type of football game that was played by teams in the rural communities in the hinterland of Nenagh. The account book of Kilruane Football

Club from 1876 to 1880 refers to games that were not recorded in the local press.[91] In it, matches between the Kilruane club and the 53rd Regiment (Nenagh Garrison) are recorded, as are matches against Carrigatoher FC and Kileen FC. At this time, clubs carried the 'football club' initials – FC – after the club name. Clanwilliam, Limerick and Clonmel were other clubs that followed this style.[92] Membership of the Kilruane club cost four shillings on 1 April 1877.[93] A match against the 53rd Regiment and a book on football, which cost seven pence, suggests that the game may have been rugby, but the exact nature of the play is unknown. The account book contains the names of all members of the club. In 1876 the club had fifty-five members; fifty members in 1877; forty-four members in 1878 and forty-two members during the season 1879–80. In 1876 the membership rate was four shillings per year. By 1 April 1877 the book recorded how much each man had paid in relation to his annual membership and how much was still outstanding for the year. Only three men had paid their fees in full by that date, with the others having various rates of underpayment. The expenses for 1877 included £1 10*s* for two half-barrels of porter and eight shillings for four gallons of ale, as well as expenses for green and white tape, footballs and caps. Expenses for the following years were £4 3*s* 9*d* for 1876; £8 8*s* 10*d* for 1877–78, and £8 0*s* 3*d* for 1878–79. The first match Kiruane played was against Carrigatoher Football Club. In all there are ten matches recorded in the account book up to 26 January, 1880. Of these the dates of seven are noted. The team lists ranged from fifteen players, on two occasions, to twenty on five occasions and twenty-five on three occasions. A cross-check of the dates recorded in the account book with reports in the local press did not yield results. This serves to highlight that there was a lot of under-recording of sporting events in the contemporary press. Similar to mid-Tipperary, the evidence suggests that, here, another nucleus of teams were accustomed to a specific version of football. Together they show that football playing among teams of local men was not unknown in the pre-GAA era.

When reports of rugby in Tipperary appeared, they featured play between the military and local teams. The early years of rugby suggest that military officers stationed in the town barracks were a common denominator in its introduction in Nenagh and Tipperary. They were not only the game's first patrons, from whom men and boys in Nenagh and Tipperary learned the rules of the game, they also supplied the opposition. Though a team was assembled in Nenagh in 1875, there was no actual rugby club until Nenagh Ormond RFC was established in 1884.[94] In the south of the county, a rugby club was established in Clonmel in 1882.[95]

On 27 December 1875, expressions of thanks were expressed to the commanding officer of the 50th (Queen's Own) Regiment 'for the kind manner in which he threw open both barracks and field to the townspeople of Nenagh with the rules of rugby, which Lieutenant Carr took great trouble to explain to the Nenagh men. This was their first attempt at the game.'[96] Reminiscent of the 79th Highlanders before them, the departure of the 50th Regiment from Nenagh was lamented in the *Guardian*. It was remarked that 'no corps ever left the town more deservedly regretted, as a most cordial relationship existed since the football matches of last season, and the courtesy of the officers on these occasions … made them well worthy of the compliment paid them yesterday on their departure'.[97]

In both Tipperary town and Clonmel, the impetus for rugby stemmed initially from the grammar schools in 1878. Grammar schools were the elite schools in the county, comparable with the public school model in England. Tipperary Grammar School, St John's College, Newport, Rockwell College and St Cronan's School, Roscrea were the only schools that appeared with any regularity in the local press where school sport was recorded. The 1871 census returns for Tipperary show that there were 12,493 boys aged between ten and fifteen living in the county.[98] Attendance levels at post-primary school were low, as the majority of families could not afford to put their children through further education, let alone public or grammar schools. In England 'less than a quarter of one per cent' of boys that went to school went to a public school.[99] On account of this, many of the school cricket and rugby teams played against old boys, where it was deemed important to keep up the links with the school. Teams were regularly permutations of various associates and pupils of the school itself. These teams were often arbitrary but it was in many cases the only course of action available, mindful that the summer holidays were a natural defining period for active school participation.

The attendance of a small number of boys at public school in England demonstrated that there was regular interaction between these educational establishments and families in Ireland. This was likely as a result of cultural ties, as some families in Tipperary identified themselves as belonging to the commonwealth of Great Britain and Ireland. They were also assisting in empire-building. A diffusion of rugby's cult ethos from the public school network in England resulted in tangential dissemination of games between like-minded young males. But the attendance of these boys at public school in England was also reflective of class and snobbery. It was the same at the grammar schools in Tipperary. That the Tipperary Grammar School played rugby matches between themselves and school old boys suggests that this was not diffusion but rather 'social separatism played out on the playing field'.[100]

In Tipperary town, a team drawn from the 15th Regiment were regular opponents of both the grammar school team and the Clanwilliam Football Club.[101] These meetings further demonstrate the level of diffusion which came from the military stimulus. In Tipperary, it was claimed that the grammar school 'fostered' the game in the town.[102] The school continued to promote the rugby code and to this extent its principal, Rev. Lindsay, sought out some of his former pupils, then residing near Newport, on the Tipperary–Limerick border, to play a match against his school team.[103] Knowledge of the game gradually extended outwards. At the time the Newport team was but a collection of men and boys brought together to play rugby without any formal club actually in existence. Though these schools were playing rugby, their overall impact was slight.

When rugby was introduced to Nenagh the military team played 'an equal number of the Nenagh Cricket Club'.[104] One of the members of Nenagh cricket team, William Chumney, who played many times for the club, subsequently lined out for the Ormond Rugby Club in the Munster Challenge Cup in 1886.[105] In Tipperary town, Thomas St

George MacCarthy, the Heuston twins and W.G. Rutherford played cricket with Clanwilliam. They also played rugby with the Clanwilliam club which, one may infer, started out as a cricket club, as had happened in Nenagh.[106] There was a literary club in Tipperary town, called the Clanwilliam Club, reputedly established in 1866 with 'officers of the Army and Navy admitted without ballot'.[107] W.G. Rutherford, prominent on both the cricket and rugby field, was a member of this club.[108] Prior to this, in 1840, 'the bachelors of the Clanwilliam Club' gave a splendid ball and supper to the '*elite* [*sic*] of this and neighbouring counties'.[109] It is quite probable that it was from this club that all other clubs and activities evolved, as it was comprised of bachelors. These men had lots of time on their hands to engage in sport and they were likely of a similar age. The club also had a strong military presence.

Thomas St George MacCarthy had an interesting and varied sporting career. Though recognised for his rugby prowess and his cricket-playing ability, he is perhaps best remembered as one of the seven men who were present when the GAA was founded in 1884.[110] A member of the Royal Irish Constabulary, his presence at this historic meeting in Thurles appears to be the only connection he had with the GAA in a public sphere. He was born in Bansha, County Tipperary on 9 June, 1862, a son of Sub-Inspector George and Margaret MacCarthy. He was educated at Tipperary Grammar School, finishing his schooling (according to his obituary) at Rockwell College. He later attended Trinity College Dublin and Cusack's Civil Service Academy, also in Dublin.[111] While attending Trinity he was selected to play for the Ireland rugby team in an international match against Wales, on 28 January, 1882, his one and only cap. He also played cricket for Clanwilliam CC and the Marist College, Dundalk. Whether he attended the foundation meeting of the GAA on police business, maintaining observations on Irish Republican Brotherhood activity, is speculative, though not implausible. However, a simpler explanation may be that he attended as a sportsman in support of Cusack, mindful of his recent association with him at Cusack's Academy. He was, after all, just fifteen kilometres away in Templemore, where he was stationed.

ASSOCIATION FOOTBALL

If the evidence for rugby is limited for the county, then that of the association game is all the less tangible. There is a difficulty in categorising this football code based on press reports alone. That problem aside, not only was Association football played in Tipperary at the latter end of the 1870s, but its presence has hitherto gone unnoticed. Its presence in the county predates by seventeen years that which was previously believed to have been the earliest example of the association code.[112] Unlike rugby, cricket and the GAA, little attention has been given to the growth or development of Association football in Ireland at a local level, apart from a recent book on soccer in Munster.[113] It is as if there has been no urgency, initiative or interest on behalf of Association football historians at a national or local level to seriously chronicle the development of the game in Ireland, as Neal Garnham has shown.[114] Garnham has provided a basis from which to redress this historical imbalance but the lack of investigative analysis at a local level continues to be an issue.[115]

As with rugby football, it was the military personnel who were the instigators of the association code in Tipperary, at Cahir and Fethard garrisons – both staffed in 1879 by members of the 7th Hussars. Based on the military personnel assigned to the various barracks in the county, there is little scope for inferring a favoured ball game among the men stationed there. The Hussars at Cahir and the infantry at Tipperary played the association game in 1875. A report of a match between the 7th Hussars (Cahir barracks) and the 15th Regiment (Tipperary) noted that the 'dribbling (that essential feature of the association game) of Corporals Murray, Urquhart' was a feature of the day's play.[116] Though specifics of the play itself are ambiguous, the reference to the 'association game' infers that it was the code sanctioned by the Football Association in 1863 which was played. In a report of a subsequent match between Cahir and Fethard, references to a goalkeeper and other characteristics not associated with the rugby code are made, from which one can infer that it was the association code that was played here.[117] Further south in the county, a notice appeared in the local press in 1880 which announced a meeting to establish the Kilcash Football Club, which would play under association rules.[118] In 1879, the Carrick-on-Suir

Amateur Athletic, Cricket and Football Club had been established. The football code which these clubs followed was the association code. The Carrick and Kilcash clubs played each other during the winter of 1879–80, with Tom Davin noted for his display as goalkeeper for the Carrick team.[119] It was to be a short-lived experience. Apart from one reference to a four-a-side football tournament, played in association with the athletic sports on Easter Monday 1882, when Carrick played against a Kilcash quartet, there were no further references to football in the club minutes.[120] The collapse of the Carrick-on-Suir club later that year put an end to sustained development of the association game.

After the foundation of the GAA the association code remained largely absent from Tipperary. There was a brief revival of interest in Association football in the latter half of the 1890s when the military were active in its promotion in the county.[121] However, though detailed consideration of this subject would take the analysis beyond 1880, the evidence shows that Association football was played in south Tipperary at a time when its progress has previously been demonstrated to have been centred on Belfast and, to some extent, Dublin.[122]

HANDBALL AND BALL COURTS

Ball playing with the hands was recorded in Ireland from the first half of the eighteen century.[123] Press reports were not specific in terms of the characteristics associated with ball-playing or indeed the type of game that was played. Where ball-playing was noted, this is inferred as playing ball with one's hands. In the Census of Ireland reports, a 'description of industrial pursuits and amusements practised' was recorded for various asylums around the country.[124] At Clonmel Asylum 'ball-playing' was permitted but in relation to the Central Criminal Asylum in Dublin, the term 'football' was used. This suggests that enumerators had a specific record sheet to differentiate various sports and recreations, and infers that there were two styles of play involved.[125] This differentiation is important as it sets a standard from which to assess the merits of ball-related activities. If a football was used, the contemporary report will refer to 'football' or 'kicking a football'.[126] Where 'ball-playing' was noted, this is inferred to be a style of play in which the participant's hands were used. Ball courts were another common feature of the Tipperary landscape throughout the nineteenth century, often tucked away behind street buildings in towns and villages. They were also found at military barracks, principally in Nenagh, Templemore and Tipperary.[127] Ball courts in County Tipperary were principally used for handball, with some leading exponents of the game originating in Clonmel.

As had happened with both hurling and football, when boys and men were found 'ball playing' on the public streets they were brought before the local magistrates. An activity like this also constituted an offence and was contrary to the law of the land.[128] In June 1857, six men were charged before the Clonmel Petty Sessions for playing ball on the public street, an instance which was not reported in the local press.[129] But where ball courts were erected, play could and did take place and most of it went unrecorded. Those recorded were games noteworthy for a couple of factors – namely the occasion itself and the degree to which open bets were offered and taken.

In 1850, two Clonmel men travelled to Limerick to compete against challengers from Cork city. The match was for '£50 aside, but several hundred pounds changed hands on the occasion', leaving the Clonmel men to return home to a rapturous welcome.[130] A match of a more local nature took place at the racket court in the County Clubhouse, Clonmel in 1858 for £10 a-side, in which Jeremiah Condon, a Clonmel victualler, defeated James Kennedy, of Carrick-on-Suir.[131] Condon then teamed up with William Bagg to challenge any men from the south of Ireland for £50 a-side. Ten years later they were still paired up together, this time to take on the Dublin champions C. Kickham and T. Waters, once more at the County Clubhouse, Clonmel, where 'as much as £1,000 was staked [on] the Clonmel boys, and *lost* [*sic*]'.[132] One reason attributed to the local men's defeat was that their ages were fifty-two and forty years, though it was not specified which was the older. It makes the claim that Bagg was the Irish professional champion from 1870 to 1880 all the more suspect.[133]

Two more men from the south of the county, P. Griffin, Carrick-on-Suir, and Edward Hickey, Clonmel, battled it out for £50 a-side at the ball alley in Kilkenny city in October 1872. As Griffin took control, 'James Laurence and John O'Connell offered *fivers* and *tenners* [*sic*] freely out of the Carrick-man, but were not taken up'.[134] The *Clonmel Chronicle* report of this fixture noted it as a 'game of fives', though this terminology was not widely used in Ireland. The main advocates for this term were the military and it was used to denote the 'skittle alley and fives-court' on the plans for Tipperary barracks. This suggests a diffusion of the sport among the military, something which also brought them into contact with civilian players.[135] At Nenagh a private in the 47th regiment defeated 'a civilian, who [was] one of the best players in this district' at the military barrack alley, where once more 'considerable stakes were laid on the issue'.[136]

Though relatively simple in concept, the game still required appropriate premises to be viable. The racket court of the County Clubhouse was a popular venue, as noted. What is less clear is the degree to which local property owners actively supported the game by renting out an alley to a local entrepreneur. That such patronage was likely may be ascertained from the details of a court case at Clonmel Borough Petty Sessions in June 1876. Thomas Cleary, Ardgeeha, charged James Goold with overholding possession of the ball alley in Peter Street. The rent due was three shillings per week, with £4 due to Cleary on account of non-payment by Goold.[137] Because of the permanence of ball alleys they can be traced on the Ordnance Survey maps of the period, an unusual feature of the Victorian landscape of Tipperary. Apart from Thurles racecourse, as previously noted, no other sporting feature attracted the attention of cartographers. On the 1874 Ordnance Survey town plan of Clonmel there were three ball courts identified. Two were at the Union Workhouse and there was one off Peter Street.[138] Of the individuals who participated, only one occupation, that of a victualler, has been identified. The physical nature of the game did not endear it to gentlemen participants. Ball courts took up a small area of land when compared to the space required for team games or horse racing. That these were recorded only on town plans is indicative of the overall lack of structure and permanence associated with sport in general in Tipperary at this time. It also demonstrates, as Paul Rouse has shown, how 'the expansion of ball courts happened at the same time as the spread of billiards, a reminder of how Ireland was influenced by international patterns of play'.[139]

CONCLUSION

The decline of hurling in the aftermath of the Famine, up to the foundation of the GAA, has been overstated. While it is acknowledged that contemporary accounts state that hurling was in decline, there was no yardstick offered by which to judge if this was actually true or if it was just believed to be true. Lack of evidence has transferred belief into fact.

An assessment of the growth and diffusion of rugby shows that it came from the military officers in the same way as Association football did. That young men played Harrow Rules football in south Tipperary was an accident of history rather than transmigration of sport. It was a football match played for sport's sake, nothing more and nothing less. The evidence from the cricket-playing fraternity emphasised this all the more. The Marylebone Cricket Club (MCC) was the *de facto* head body of cricket. Yet there was no national organisational structure to oversee cricket's growth in Ireland. This undermined the continued development of the game. The very nature of the game as it developed in Tipperary was one that was diffused down through all classes. This resulted in many games taking place on a Sunday afternoon. With the foundation of the GAA in 1884 all the main ball sports in the country now had a national body to oversee their growth and development. All, that is, except cricket. It was one of the reasons for its decline in the opening years of the twentieth century. Ball games in County Tipperary were diffused through the classes. This ranged from the landowner, clerk, and shop assistant with cricket, to the farm labourer with hurling.

CONCLUSION

The evolution and growth of sport in County Tipperary between 1840 and 1880 was predicated along class lines. It was the landed, propertied and military classes who controlled, patronised and participated in sport in the county. The spread and participation level of sport demonstrated a strong element of social exclusion. This was not by design. The individuals in question belonged to a narrow social class and operated within a confined network of relationships, and diffusion was not part of their agenda. It was by the nature of their close association and cultural ties that like-minded individuals and families invited their friends, associates and visitors to their homes and demesnes to participate in some form of sport. This maintained familial links and cultural ties in what was a predominantly rural society.

Sport that took place in the demesnes and estates required an organisational structure, which would not have happened were it not for patronage from above, that is from the landlord or lessee, or in the case of the military, the officer class. Structures put in place, under the direction of these men or their appointed officials, ensured that a calendar of events could be drawn up for the successful completion of whatever sporting season was in vogue. Because the elite had time, social position and money, a variety of sports were organised and sustained. This was sport for the elite, organised by the elite. The diffusion of various sports emanated from the demesne and garrison out into the countryside.

Critical to the development and growth of sport in Tipperary during the period 1840–1880 was the large-scale presence of officers in Tipperary's numerous military barracks. Many of these officers were born outside Ireland and were already familiar with modern and codified forms of sport. The level of support the officer class gave to all sports was an indication of the relative security they enjoyed in rural Ireland. A posting to southern Ireland was one of three which artillery field officers could receive,[1] the other two being India or the south of England, alternating between Woolwich, Aldershot and Salisbury Plain. Officers sent to southern Ireland 'enjoyed hunting and all sports'. A combination of key individuals and military officers ensured that sport would continue to prosper. That this happened in Tipperary in the middle of the 1860s was a reflection of the diffusion of sport nationally and internationally. This was also clearly evident in County Westmeath. The military, in promoting and sustaining the growth of sport in Tipperary, were in essence replicating what was happening elsewhere in the country. As well as being agents of law and order, they were also agents of sporting diffusion. They were as instrumental in this diffusion in Tipperary as they were in Westmeath, or indeed in any part of the British Empire.[2] Officers soon discovered that life in the army varied little, no matter the location. Percival Marling of the 18th Hussars recounted that there was hunting six days a week in Cahir, with a drag on Sunday, in the 1880s. When he was transferred to Aldershot, apart from one route march per week, they 'were hunting five and six days a week'.[3]

Alongside this was the development of an integrated rail network covering most of the county that allowed for the cheap and easy construction of sporting networks. The post-Famine boom (and the end of the social and economic dislocation of the 1845–51 period) created the societal stability that allowed sport to prosper. The estate system experienced a period of sustained economic certainty during this period, including new investment in landed estates. It was no surprise that cricket was described in the Tipperary press as 'a republican game' – that is, a game that had truly spread countywide and was diffused among all the classes. However, despite the often-held view that hurling had died out due to the effects of the Famine and its consequences, the game continued to be widely played, although not in a readily recognised codified form as is apparent in modern times.

The period between 1840 and 1880 also witnessed the emergence of the first sports stars (such as Henry, 3rd Marquis of Waterford, Lord Waterford) who captivated the public at large. To document such individuals there emerged a commercialised sporting journalism, with, for example, 'Larky Grigg' supplying weekly columns to the Tipperary press on hunting to hounds. Other pseudonymous writers followed, but 'Grigg' was to continue with his reporting of hunt meets to the end of the century. He may have been a correspondent, but he was certainly knowledgeable. This suggests he was an insider.

For the first time in Irish history, female participation in sport became widespread and recorded during this period, notably in hunting to hounds, archery, croquet and lawn tennis. These factors combine to show that there was a clearly defined take-off period for sport in the county in the mid-1860s, when there was a transition from occasional fixtures and contests to a more frequent 'calendar' of competition in a range of sports. Increased participation in cricket, with four cricket clubs established in Clonmel alone in 1864, and an upturn in the number of horse race meetings and fox/hare hunting meetings, serves to indicate that a defining period had arrived in the evolution of Tipperary sport. There was an appetite for sport and this was also evident in the level of reporting.

The period saw a steady growth in the business surrounding sport, including the employment of professionals (in a range of capacities and sports), such as the hiring of English trainers by the Clonmel Rowing Club, which demonstrated a winning mentality in the club, which was only of recent foundation. Social and business interaction conducted in the course of daily life now found expression on the playing field, the cricket ground or the tennis court. The associational ties ran deep through society. The strong bond of friendship was critical in the world of the elite, frequently cultivated at public school. Working through local committees, this cohesive element brought to bear by the elite in the promotion and organisation of sport was a crucial factor. There were four sports which retained a significant presence in Tipperary throughout the whole period – hunting, horse racing, cricket and hurling.

Close social networks resulted in some of the same family names appearing at various sports right through the 1840–1880 period. Bagwell, Barton, Bassett Holmes, Carden, Charteris, Earl of Donoughmore, Going, Grubb, Langley, Viscount Lismore, Moore, Palliser, Perry, Smithwick, Trant, Trench and Lord Waterford were names which typically appeared at various sporting occasions county-wide. While there were 1,706 owners of land of one acre and upwards in Tipperary in 1876, the number of those at the fore of sporting promotion was much smaller.[4] Given that there were forty-four hunt packs, two hundred and seven cricket teams, seven archery societies, twenty-six horse racing venues, twenty-six athletics sport venues and twenty-nine lawn tennis venues, the total sum of 339 specific team or venue locations suggests a large number of people were required to support the growth of these sports.

While the Great Famine had a devastating effect on society, sports such as hunting to hounds, horse racing and cricket continued. Fox hunting and horse racing were, by then, integral elements in the social and sporting activities of a class that was able to maintain its standard of living. Having fulfilled their moral obligations by contributing to funds dedicated to alleviating distress caused by the Famine, life could – and for the most part did – continue as normal for the patrons of Irish sport. The sports of hunting to hounds, horse racing and cricket enjoyed the patronage of the landed, propertied and military classes, in contrast to hurling. Hurling was frequently violent and without any permanent or prescribed playing area. Whereas the three former sports, and other lawn games which emerged during the era, followed a structure and format that were in many ways the building blocks of codification, hurling was still volatile and unregulated.

For the most part, the growth of sport in Tipperary was similar to that which took place on the British mainland. An example of this is the initial promotion of archery, which gave way to croquet, which in turn gave way to lawn tennis. This also happened in central Scotland, where 'at one time or another most of the region's major sporting activities were affected adversely by competition from a temporarily more successful rival'.[5] Much of the sporting influences in Tipperary had their origin in England. This was especially so with country house sport, which was reflective of that which took place in estates and demesnes in Britain.

As noted in the Introduction, the main feature of pre-codified sport in Tipperary was that it was organised along class lines, and was as much 'a product and a reflection of social class' as it was in Great Britain.[6] Sport was principally for the moneyed leisured. The shift came with the transition from pre-modern to modern sport, which resulted in some class elements becoming weakened, though remaining strong in lawn tennis, rugby football and golf. Once sport became codified, other pastimes took note and in order to attract participants, also began to draw up codes. Cycling is a prime example of this process.[7] What sport also gave to many was a sense of identity. Townland names typically became a feature of cricket-playing, denoting the origin or base of a team. This was at a level beneath that of the parish, which became and still remains a core element of club toponymy in the GAA. As Tom Hayes has noted, sport 'enhanced a growing appreciation of borders and divisions between parishes, districts, unions, counties, provinces and countries'.[8]

In Victorian Tipperary there was a very limited industrial base and therefore little in the way of factory life to prompt the working class to seek the escape of sporting recreation. This was a situation unlike that of the mill workers of Leeds and Bolton, who found respite on the soccer field, or unlike the assembly line workers in America, who had baseball as a relief.[9] In Tipperary, and throughout much of rural Ireland, the tenant farmer class dominated the Gaelic fields, participating in sports that were derived from a nationalist ideology. The ideological differences meant that the newly codified Irish sports were to become virtually unique among international games, which, as Richard Holt has commented, are 'arguably the most striking instance of politics shaping sport in modern history'.[10]

In common with the findings of Tom Hunt for Westmeath, female participation was drawn from the upper and middle classes of Victorian

Tipperary.[11] While the nature of the language used in the papers at that time appears sexist by the standards of today, this was typical of the style of reporting in the nineteenth-century press. Sport was a social occasion and for many families it presented ideal opportunities not only to maintain links with peers, but also to cultivate new links with potential marriage partners. The pioneering paths made by these women paved the way for sport to become acceptable and fashionable for their female descendants. One of these was Lena Rice, Marlhill, New Inn. She had commenced playing lawn tennis tournaments around the county in conjunction with other members of her family.[12] As has been shown, this resulted in her victory at Wimbledon in 1890, the only female from Ireland to win the Wimbledon lawn tennis tournament.[13]

It is clear that sport evolved in a rural community like Tipperary very differently from how it did in the industrialised and urban communities of mainland Britain. In Britain sport developed with the promotion and encouragement of a wide spectrum: mill owners, publicans, public schools, businessmen, estate owners, Christian groups, etc. In Tipperary, in contrast, the spectrum of support was much narrower and in addition was increasingly politically suspect. As Vincent Comerford observed, 'the institutionalisation of sport occurred within a society constructed along lines of entrenched social class'.[14] Emulation, the lower classes copying their 'betters' in sport as in life, was an important aspect of diffusion. It could equally be drinking tea out of china cups as much as it was the promotion of sport.

In County Tipperary, sports were refined and codified before they made the jump to general acceptance among the masses. A Victorian dislike of cruel, barbaric recreations such as bull-baiting and cock-fighting meant that these were removed from the new social order, even though those who were objecting to them – the elite – were, in the eighteenth century, regularly some of their principal supporters.[15] Essentially, the picture that emerged in Tipperary in the mid-nineteenth century was reflective of the ongoing development of sport in Great Britain. The appearance of rugby and Association football, croquet and lawn tennis in England was quickly replicated in Tipperary. The biggest mystery surrounds cricket. Though there was no formally instituted

County Championship until 1890, there were unofficial county champions from 1864. With cricket in Tipperary, from 1864 to 1878, at a height never seen again, it is intriguing to think what might have happened had a national body been put in place, as occurred with rugby and Association football.

Issues around hunting to hounds went much deeper than just simply objecting to hunting. Hunting during the long winter months was a way of life for many families. The evidence from County Tipperary shows that the hunt grew ever more powerful and influential as the 1870s progressed. By stopping the hunt at the onset of the Land War, the protestors hit at the very heart of a particular strand of rural society. For many of them, it was the beginning of the end of a way of life that had existed for over a century. With political and social movements shaping the future of the country, it was something from which the landed elite would not recover.

In the context of the evolution of sport in Ireland at a micro-level, this book has embraced all aspects of social life in Victorian Tipperary. It has shown how the elite were responsible for the proliferation and promotion of sport and its ethos. The appetite for sport that these men and women displayed laid the foundation for their associates and subordinates to follow. In the private setting of a demesne, the building blocks of sport were unwittingly laid. As sport crossed the divide from private to public, its diffusion to the wider community of Tipperary coincided with the emergence of codified team sports in England. The appearance of these team sports in Tipperary, and in Ireland generally, would lead to the awakening of national consciousness which, in turn, would result in the codification of the uniquely Irish field games of hurling and Gaelic football and the foundation of the Gaelic Athletic Association.

NOTES AND REFERENCES

INTRODUCTION

1   Paul Rouse, *Sport and Ireland: a history* (Oxford: Oxford University Press, 2015). See especially Chapter 2, 'The Modernisation of Irish Sport: 1800–1880', pp. 84–148.

2   J.G.A. Prim, 'Olden Popular Pastimes in Kilkenny', *Transactions of the Kilkenny Archaeological Society* vol. II, 1852–53 (Dublin, 1855), pp. 319–35; James Kelly, 'The Pastime of the Elite: clubs and societies and the promotion of horse racing', in James Kelly and Martyn J. Powell (eds), *Clubs and Societies in Eighteenth-century Ireland* (Dublin: Four Courts Press, 2010), pp. 409–24.

3   James Kelly, *Sport in Ireland, 1600–1840* (Dublin: Four Courts Press, 2014).

4   M.M. O'Hara, *Chief and Tribune: Parnell and Davitt* (Dublin and London: Maunsel & Co., 1919), p. 64.

5   L.P. Curtis Jr., 'Stopping the Hunt, 1881–1882: an aspect of the Irish land war', in C.H.E. Philpin (ed.), *Nationalism and Popular Protest in Ireland* (Cambridge: Cambridge University Press, 2002), pp. 349–402.

6   Thomas F. O'Sullivan, *The Story of the GAA* (Dublin: Thomas F. O'Sullivan, 1916); Canon Philip Fogarty, *Tipperary's GAA Story* (Thurles: The Tipperary Star, 1960); Marcus de Búrca, *The GAA: a history of the Gaelic Athletic Association* (Dublin: Cumann Lúthchleas Gael, 1980); Pádraig Puirséal, *The GAA in Its Time* (Dublin: Ward River Press, 1982); W.F. Mandle, *The Gaelic Athletic Association and Irish Nationalist Politics, 1884–1924* (Dublin and London: Gill & Macmillan, 1987); Dónal McAnallen, David Hassan and Roddy Hegarty, *The Evolution of the GAA: Ulaidh, Éire agus eile* (Belfast: Ulster Historical Foundation, 2009).

7   Tom Hunt, *Sport and Society in Victorian Ireland: the case of Westmeath* (Cork: Cork University Press, 2007).

8   *Return of Owners of Land of One Acre and Upwards, in the Several Counties, Counties of Cities, and Counties of Towns in Ireland* (Dublin: A. Thom for HM Stationery Office, 1876), pp. 159, 162.

9   Mike Huggins, 'Sport and the Upper Classes: introduction', *Sport in History*, vol. 28, no. 3 (September 2008), p. 356.

10 Edward Walford, *The County Families of the United Kingdom* (London: Robert Hardwicke, 1860), pp. 840–1.

11 Ibid., pp. 814–15.

12 Ibid., pp. 809, 826, 829.

13 *Return of Owners of Land*, pp. 163, 165, 167.

14   *Debrett's Illustrated Peerage and Baronetage of the United Kingdom of Great Britain and Ireland, 1864* (London: Bostworth & Harrison, 1864), pp. 108, 129, 156.

15   U.H. Hussey de Burgh, *The Landowners of Ireland* (Dublin: Hodges, Foster & Figgis, 1878), pp. 158–72.

16   T. Jones Hughes, 'Landholding and Settlement in County Tipperary in the Nineteenth Century', in William Nolan (ed.), *Tipperary: history and society* (Dublin: Geography Publications, 1985), p. 340.

17   £100 in 1880 equates to £9,135 (€10,791.43) in 2016, while £5,000 in 1880 equates to £456,800 (€539,650.72) in 2016. Calculations carried out on Measuringworth.com website, http://www.measuringworth.com/ukcompare/ (Accessed 13 May 2017).

18   Tom Hunt, 'The Development of Sport in County Westmeath, 1850–1905', unpublished PhD thesis, De Montfort University, Leicester, 2005, pp. 5–6.

19   Patrick Bracken, 'The Emergence of Hurling in Australia, 1877–1917', *Sport in Society: cultures, commerce, media, politics*, vol. 19, no. 1 (January 2015), pp. 62–73.

20   Joseph C. Hayes, 'Guide to Tipperary Newspapers, 1770–1989', *Tipperary Historical Journal 1989*, p. 8.

21   Rouse, *Sport and Ireland*, pp. 7–8.

22   M.E. Daly, 'The Development of the National School System, 1831–40', in Art Cosgrove and Donal McCartney (eds), *Studies in Irish History, Presented to R. Dudley Edwards* (Dublin: University College Dublin, 1979), pp. 150–63.

23   J.S. Donnelly and Kerby A. Miller, *Irish Popular Culture 1650–1850* (Dublin and Portland: Irish Academic Press Ltd., 1999), p. 24.

24   *Clonmel Chronicle*, 15 April 1874; *Nenagh Guardian*, 29 December 1875.

25   *Tipperary Free Press*, 22 April 1856, 19 March 1858, 15 February 1859.

26   W.E. Vaughan and A.J. Fitzpatrick, *Irish Historical Statistics: population, 1821–1971*, (Dublin: Royal Irish Academy, 1978), pp. 306–7.

27   Joel Mokyr, *Why Ireland Starved: a quantitative and analytical history of the Irish economy, 1800–1850* (London: Allen & Unwin, 1983), p. 267.

28   John Crowley, William J. Smyth and Mike Murphy (eds), *Atlas of the Great Irish Famine* (Cork: Cork University Press, 2012), p. 12.

29   Cormac Ó Gráda, *Ireland: a new economic history, 1780–1939* (Oxford: Oxford University Press, 1994), pp. 224–5.

30   Ibid., p. 273.

31   Ibid.

32   George Henry Bassett, County *Tipperary One Hundred Years Ago: a guide and directory, 1889* (reprint Belfast: Friars Bush Press, 1991), p. 23.

33   John Murray, *Handbook for Travellers in Ireland*, 2nd revised edn (London:

John Murray, 1866), p. 273.

34   Sean O'Donnell, *Clonmel, 1840–1900: anatomy of an Irish town* (Dublin: Geography Publications, 1999), p. 23.

35   Bassett, *Tipperary: a guide and directory, 1889*, p. 369.

36   Crowley, Smyth and Murphy, *Atlas of the Great Irish Famine*, p. 240.

37   Vaughan and Fitzpatrick, *Population, 1821–1971*, p. 34.

38   Kevin O'Connor, *Ironing the Land: the coming of the railways to Ireland* (Dublin: Gill & Macmillan, 1999), p. 48.

39   Ibid., p. 49.

40   *Tipperary Free Press*, 12 May 1847.

41   K.A. Murray and D.B. McNeill, *The Great Southern & Western Railway* (Dublin: Irish Railway Record Society, 1976), p. 186.

42   Ibid., p. 15.

43   Ibid., p. 110.

44   *Tipperary Free Press*, 2 December 1846.

45   Murray and McNeill. *Great Southern & Western Railway*, pp. 186–8.

46   *Nenagh Guardian*, 20 October 1860, p. 2.

47   Hunt, *Sport and Society*, p. 8.

48   Fergus D'Arcy, *Horses, Lords and Racing Men: the Turf Club, 1790–1990* (The Curragh: The Turf Club, 1991), p. 145. For a further insight into the railways and horse racing see John Tolson and Wray Vamplew, 'Derailed: railways and horse-racing revisited', *The Sports Historian*, vol. 18, no. 2 (November 1998), pp. 34–49 and John Tolson and Wray Vamplew, 'Facilitation Not Revolution: railways and British flat racing, 1830–1914', *Sport in History*, vol. 23, no. 1 (Summer 2003), pp. 89–106.

49   Córas Iompair Éireann archives, Dublin: Meeting of the Great Southern and Western Railway Board, 27 September 1850; Great Southern and Western Railway minute book no. 5, pp. 234–5.

50   *Clonmel Chronicle*, 5 July 1862.

51   Ibid., 15 January 1873.

52   Ibid., 29 July 1863.

53   New national schools include Littleton (1847), Moycarkey (1847), Dromakeenan (1851), Clonlisk (1857).

54   G.P.T. Finn, 'Trinity Mysteries: university, elite schooling and sport in Ireland', *The International Journal of the History of Sport*, vol. 27, no. 13 (September 2010), p. 2274; Mike Cronin, '"Trinity Mysteries": responding to a chaotic reading of Irish history', *The International Journal of the History of Sport*, vol. 28, no. 18 (December 2011), p. 2757.

55   Allen Guttman, *From Ritual to Record: the nature of modern sports* (New York: Columbia University Press, 1978).

CHAPTER 1

1   See especially Tony Mason and Eliza Reidi, *Sport and the Military: the British armed forces, 1880–1960* (Cambridge: Cambridge University Press, 2010).

2   Ibid., pp. 16–17.

3   E.M. Spiers, 'Army Organisation and Society in the Nineteenth Century' in Thomas Bartlett and Keith Jeffery (eds), *A Military History of Ireland* (Cambridge: Cambridge University Press, 1996), p. 337.

4   Crowley, Smyth and Murphy, *Atlas of the Great Irish Famine*, p. 54.

5   Samuel Lewis, *A Topographical Dictionary of Ireland*, vol. II (London: S. Lewis & Co., 1837), pp. 609–10.

6   Samuel Lewis, *A Topographical Dictionary of Ireland*, vol. I (London: S. Lewis & Co., 1837), p. 238.

7   Ibid., p. 341.

8   Ibid., p. 369.

9   Ibid., p. 276.

10   Ibid., p. 285.

11   Ibid., p. 626.

12   Lewis, *Topographical Dictionary*, vol. II, p. 635.

13   Ibid., p. 423.

14   Ibid., p. 527.

15   Ibid., p. 610.

16   Virginia Crossman, 'Irish Barracks in the 1820s and 1830s: a political perspective', *The Irish Sword*, vol. XVII, no. 68 (1989), p. 212.

17   Noreen Higgins, *Tipperary's Tithe War, 1830–1838: parish accounts of resistance against a church tax* (Tipperary: St Helen's Press, 2002), p. 25.

18   Ciarán Reilly, *The Irish Land Agent, 1830–60: the case of King's County* (Dublin: Four Courts Press, 2014), p. 69.

19   Paul M. Kerrigan, 'Barracks in Ireland, 1847', *The Irish Sword*, vol. XIX no. 77 (Summer 1995), p. 232.

20   Martin Loft, *Lieutenant Harry Loft of Louth and the 64th Regiment of Foot (Second Staffordshire)* (Leek: Churnet Valley Books, 2003), p. 65.

21   O'Donnell, *Clonmel 1840–1900*, p. 28.

22   Ibid., p. 29.

23   *Clonmel Chronicle*, 1 December 1855.

24   *Tipperary Free Press*, 15 November 1854.

25   Ibid., 2 June 1855.

26   Ibid., 9 January 1855.

27   Ibid., 7 October 1856.

28   Ibid., 9 June 1857.

29   *Clonmel Chronicle*, 28 January 1865.

30 *Census of Ireland 1871: Part 1 area, houses and population: also the ages, civil condition, occupations, birthplaces, and education of the people, vol. II, province of Munster, no. 5 county of Tipperary* (Dublin: A. Thom for Her Majesty's Stationery Office, 1874), p. 770.

31 The military and dependants figure is 2,231. The total town returns, where census returns for the eight military barracks are available, was 30,931.

32 The impact of the garrison is still evident in these towns today.

33 *Tipperary Free Press*, 22 April 1840.

34 Ibid., 18 May 1875; *Clonmel Chronicle*, 30 June 1880.

35 Chapter 6 also deals with some transference aspects of sport from the United Kingdom to Ireland by way of returning public school pupils.

36 The Palliser and Gough families from south Tipperary and the Carden or Trant families in north Tipperary being some examples.

37 Peter Wynne-Thomas, *The History of Cricket: from the Weald to the world* (Norwich: Stationery Office, 1997), p. 35.

38 Con Costello, *A Most Delightful Station: the British Army on the Curragh of Kildare, Ireland, 1855–1922* (Cork: The Collins Press, 1996), p. 199.

39 Mason and Reidi, *Sport and the Military*, p. 24.

40 *Tipperary Free Press*, 19 July 1843.

41 After Colonel Charteris died on 15 August 1961, the grounds of Cahir House were subsequently sold and the cricket club was disbanded.

42 Denis Judd, *Empire: the British imperial experience from 1765 to the present* (London: Harper Collins, 1996), pp. 40–1.

43 Loft, *Lieutenant Harry Loft*, p. 65.

44 Ashbrook Union Cricket Club scorebook, 1846–9, ff 42, 61.

45 *Tipperary Advocate*, 12 July 1862.

46 Jeff Hancock, librarian/archivist Surrey CCC, personal communication 10 May 2002.

47 Mason and Riedi, *Sport and the Military*, p. 7.

48 Costello, *A Most Delightful Station*, p. 178.

49 *Nenagh Guardian*, 1 September 1849, 12 September 1849.

50 *Clonmel Chronicle*, 15 September 1875.

51 Hunt, *Sport and Society*, p. 15.

52 Spiers, 'Army Organisation', p. 342.

53 Elizabeth A. Muenger, *The British Military Dilemma in Ireland* (Dublin: Gill & Macmillan, 1991), p. 26.

54 *Nenagh Guardian*, 30 December 1865

55 Ibid.

56 *Clonmel Chronicle*, 22 September 1866.

57 Ibid., 25 August 1866.

58   Ibid., 6 August 1864.

59   *Tipperary Free Press*, 28 November 1856.

60   Ibid., 19 December 1856.

61   Ibid., 6 December 1859; 9 December 1859.

62   *Clonmel Chronicle*, 27 June 1868.

63   *Nenagh Guardian*, 11 May 1870.

64   Ibid., 15 June 1870.

65   Ibid., 6 August 1870.

66   Ibid., 3 April 1850.

67   Ibid.

68   Ibid., 10 April 1850.

69   Ibid.

70   *Clonmel Chronicle*, 4 April 1871, 24 April 1872, 16 April 1873, 18 April 1874, 10 April 1875, 19 April 1876, 25 April 1877, 24 April 1878, 19 April 1879, 3 April 1880.

71   Sir Bernard Burke, *A Genealogical and Heraldic History of the Landed Gentry of Ireland* (London: Burke's Peerage, 1904), p. 620.

72   *Clonmel Chronicle*, 19 April 1876.

73   Ibid., 15 April 1876.

74   Costello, *A Most Delightful Station*, p. 177.

75   J.D. Campbell. "'Training for Sport Is Training for War': sport and the transformation of the British Army, 1860–1914', *The International Journal for the History of Sport*, vol. 17, no. 4 (December 2000), p. 22.

76   Sample prizes at Carabineers regimental steeplechases at Cahir in April 1867, *Clonmel Chronicle*, 24 April 1867.

77   Campbell, "'Training for Sport Is Training for War'", p. 23.

78   *Tipperary Constitution*, 5 February 1841.

79   *Tipperary Free Press*, 14 October 1846; 7 July 1857.

80   Ibid., 13 July 1850; *Nenagh Guardian*, 2 February 1850, 24 April 1861.

81   *Clonmel Chronicle*, 25 May 1861.

82   *Nenagh Guardian*, 5 June 1858, 30 May 1860; *Clonmel Chronicle*, 17 August 1861, 17 September 1862.

83   *Nenagh Guardian*, 12 May 1858.

84   Ibid., 5 June 1858.

85   Ibid., 11 June 1859.

86   *Clonmel Chronicle*, 27 March 1878.

87   *Nenagh Guardian*, 14 September 1878.

88   Ibid., 8 September 1875, 9 August 1879; *Clonmel Chronicle*, 1 October 1879.

89   Tom Hayes, 'God Save the Green, God Save the Queen and the Usual Loyal Toasts: sporting and dining for Ireland and/or the Queen', in Peter Gray (ed.),

Victoria's Ireland? Irishness and Britishness, 1837–1901 (Dublin: Four Courts Press, 2004), p. 82.

90   Sir Bernard Burke, *A Genealogical and Heraldic History of the Landed Gentry of Ireland*, volume II (London: Burke's Peerage, 1904), p. 924.

91   Ibid., p. 966.

92   Ibid., p. 1123.

93   Lists of names included with archery reports permit some form of quantification. 190 names were mentioned in the report of the Kilcommon Archers (Cahir) meet, in August 1861 (*Clonmel Chronicle*, 31 August 1861). 108 people were recorded at a meeting of the South Tipperary Bowmen in June 1863 (*Clonmel Chronicle*, 20 June 1863).

94   *Clonmel Chronicle*, 31 August 1861.

95   *Nenagh Guardian*, 29 December 1875.

96   Ibid., 10 June 1876.

97   National Library of Ireland Ms. 9515: Account book and records of Kilruane Football Club 1876–1880.

98   *Clonmel Chronicle*, 26 November 1879.

99   Ibid., 8 August 1868.

100 Hone, *Cricket in Ireland*, p. 34.

101 *Clonmel Chronicle*, 3 April 1880.

102 Horace A. Laffaye, *Polo in the United States: a history* (Jefferson, NC: McFarland & Co., 2011), pp. 20–2; *Polo: players edition*, vol. 15, no. 4 (December 2011), p. 63.

103 *Clonmel Chronicle*, 13 August 1887.

104 *Nenagh Guardian*, 10 September 1890.

105 Ramachandra Guha, *A Corner of a Foreign Field: the Indian history of a British sport* (London: Picador, 2002), p. 13.

106 See Mark Tierney, *Croke of Cashel: the life of Archbishop Thomas William Croke, 1823–1902* (Dublin: Gill & Macmillan, 1976), p. 195.

107 Mason and Riedi, *Sport and the Military*, p. 253.

108 Tom Hunt has shown how sporting recreation offered military personnel 'a seamless introduction and a means of integration into local elite society', Hunt, *Sport and Society*, p. 15.

CHAPTER 2 COUNTRY HOUSE SPORT
SPORT AND THE MILITARY

1   As has been pointed out by Terence Dooley, the terms 'country house' and 'big house' were interchangeable when houses were being described. For the

purposes of this book, the term 'country house' is used for the period under review. Terence Dooley, *The Decline of the Big House in Ireland* (Dublin: Wolfhound Press, 2001), p. 9. The term 'big house' has also been used in an exposition of archery: Brian Griffin, 'The Big House at Play: archery as an elite pursuit from the 1830s to the 1870s', in Ciaran O'Neill (ed.), *Irish Elites in the Nineteenth Century* (Dublin: Four Courts Press, 2013), pp. 153–171.

2 William Nolan, 'Patterns of Living in County Tipperary from 1770 to 1850', in William Nolan (ed.), *Tipperary: history and society* (Dublin: Geography Publications, 1985), pp. 295, 302.

3 Jones Hughes, 'Landholding and Settlement', p. 354.

4 David Underdown, *Start of Play: cricket and culture in eighteenth-century England* (London: Penguin Books, 2000), p. 47.

5 Nolan, 'Patterns of Living', p. 302.

6 *Nenagh Guardian*, 2 April 1873; John Lawrence, *Handbook of Cricket in Ireland 1873–74* (Dublin: John Lawrence, 1874), p. 151. Going had an estate of 2,522 acres in 1878: Hussey de Burgh, *The Landowners of Ireland*, p. 195.

7 *Cashel Gazette*, 5 August 1871; *Clonmel Chronicle*, 6 July 1872.

8 Neil Tranter, *Sport, Economy and Society in Britain, 1750–1914* (Cambridge: Cambridge University Press, 1998), p. 5.

9 Dooley, *The Decline of the Big House*, p. 18.

10 See Chapter 5, 'Women and the Masculine Kingdom of Sport', in Tony Collins, *Sport in Capitalist Society* (London: Routledge, 2013), pp. 38–47.

11 *Tipperary Free Press*, 4 June 1834.

12 Wynne-Thomas, *The History of Cricket*, pp. 7–8; Tranter, *Sport, Economy and Society*, p. 14.

13 *Tipperary Free Press*, 6 June 1849; *Clonmel Chronicle*, 1 June 1850.

14 *Tipperary Advocate*, 20 September 1862; *Nenagh Guardian*, 30 August 1873.

15 Ashbrook Union Cricket Club scorebook, 1846–9, match dates 24 July 1847, 31 July 1847, 26 August 1847.

16 Ibid., 'Rules and Regulations for the Season 1847', n.p.

17 *Clonmel Chronicle*, 18 September 1852.

18 Ibid., 14 May 1864.

19 *Nenagh Guardian*, 9 September 1865.

20 Ibid., 2 May 1860.

21 Ibid., 6 June 1866.

22 *Cashel Gazette*, 23 June 1866.

23 *Clonmel Chronicle*, 28 July 1866.

24 Ibid., 26 February 1870.

25 Ibid., 19 July 1876.

26 *Nenagh Guardian*, 17 August 1864.

27   *Clonmel Chronicle*, 29 June 1864; *Tipperary Free Press*, 21 April 1871.

28   *Tipperary Free Press*, 9 June 1865.

29   Seán O'Donnell, 'John Bagwell: politician and landlord (1811–1883)', *Tipperary Historical Journal 2017*, p. 33.

30   Albert Barry, CSSR *The Life of Count Moore* (Dublin: Gill & Son Ltd., 1905), p. 11; William Hayes and Art Kavanagh, *The Tipperary Gentry*, vol. 1 (Dublin: Irish Family Names, 2003), p. 24.

31   *Return of Owners of Land*, p. 158.

32   Mark Bence-Jones, *Twilight of the Ascendancy* (reprint London: Constable, 1993), p. 19.

33   Randall MacDonnell, *The Lost Houses of Ireland* (London: W&N, 2002), p. 152.

34   *Tipperary Vindicator*, 2 October 1844.

35   Jones Hughes, 'Landholding and Settlement', p. 340.

36   Ibid., p. 343.

37   Andrew Tierney, 'Architecture of Gentility in Nineteenth-century Ireland' in Ciaran O'Neill (ed.), *Irish Elites in the Nineteenth Century* (Dublin: Four Courts Press, 2013), p. 34. See also Thomas Power, *Land, Politics and Society in Eighteenth-century Tipperary* (Oxford: Clarendon Press, 1993), pp. 113–14.

38   Nolan, 'Patterns of Living', p. 302.

39   *Tipperary Advocate*, 20 September 1862.

40   *Clonmel Chronicle*, 12 October 1861. In 1875 the figure quoted for the improvements was 'about £40,000', *Clonmel Chronicle*, 10 February 1875.

41   *Return of Owners of Land*, p. 159.

42   Mary Cecelia Lyons, *Illustrated Incumbered Estates* (Whitegate, Co. Clare: Ballinakella Press, 1993), p. xiii.

43   Ibid., p. xlvi.

44   Ibid., pp. 49, 69–76.

45   *Finn's Leinster Journal*, 8–12 July 1869; 24-27 October 1770.

46   *Nenagh Guardian*, 23 July 1873.

47   Reference to summer and hunting by J.P. Mahaffy as quoted in Dooley, *The Decline of the Big House*, p. 56.

48   *Clonmel Chronicle*, 31 May 1851.

49   Tranter, 'Organised Sport and the Middle-class Woman', p. 36.

50   *Nenagh Guardian*, 13 August 1879.

51   Ibid., 9 August 1862.

52   *Cashel Gazette*, 21 August 1869.

53   Ibid.

54   Collins, *Sport in Capitalist Society*, p. 81.

55   *Clonmel Chronicle*, 16 August 1873.

56   The term 'gentle sex' or the 'fair sex' was widely used in reports and accounts of matches.

57   Martin Johnes, 'Archery, Romance and Elite Culture in England and Wales, *c.*1780–1840', *History*, vol. 89 (2004), p. 197.

58   *Tipperary Free Press*, 13 July 1844.

59   *Nenagh Guardian*, 12 May 1858, 5 June 1858, 7 August 1858.

60   Griffin, 'Archery as an Elite Pursuit', p. 154.

61   Ibid., p. 164.

62   *Nenagh Guardian*, 12 May 1858, 5 March 1859; *Clonmel Chronicle*, 25 May 1861; 1 June 1861, 18 September 1861.

63   Griffin, 'Archery as an Elite Pursuit', p. 164.

64   *Clonmel Chronicle*, 25 May 1861, 3 July 1861.

65   Johnes, 'Archery in England and Wales', p. 196.

66   *Nenagh Guardian*, 9 October 1858.

67   *Clonmel Chronicle*, 31 August 1861.

68   Toxophilite is a noun to denote a student or lover of archery.

69   *Clonmel Chronicle*, 3 July 1861.

70   *Clonmel Chronicle*, 13 July 1861, 17 August 1861; *Nenagh Guardian*, 31 August 1861; *Clonmel Chronicle*, 30 July 1862.

71   *Clonmel Chronicle*, 15 August 1862, 28 August 1866.

72   *Nenagh Guardian*, 3 August 1861; *Clonmel Chronicle*, 20 June 1863.

73   *Clonmel Chronicle*, 12 September 1863, 3 September 1864.

74   *Freeman's Journal*, 8 August 1850.

75   Ibid., 9 August 1851.

76   *Clonmel Chronicle*, 12 September 1863, 19 March 1864.

77   Ibid., 18 June 1864.

78   Ibid., 19 March 1864.

79   Ibid., 31 August 1861.

80   Ibid., 27 July 1864, 8 October 1864.

81   Ibid., 3 June 1865; Brian Griffin, 'Cecilia Betham (1843–1913): Ireland's first female international sports star', *History Ireland*, vol. 24 no. 3 (May–June 2016), pp. 30–3.

82   *Leinster Express*, 17 November 1866, p. 3.

83   *Freeman's Journal*, 5 September 1866, p. 3.

84   Johnes, 'Archery in England and Wales', p. 201.

85   Griffin, 'Archery as an Elite Pursuit', p. 163.

86   *Clonmel Chronicle*, 19 March 1864.

87   Ibid., 3 July 1861.

88   Ibid., 5 July 1871.

89   Tom Hunt, 'Women and Sport in Victorian Westmeath', *Irish Economic and Social History*, vol. xxxiv (2007) p. 35.

90   Neil L. Tranter, 'Organised Sport and the Middle-class Woman in Nineteenth-century Scotland', *The International Journal of the History of Sport*, vol. 6, no. 1 (1989), p. 44.

91   *Clonmel Chronicle*, 16 September 1871.

92   *Nenagh Guardian*, 24 July 1879; *Clonmel Chronicle*, 11 September 1869, 13 July 1872.

93   Griffin, 'Archery as an Elite Pursuit,' pp. 170–1.

94   Ibid., p. 171.

95   Ibid.

96   *Clonmel Chronicle*, 7 July 1869.

97   *Nenagh Guardian*, 4 August 1869, 17 August 1870; *Cashel Gazette*, 11 September 1869; 13 August 1870; *Clonmel Chronicle*, 23 July 1870, 13 July 1872.

98   This assertion is based on a lack of documentary evidence in the contemporary press. As accounts of the South Tipperary Bowmen disappear from the press no data is provided to suggest that a croquet club or society was established in south Tipperary, apart from the Rock Archery and Croquet Club.

99   *Nenagh Guardian*, 5 March 1859.

100 The last reference for the Ormond Archery Club identified was in the *Nenagh Guardian*, 11 August 1860. Press reports do not extend further than two years for the club.

101 *Nenagh Guardian*, 2 July 1859, 8 September 1875.

102 Ibid., 28 August 1875.

103 The term 'reunion' was widely used at this time when a croquet gathering took place. It was subsequently used for lawn tennis meetings.

104 Hiner Gillmeister, *Tennis: a cultural history* (London: Leicester University Press, 1998), pp. 172–7.

105 J.G. Smyth, *Lawn Tennis* (London: B.T. Batsford Ltd., 1953), p. 2.

106 Tom Higgins, *The History of Irish Tennis*, vol. 1 (Sligo: Sligo Tennis Club, 2006), p. 7.

107 *Nenagh Guardian*, 8 September 1875.

108 Hunt, *Sport and Society*, p. 79.

109 The term 'at home' was applied to a meeting which took place at Willington, Nenagh: *Nenagh Guardian*, 19 August 1876.

110 *Nenagh Guardian*, 29 July 1876, 12 August 1876, 19 August 1876, 26 August 1876, 30 August 1876.

111 Hunt, *Sport and Society*, p. 79.

112 *Nenagh Guardian*, 14 September 1878.

113 For a comparative list of names for those in attendance at a lawn tennis meet in 1878 and those who followed the Ormond Hunt in 1877, see *Nenagh Guardian*, 8 December 1877, 14 September 1878.

114 *Nenagh Guardian*, 2 July 1879, 10 June 1880.

115 Ibid., 12 July 1879.

116 Ibid., 23 August 1879.

117 Ibid., 28 March 1877.

118 Ibid., 26 April 1879.

119 Ibid., 28 June 1879.

120 Hunt, *Sport and Society*, p. 78.

121 *Nenagh Guardian*, 23 July 1881.

122 Ibid., 27 July 1881.

123 *Clonmel Chronicle*, 15 June 1878, 19 June 1878.

124 *Tipperary Free Press*, 1 October 1878.

125 *Clonmel Chronicle*, 8 October 1879.

126 *Freeman's Journal*, 20 July 1897, p. 7; *Clonmel Chronicle*, 13 August 1898; *Nenagh Guardian*, 27 August 1898; *Freeman's Journal*, 2 August 1899, p. 7.

127 Higgins, *Irish Tennis*, vol. 1, p. 228.

128 *Clonmel Chronicle*, 5 July 1890; Virginia Wade and Jean Rafferty, *Ladies of the Court: a century of women at Wimbledon* (London: Pavilion, 1984), p. 189; Eileen Bell, 'Lena Rice of New Inn: the only Irish ladies Wimbledon champion', *Tipperary Historical Journal 1988*, pp. 13–14.

129 Smyth, *Lawn Tennis*, p. 2.

130 Dooley, *The Decline of the Big House*, p. 49.

131 For an overview of resident magistrates in Ireland see Penny Bonsall, *The Irish RMs: the resident magistrates in the British administration in Ireland* (Dublin: Four Courts Press, 1997).

132 *Tipperary Weekly News*, 23 January 1858.

133 *Tipperary Free Press*, 9 November 1844.

134 Ibid., 2 April 1851.

135 Ibid., 19 July 1845.

136 'An act for the protection and improvement of the salmon, trout, and other inland fisheries of Ireland [31 August 1848]', in *A Collection of the Public General Statutes, Passed in the Eleventh and Twelfth Year of the Reign of Her Majesty Queen Victoria* (London: George E. Eyre & William Spottiswoode, 1848), pp. 518–28; *Tipperary Free Press*, 24 January 1849.

137 *Tipperary Free Press*, 24 January 1849.

138 Ibid., 13 October 1857.

139 Ibid., 13 October 1857, 17 July 1860.

140 Ibid., 9 November 1858.

141 Ibid., 9 October 1857.

142 Ibid.

143 *Clonmel Chronicle*, 6 November 1861.

144 Ibid., 17 February 1864.

145 Ibid.

146 *Tipperary Free Press*, 9 December, 1856, 16 October 1857, 10 November 1857, 15 November 1859.

147 Ibid., 16 October 1857.

148 Game Certificates (Ireland) Act, 1842, 5th and 6th Vic. Chap. 81. Sec. 5; *Tipperary Free Press*, 31 December 1845.

149 Game Licences Act 1860, 15 & 16 Vic. C. 81, Sec. 8; *Tipperary Free Press*, 12 October 1860.

150 Hussey de Burgh, *The Landowners of Ireland*, p. 60. John Bateman, *The Great Landowners of Great Britain and Ireland* (reprint New York: A.M. Kelley, 1970), p. 65; Mark Bence-Jones, *Burke's Guide to Country Houses. Volume 1: Ireland* (London: Burke's Peerage, 1978), p. 130.

151 *Clonmel Chronicle*, 6 September 1873.

152 Ibid., 1 September 1875.

153 *Tipperary Free Press*, 19 September 1849, 26 March 1851, 22 April 1856, *Clonmel Chronicle*, 11 March 1875, 12 April 1876.

154 *Clonmel Chronicle*, 15 September 1869, 13 November 1869; 21 September 1870.

155 *Nenagh Guardian*, 19 December 1868.

156 *Clonmel Chronicle*, 13 February 1869.

157 Ibid., 23 July 1870.

158 Ibid., 18 March 1865, 26 April 1865, 30 May 1866, 20 February 1869, *Nenagh Guardian*, 25 April 1868.

159 *Clonmel Chronicle*, 1 March 1873.

160 Ibid., 5 May 1875.

161 Ibid., 19 May 1880, 29 May 1880, 28 July 1880.

162 Brian Lalor (ed.), *The Encyclopaedia of Ireland* (Dublin: Gill & Macmillan, 2003), p. 647.

163 William Stokes, *Pictorial Survey and Tourists Guide to Lough Derg and the River Shannon* (London: Schulze & Co., 1842), p. 6.

164 Peter Heaton, *Yachting: a history* (London: B.T. Batsford, 1955), pp. 57–8; Douglas Phillips-Birt, *The History of Yachting* (London: Elm Tree Books, 1974), pp. 21–2.

165 Phillips-Birt, *History of Yachting*, p. 22.

166 Hardress Waller, 'Lough Derg Yacht Club', *Cois Deirge* (Summer 1980), p. 8. The current club flag bears an inception date of 1835, though Waller has

noted that 'no records of the LDYC have survived prior to 1883.

167 *Nenagh Guardian*, 21 July 1865, 29 August 1866, 30 August 1871.

168 Ibid., 13 July 1859, 6 September 1862.

169 Ibid., 14 August 1872.

170 The title of Commodore is that given to the president of a yacht club: *Nenagh Guardian*, 9 August 1845, 27 June 1846, 5 July 1854, 10 September 1856, 2 August 1873, 29 July 1876.

171 The 'burgee' was a small red triangular flag, emblazoned with three gold-coloured shamrock sprigs: *Nenagh Guardian*, 5 July 1854.

172 Waller, 'Lough Derg Yacht Club', p. 8.

173 *Nenagh Guardian*, 11 August 1852.

174 Ibid., 21 June 1865.

175 Ibid.

176 Ibid., 29 August 1866.

177 Ibid., 30 August 1871.

178 Ibid., 17 August 1878.

179 Ibid., 11 August 1852.

180 Ibid., 2 July 1859, 17 August 1872, 8 September 1875.

181 Ibid., 30 August 1876, 13 August 1879.

CHAPTER 3 THE HUNT COMMUNITY

1 Colin A. Lewis, *Hunting in Ireland: an historical and geographical analysis* (London: J.A. Allen, 1975), p. 67.

2 Marjorie Quarton, *The North Tipperary Foxhounds: hunting in north Tipperary over two centuries* (Nenagh: Marjorie Quarton, 2010), p. 1, gives a date of 1738 for the foundation of the hunt.

3 *Finn's Leinster Journal*, 16 February 1771.

4 Ibid., 13 June 1772.

5 *Nenagh Guardian*, 1 January 1873.

6 Iris M. Middleton, 'The Origins of English Fox Hunting and the Myth of Hugo Meynell and the Quorn', *Sport in History*, vol. 25, no. 1 (April 2005), p. 9.

7 Muriel Bowen, *Irish Hunting* (Tralee: The Kerryman, 1954), p. 154.

8 *British Hunts and Huntsmen in England (North), Scotland and Ireland: compiled in conjunction with* The Sporting Life (London: Biographical Press, 1911), p. 516.

9 See Table 3.1, pp. 83-4. The data has been compiled from *The Tipperary Free Press, Nenagh Guardian, Clonmel Chronicle, Tipperary Advocate, Cashel Gazette*

and *The Tipperary Constitution* and the hunting journal of the 3rd Marquis of Waterford.

10   *Clonmel Chronicle*, 21 March 1863.

11   Ibid., 30 November 1872, 19 February 1873, 23 December 1874, 31 March 1877, 12 March 1879.

12   *Nenagh Guardian*, 3 December 1856.

13   Ibid., 22 June 1870, 29 June 1870, 6 July 1870.

14   Ibid., 15 April 1871.

15   Rawdon B. Lee, *A History and Description of the Modern Dogs of Great Britain and Ireland, sporting division: vol. 1* (London: Horace Cox, 1897), p. 166.

16   *Clonmel Chronicle*, 22 March 1873.

17   *Nenagh Guardian*, 23 December 1876.

18   Ibid., 7 April 1877.

19   This is a baseline figure derived from hunt meet notifications in the contemporary press. As every issue of every paper has not been analysed, the data from across the whole time frame is representative and can be seen to be a true reflection of hunting in Tipperary from 1840 to 1880.

20   It was typical for meets to be cancelled when a relative of the MFH, or indeed the MFH himself, died, as was the case with John Going, late MFH, Tipperary Hunt, in 1873. *Clonmel Chronicle*, 29 October 1873.

21   Due to the paucity of evidence for some packs it is difficult to quantify whether they were subscription packs or not.

22   *Nenagh Guardian*, 5 December 1849, 13 December 1868.

23   Ibid., 25 April 1874.

24   *Clonmel Chronicle*, 30 December 1868.

25   This tally does not allow for the highly probable non-recording of scheduled hunt meets in the preceding thirty-five years in the local press. The data quantified for the whole period is that which has been derived from the regular hunt notices in the various local newspapers.

26   For a detailed insight into the plan of campaign against the various hunt meets see Curtis Jr., 'Stopping the Hunt', pp. 349–401; Dooley, *The Decline of the Big House*, pp. 260–4.

27   'From 1882 to 1896, I can only find a couple of references to them, mainly meetings': Quarton, *North Tipperary Foxhounds*, p. 7.

28   *Clonmel Chronicle*, 7 June 1882, 20 September 1882.

29   *Tipperary Free Press*, 18 November 1854.

30   Quarton, *North Tipperary Foxhounds*, p. 3.

31   *Clonmel Chronicle*, 5 March 1879, 2 April 1879, 12 April 1879, 3 December 1879. Attempts to identify the identity and residential area of this man have proved fruitless. He was very close to the hunt, and a likely participant, an

early version of a public relations officer for the MFH, or pack owner. In 1897 he was contributing articles on the Tipperary Hounds to the *Clonmel Nationalist*, a rival paper in political outlook to the *Clonmel Chronicle*. *Clonmel Nationalist*, 8 September 1897.

32 *Nenagh Guardian*, 28 February 1872.

33 *Clonmel Chronicle*, 1 April 1874.

34 *Tipperary Free Press*, 6 June 1840.

35 Ibid., 24 October 1840. This village is New Inn, and it appears on the 1840 Ordnance Survey map under this name.

36 Ibid., 10 April 1841.

37 *British Hunts and Huntsmen*, p. 518.

38 Col. S.J. Watson, *Between the Flags: a history of Irish steeplechasing* (Dublin: Allen Figgis, 1969), p. 51.

39 *Tipperary Free Press*, 6 August 1842.

40 Ibid., 19 April 1843, Michael MacEwan, *Tipperary: the people, the horses, the hounds* (Dublin: Bookconsult, 2003), p. 14.

41 *Tipperary Free Press*, 8 January 1842.

42 Ibid., 26 January 1842.

43 Ibid., 1 November 1843

44 Ibid., 11 November 1843.

45 Ibid., 8 November 1843.

46 *Clonmel Chronicle*, 8 May 1872.

47 David C. Itzkowitz, *Peculiar Privilege: a social history of English fox hunting, 1753–1885* (Hassocks: Harvester Wheatsheaf, 1977), p. 76.

48 Ibid., p. 77.

49 Ibid.,

50 *Nenagh Guardian*, 30 March 1844.

51 Itzkowitz, *Peculiar Privilege*, p. 31.

52 *Nenagh Guardian*, 5 November 1842.

53 *Clonmel Chronicle*, 21 March 1863.

54 Nicola Drücker, 'Hunting and Shooting: leisure, social networking and social complications', in Terrence McDonough (ed.), *Was Ireland a Colony? Economics, politics and culture in nineteenth-century Ireland* (Dublin: Irish Academic Press, 2005), p. 126.

55 *Clonmel Chronicle*, 7 May 1864.

56 Itzkowitz, *Peculiar Privilege*, p. 32.

57 *Tipperary Free Press*, 24 October 1856. The following year also saw sale prices in much the same range bracket: *Tipperary Free Press*, 30 October 1857.

58 Ibid., 1 April 1859.

59 Ibid., 28 June 1859.

60   *Tipperary Examiner*, 29 June 1859.

61   *Clonmel Chronicle*, 29 April 1865.

62   *Tipperary Examiner*, 29 June 1859.

63   *Clonmel Chronicle*, 11 December 1869.

64   *Nenagh Guardian*, 3 May 1871.

65   For instance Tipple Cider stood at Clonmel and Carrick-on-Suir in 1855 (*Tipperary Free Press*, 14 April 1855) and at the Glengall Arms stables, Cahir, in 1856, at a rate of £2 10*s* for gentlemen and gentlemen farmer mares. Farmers who held not more than twenty acres were charged £1 10*s*, with it being noted that the horse was 'purchased from Baron Rothschild in England': *Tipperary Free Press*, 26 February 1856.

66   F.P. Delmé Radcliffe, *The Noble Science: a few general ideas on fox-hunting, for the use of the rising generation of sportsmen, and more especially those of the Hertfordshire Hunt Club* (London: Rudolph Ackermann, 1839), p. 283.

67   Ibid., *The Noble Science*, p. 285.

68   *Clonmel Chronicle*, 13 May 1863.

69   Bernard Burke, *A Genealogical and Heraldic History of the Landed Gentry of Ireland* (London: Burke's Peerage, 1912), p. 270; Rev. C.C. Ellison. 'Going of Munster', *The Irish Ancestor*, vol. IX, no. 1 (1977), p. 31.

70   Burke, *Landed Gentry*, p. 269.

71   *Clonmel Chronicle*, 25 October 1871.

72   Ibid., 8 June 1872.

73   Ibid., 14 March 1866.

74   Ibid., 7 May 1864.

75   Ibid., 8 May 1872.

76   Ibid.

77   Details of land holdings are sourced from *Return of owners of land of one acre and upwards, in the several counties, counties of cities, and counties of towns in Ireland* (Dublin: A. Thom for H.M. Stationery Office, 1876). Geoffrey Watkins Grubb, *The Grubbs of Tipperary: studies in heredity and character* (Cork: Mercier Press, 1972), p. 115.

78   *Clonmel Chronicle*, 8 June 1872.

79   Hunt, *Sport and Society*, p. 28.

80   Itzkowitz, *Peculiar Privilege*, pp. 23–9.

81   Curtis Jr., 'Stopping the Hunt', pp. 349–401.

82   *Clonmel Chronicle*, 7 May 1873.

83   Ibid., 7 June 1873.

84   Ibid.

85   Ibid.

86   Ibid.

87 In the *Tipperary Free Press* report of this meeting, the name of the gentlemen enquiring about the position of Master of the Tipperary Hunt was given as 'Wm. T. Lugar'. *Tipperary Free Press*, 4 June 1875.

88 *Clonmel Chronicle*, 5 June 1875.

89 Ibid.

90 Richard Holt, *Sport and the British: a modern history* (Oxford: Clarendon Press, 1989), p. 53.

91 Itzkowitz has outlined the fees incurred by four hunt packs in England in the mid 1870s, with the Meynell costing just over £3,889 at the top end and at the bottom of the four, the Braes of Derwent having fees of just over £253: Itzkowitz, *Peculiar Privilege*, p. 79.

92 *Clonmel Chronicle*, 1 May 1875.

93 Ibid., 9 June 1877.

94 Ibid., 6 March 1878.

95 'The chronicles of Ashley Park commenced A.D. 1866 by James N. Atkinson': Entry for 1 November 1867.

96 Ibid.

97 *Nenagh Guardian*, 7 February 1872.

98 Ibid., 6 March 1872.

99 Ibid., 7 February 1872.

100 Ibid., 8 February 1873.

101 Ibid., 1 January 1873.

102 Ibid., 8 January 1873.

103 Ibid., 22 February 1873.

104 Ibid., 25 April 1874.

105 Ibid.

106 Ibid., 5 April 1876.

107 Ibid., 25 March 1876.

108 Ibid., 5 April 1876.

109 Ibid., 29 April 1876.

110 Hunt, *Sport and Society*, p. 23.

111 John A. Daly. 'A new Britannia in the Antipodes: sport, class and community in colonial South Australia', in J.A. Mangan (ed.), *Pleasure, Profit, Proselytism: British culture and sport at home and abroad, 1700–1914* (London: Frank Cass, 1988), p. 167.

112 *Clonmel Chronicle*, 18 January 1879.

113 Hunt, *Sport and Society*, p. 15.

114 *Clonmel Chronicle*, 2 January 1878.

115 It is also likely that this happened in the years preceding 1874, though sales or advertisement notices have not been identified.

116 *Clonmel Chronicle*, 15 April 1874.

117 Ibid., 1 May 1875.

118 Ibid., 13 May 1876.

119 Ibid., 28 May 1864.

120 *Nenagh Guardian*, 20 January 1864, 11 January 1865, *Clonmel Chronicle*, 16 November 1864.

121 *Clonmel Chronicle*, 2 March 1870, 30 April 1873.

122 Itzkowitz, *Peculiar Privilege*, p. 55.

123 *Nenagh Guardian*, 10 March 1849.

124 The brush is the term used to denote the tail of a fox.

125 Itzkowitz, *Peculiar Privilege*, p. 14.

126 *Nenagh Guardian*, 2 January 1867.

127 *Clonmel Chronicle*, 20 November 1861, 21 March 1863. Evidence of female participation in the hunt in the 1860s from County Westmeath mirrors that from Tipperary, see Hunt, *Sport and Society*, p. 17.

128 *Clonmel Chronicle*, 27 June 1868.

129 Ibid., 14 November 1874. It is unknown if this Miss Quin is the same person as Lucy Quin who featured in the archery reports in Chapter 2.

130 Ibid., 17 February 1875. Italics are as appeared in the original text.

131 Ibid., 2 January 1878.

132 Itzkowitz, *Peculiar Privilege*, p. 56.

133 *Tipperary Free Press*, 4 January 1845.

134 Ibid., 10 November 1845.

135 Ibid., 2 December 1846; *Tipperary Vindicator*, 2 December 1846.

136 *Tipperary Free Press*, 6 March 1847.

137 *Nenagh Guardian*, 30 January 1867.

138 Ibid., 1 April 1840.

139 *Tipperary Free Press*, 24 July 1857; *Clonmel Chronicle*, 25 March 1863.

140 Itzkowitz, *Peculiar Privilege*, pp. 5–56; Emma Griffin, *Blood Sport: hunting in Britain since 1066* (New Haven and London: Yale University Press, 2007), pp. 166–7.

141 Griffin, *Blood Sport*, p. 167.

142 *Nenagh Guardian*, 28 April 1875.

143 This is based only on the figures for the Ormond Hunt season returns of 1874–5, as similar reports from other seasons of each respective Hunt have not yet come to light.

144 *Clonmel Chronicle*, 27 June 1868.

145 *Nenagh Guardian*, 15 November 1876.

146 *Sport*, 10 March 1883; *Nenagh Guardian*, 6 February 1884.

147 *Clonmel Chronicle*, 8 May 1872.

148 Ibid.

149 *Nenagh Guardian*, 1 February 1879.

150 Ibid.

151 Ibid., 26 February 1851.

152 Watson, *Between the Flags*, p. 49; John Welcome, *Irish Horse-racing: an illustrated history* (London: Gill & Macmillan, 1982), p. 37.

153 Griffin, *Blood Sport*, p. 135.

154 This was a feature of the hunt. In 1912, when the Tipperary Hunt were out it was not unusual for foxes to be left once they got to cover: *Nationalist*, 2 November 1912, p. 5.

CHAPTER 4
THE TURF: HORSE RACING
DEVELOPMENT AND COMMERCIALISATION

1   Hunt, *Sport and Society*, p. 31.

2   D'Arcy, *Horses, Lords and Racing Men*, p. 16.

3   *Pue's Occurrences*, 22 July 1732, quoted in Kelly, 'The Pastime of the Elite', p. 414.

4   James Weatherby, *Racing Calendar: containing an account of the plates, matches, and sweepstakes run for in Great-Britain and Ireland in the year 1775*, vol. 3 (London: James Weatherby, 1775), p. 203.

5   D'Arcy, *Horses, Lords and Racing Men*, pp. 16, 18.

6   Kelly, 'The Pastime of the Elite', p. 414.

7   *General Alphabetical Index to the Townlands and Towns, Parishes and Baronies of Ireland* (Baltimore: Genealogical Publishing Co., Inc, 1984), p. 767.

8   Cronin and Higgins., *Places We Play*, pp. 251, 253.

9   Kelly, *Sport in Ireland*, p. 21.

10 Watson, *Between the Flags*; G. St J. Williams and F.P. Hyland, *The Irish Derby, 1866–1979* (London: J.A. Allen, 1980); Welcome, *Irish Horse-racing*; John O'Flaherty, *Listowel Races, 1858–1991* (Listowel: John O'Flahery, 1992); Stan McCormack, *Against the Odds: Kilbeggan races, 1840–1994* (Westmeath: Stan McCormack, 1994); G. St J. Williams and F.P. Hyland, *Jameson Irish Grand National: a history of Ireland's premier steeplechase* (Dublin: The Organisation, 1995).

11 Pat Maher, 'The Cashel Racecourse Stand House', *Boherlahan Dualla Historical Journal 2000*, pp. 40–5.

12 D'Arcy, *Horses, Lords and Racing Men*, p. 9.

13 Ibid., p. 10.

14 Ibid., p. 12.

15 James Weatherby, *Racing Calendar containing and account of the plates, matches and sweepstakes run for in Great Britain and Ireland in the year 1786*, vol. 14 (London: James Weatherby, 1786), pp. 177–9, 181–3, 199–201, 205–6.

16 Weatherby, *Racing Calendar 1775*, pp. 174–8; 187–9.

17 *Tipperary Free Press*, 25 June 1845. I inferred that the term 'pounding match' refers to two horses racing fast across a field. In the press report the term 'Jockey Club' was used, by which, I believe, is meant the Turf Club.

18 *Tipperary Free Press*, 8 January 1840; *Nenagh Guardian*, 18 January 1840.

19 *Nenagh Guardian*, 1 April 1840, 27 April 1842, 29 April 1843; *Tipperary Free Press*, 28 April 1841; *Tipperary Vindicator*, 10 April 1844, 5 April 1845, 21 February 1846.

20 *Nenagh Guardian*, 17 April 1844.

21 Hunt, *Sport and Society*, p. 40.

22 *Nenagh Guardian*, 1 April 1840, 29 April 1843, 22 April 1868, 4 May 1872, 10 May 1876.

23 *Clonmel Chronicle*, 19 November 1862, 25 March 1863, 23 April 1864.

24 Ibid., 29 April 1874.

25 *Nenagh Guardian*, 15 September 1880.

26 *Nenagh Guardian*, 3 May 1873; 4 April 1874.

27 Itzkowitz, *Peculiar Privilege*, p. 104; Hunt, *Sport and Society*, p. 31.

28 *Clonmel Chronicle*, 1 May 1872, 29 April 1874, 9 May 1874; *Nenagh Guardian*, 6 September 1879.

29 *Nenagh Guardian*, 1 April 1840; *Tipperary Constitution*, 5 February 1841; *Tipperary Free Press*, 12 February 1851.

30 *Tipperary Free Press*, 29 December 1841.

31 Iris Maud Middleton, 'The Developing Pattern of Horse Racing in Yorkshire, 1700–1749: an analysis of the people and the places', unpublished PhD thesis, De Montfort University, Leicester, 2000, p. 66.

32 *Nenagh Guardian*, 27 April 1842.

33 *Tipperary Free Press*, 23 February 1848, 1 April 1848.

34 *Clonmel Chronicle*, 18 September 1872.

35 The first edition Ordnance Survey was on a scale of six inches to the mile.

36 *Index to the townlands and towns, parishes and baronies of Ireland*, p. 767.

37 The race articles were published in the *Nenagh Guardian*, 29 January 1840. A report of the three-day meeting was published in the *Nenagh Guardian*, 11 March 1840.

38 *Tipperary Free Press*, 28 October 1840.

39 Ibid., 16 October 1840.

40   *Tipperary Vindicator*, 4 October 1845; *Tipperary Free Press*, 23 October 1852, 15 October 1853.

41   *Nenagh Guardian*, 11 November 1843.

42   The rental from which these figures are obtained are filed at Tipperary Studies as Beere estate rental 1839–1843 TL/F/13. I believe this to be incorrect. Usher Beere, the first name on the rental, had land on rental from Nicholas V. Maher, as did many of the other names in this estate rental, when cross-referenced with the Richard Griffith valuation books for the Barony of Eliogarty. Based on this, I am of the opinion that this rental is from the Nicholas V. Maher estate, Turtulla.

43   *Nenagh Guardian*, 18 November 1843.

44   *Tipperary Free Press*, 26 September 1849, 29 September 1849, 3 October 1849.

45   *Tipperary Vindicator*, 10 April 1844, 5 April 1845, 21 February 1846; *Tipperary Free Press*, 18 April 1849.

46   *Nenagh Guardian*, 13 February 1850, 3 April 1850, 22 March 1854.

47   Ibid., 3 April 1850.

48   *Tipperary Free Press*, 15 March 1841, 15 July 1843. *Clonmel Chronicle*, 16 May 1863, 7 May 1864, 17 January 1866.

49   *Tipperary Free Press*, 28 December 1842, 4 January 1843; *Nenagh Guardian*, 7 June 1865.

50   *Nenagh Guardian*, 30 June 1855.

51   This is based on a lack of evidence in the local press.

52   *Nenagh Guardian*, 26 February 1859, 24 March 1860.

53   Ibid., 22 March 1873.

54   Ibid., 2 August 1876, 12 July 1879

55   Ibid., 22 March 1873.

56   Ibid., 22 November 1879, 8 October 1879.

57   Ibid., 5 June 1872, 22 March 1873.

58   Ibid., 10 May 1873, 12 May 1873, 28 May 1879.

59   Ibid., 8 October 1873, 11 October 1873.

60   Ibid., 15 November 1873.

61   Ibid., 13 September 1876, 10 September 1879; *Clonmel Chronicle*, 10 September 1879.

62   *Tipperary Free Press*, 5 February 1845, 21 June 1845, 24 March 1849.

63   *Clonmel Chronicle*, 14 October 1871.

64   Ibid.

65   Ibid.

66   Ibid., 16 March 1872.

67   Ibid.

68 Ibid., 16 December 1871.

69 Ibid., 6 January 1872.

70 Ibid., 30 May 1877.

71 Ibid., 16 April 1879.

72 Murray and McNeill, *Great Southern and Western Railway*, pp. 15–18.

73 *Tipperary Free Press*, 1 April 1848; Ernie Shepherd, *Waterford, Limerick and Western Railway* (Hersham, Surrey: Ian Allan Ltd., 2006), p. 11.

74 *Tipperary Free Press*, 12 May 1852, 10 September 1853, 20 May 1854, 29 May 1860.

75 Ibid., 30 March 1850.

76 Ibid., 14 September 1853.

77 *Clonmel Chronicle*, 25 May 1870.

78 His eldest son, Michael, died in January 1879: *Nenagh Guardian*, 13 January 1879.

79 Fifty sovereigns in 1840 equates to £4,350 (€5,128.26) in 2016. Ten sovereigns is the equivalent of £870.10 (€1,025.77) in 2016, calculations carried out on Measuringworth.com website, http://www.measuringworth.com/ukcompare/ (Accessed 13 May 2017). *Tipperary Free Press*, 5 June 1841, 6 October 1841, 30 October 1841; 13 November 1841.

80 Ibid., 12 February 1853.

81 John W. Boyle, 'A Marginal Figure: the Irish rural labourer', in Samuel Clark and James J. Donnelly Jnr (eds), *Irish Peasants: violence and political unrest, 1780–1914* (Manchester: Manchester University Press, 1983), p. 313.

82 *Tipperary Free Press*, 14 April 1849. £250 in 1850 equated to £24,530 (€28,918.67) in 2016. £100 in 1850 equated to £9,814 (€11,569.83) in 2016, calculations carried out on Measuringworth.com website, http://www. measuringworth.com/ukcompare/ (Accessed 13 May 2017).

83 Ibid., 2 October 1850.

84 Ibid., 2 September 1843, 21 May 1845; *Nenagh Guardian*, 13 April 1844.

85 *Tipperary Free Press*, 2 November 1842.

86 Ibid., 30 November 1842.

87 D'Arcy, *Horses, Lords and Racing Men*, pp. 347–8.

88 *Tipperary Free Press*, 13 November 1841.

89 Mike Huggins, *Flat Racing and British Society, 1790–1914: a social and economic history* (London: Routledge, 2000), p. 25.

90 Vamplew, *The Turf*, pp. 31–2. Rouse, *Sport and Ireland*, pp. 107–8.

91 In 1850, the Racecourse demesne was held by Avary Jordan from Cashel Town Commissioners. Richard Griffith, *General Valuation of Rateable Property in Ireland: county of Tipperary, south riding, barony of Middlethird* (Dublin: Valuation Office, 1851), p. 159. See also Denis G. Marnane, 'John Davis

White's Sixty Years in Cashel', *Tipperary Historical Journal 2001*, p. 69.

92   *Freeman's Journal*, 21 October 1788.

93   Ibid., 29 September 1789.

94   Edward and James Weatherby, *Racing Calendar Containing an Account of the Plates, Matches and Sweepstakes Run for in Great Britain and Ireland in the Year 1797* (London: James Weatherby, 1798), pp. 178–80.

95   *Tipperary Free Press*, 19 October 1844.

96   *Clonmel Chronicle*, 26 September 1873.

97   *Tipperary Free Press*, 14 November 1840.

98   *Nenagh Guardian*, 19 October 1844; *Tipperary Free Press*, 19 October 1844.

99   Richard Griffith, *General Valuation of Rateable Property in Ireland: county of Tipperary, north riding, barony of Eliogarty* (Dublin: Valuation Office, 1852), p. 97.

100   Catherine Fogarty, 'The Disenfranchisement of the Boroughs of Cashel and Sligo', unpublished MA thesis, National University of Ireland Maynooth, 2000, pp. 143–64.

101   Fogarty, 'The Boroughs of Cashel and Sligo', p. 47.

102   Griffith, *General Valuation: barony of Middlethird*, pp. 170–1. For the Earl of Normanton see *Debrett's Illustrated Peerage and Baronetage* (London: Bosworth & Harrison, 1864), p. 260.

103   *Tipperary Free Press*, 2 October 1841; 4 September 1844.

104   Ibid., 19 September 1846.

105   Huggins, *Flat Racing*, p.159.

106   An ordinary was an after-race function, inclusive of a meal, which typically took place at a local hotel.

107   There are no race meetings from County Tipperary recorded in W. Ruff, *Guide to the Turf for 1847: spring edition* (London: R. Ackermann, 1847), pp. 139–56. The Cashel results for 1847 appear in W. Ruff, *Guide to the Turf for 1848* (London: R. Ackermann, 1847), p. 144.

108   *Tipperary Free Press*, 3 October 1846.

109   Ibid., 4 December 1844.

110   Huggins, *Flat Racing*, p. 144.

111   *Tipperary Free Press*, 19 September 1846.

112   Ibid., 23 October 1852, 15 October 1853, 18 October 1854, 26 September 1855.

113   *Clonmel Chronicle*, 6 May 1865, 12 May 1866.

114   *Tipperary Free Press*, 23 October 1852.

115   Ibid.

116   *Nenagh Guardian*, 5 October 1867; *Clonmel Chronicle*, 4 October 1871.

117   *Tipperary Free Press*, 2 October 1847.

118 *Tipperary Examiner*, 28 August 1858.

119 *Tipperary Free Press*, 5 August 1859.

120 *Tipperary Examiner*, 23 January 1858.

121 *Clonmel Chronicle*, 9 August 1865.

122 *Tipperary Free Press*, 30 September 1859.

123 *Clonmel Chronicle*, 28 September 1861.

124 Huggins, *Flat Racing*, p. 149.

125 *Clonmel Chronicle*, 1 October 1862.

126 Ibid.

127 Huggins, *Flat Racing*, p. 24.

128 *Clonmel Chronicle*, 30 September 1863.

129 Ibid., 3 October 1863.

130 Ibid., 12 October 1861.

131 Ibid., 30 September 1865; *Clonmel Chronicle*, 5 October 1869.

132 *Clonmel Chronicle*, 28 October 1865.

133 *Tipperary Free Press*, 7 August 1850; *Nenagh Guardian*, 11 May 1862, 5 August 1868; *Clonmel Chronicle*, 16 June 1868.

134 *Clonmel Chronicle*, 9 September 1865.

135 Ibid., 23 September 1868.

136 Ibid., 5 October 1869.

137 Ibid., 12 October 1870.

138 Ibid., 4 October 1871.

139 Ibid., 2 May 1874, 9 May 1874.

140 Ibid., 19 August 1874.

141 Ibid., 15 November 1873.

142 Tolson, 'The Railway Myth', p. 352.

143 *Clonmel Chronicle*, 25 April 1877, 15 May 1878.

144 Murray and McNeill, *Great Southern and Western Railway*, p. 15; Denis Marnane, 'The Coming of the Railway to County Tipperary in 1848', *Tipperary Historical Journal 1998*, pp. 139–40.

145 Bassett, *Tipperary: a guide and directory 1889*, p. 209.

146 *Clonmel Chronicle*, 15 August 1877, 3 November 1880.

147 D'Arcy, *Horses, Lords and Racing Men*, p. 197.

148 *Tipperary Free Press*, 18 April 1849.

149 *Tipperary Vindicator*, 4 October 1845, 3 October 1846; *Tipperary Free Press*, 2 October 1847, 23 September 1848, 26 September 1849, 29 September 1849, 3 October 1849.

150 For instance, John Bagwell and the Malcolmson brothers contributed £100 each to the Clonmel Relief Fund in February 1847. *Tipperary Free Press*, 6 February 1847: The Marquis of Waterford gave £100 to the destitute of

Dungarvan, County Waterford, while also contributing to the poor in other districts where he had property: *Tipperary Free Press*, 16 May 1846.

151 Quoted in Denis Marnane, *Cashel: history and guide* (Dublin: Nonsuch Publishing, 2007), p. 92.

152 *Tipperary Free Press*, 19 March 1853.

153 D'Arcy, *Horses, Lords and Racing Men*, pp. 38–41, 354.

154 *Clonmel Chronicle*, 23 August 1865, 11 August 1866, 1 September 1869; *Nenagh Guardian*, 5 June 1872.

155 *Clonmel Chronicle*, 13 April 1870, 11 September 1872.

156 Ibid., 4 October 1871.

157 Watson, *Between the Flags*, p. 73; Welcome, *Irish Horse-racing*, pp. 43, 45, 104–5; Francis P.M. Hyland, *History of Galway Races* (London: Robert Hale, 2008), p. 45.

158 *Clonmel Chronicle*, 5 October 1872; *Nenagh Guardian*, 23 October 1872.

159 *Clonmel Chronicle*, 5 October 1872, 7 June 1873, 28 April 1877; *Nenagh Guardian*, 17 March 1877.

160 Welcome, *Irish Horse-racing*, p. 56.

161 *Nenagh Guardian*, 17 May 1873.

162 Ibid., 28 May 1879.

163 Ibid.

164 *Tipperary Free Press*, 14 March 1853; *Nenagh Guardian*, 2 September 1876; D'Arcy, *Horses, Lords and Racing Men*, pp. 39–40.

165 Huggins, *Flat Racing*, pp. 117–22.

166 *Tipperary Free Press*, 4 March 1843, 28 March 1849; *Nenagh Guardian*, 1 May 1867; *Clonmel Chronicle*, 23 September 1868.

167 *Nenagh Guardian*, 22 April 1843; *Tipperary Free Press*, 4 April 1849, 27 July 1850.

168 *Nenagh Guardian*, 3 March 1864, 11 April 1864, 19 April 1865.

169 Ibid., 13 February 1850.

170 *Clonmel Chronicle*, 29 May 1861.

171 *Nenagh Guardian*, 22 April 1843.

172 Ibid., 13 February 1850, 30 April 1862, 1 May 1867; *Clonmel Chronicle*, 25 May 1870. For an account of factionalism in Ireland see Patrick D. O'Donnell, *The Irish Faction Fighters of the 19th Century* (Dublin: Anvil Books, 1975).

173 For example, at the Cashel races in 1859 'there was a large force of constabulary present', yet there is no indication as to how their presence was financed: *Tipperary Free Press*, 30 September 1859.

174 Ibid., 4 April 1856.

175 *Nenagh Guardian*, 2 August 1856.

176 Ibid., 26 July 1862.

177 *Tipperary Vindicator*, 2 November 1844; *Nenagh Guardian*, 11 May 1862; *Clonmel Chronicle*, 16 June 1878.

178 *Tipperary Free Press*, 16 April 1841.

179 Huggins, *Flat Racing*, p. 20.

180 See for instance Tipperary races report in *Nenagh Guardian*, 28 May 1873, 24 May 1876.

181 *Tipperary Free Press*, 30 September 1859.

182 *Clonmel Chronicle*, 18 December 1861; 12 February 1862, 31 March 1866, 15 April 1868.

183 *Nenagh Guardian*, 8 October 1879.

184 *Clonmel Chronicle*, 23 September 1868. See also Huggins, *Flat Racing*, p. 27.

185 *Cashel Gazette*, 9 September 1865.

186 *Clonmel Chronicle*, 6 January 1864.

CHAPTER 5 THE ADVENT OF ORGANISED ATHLETICS AND ROWING

1 *United Ireland*, 11 October 1884.

2 Marcus de Búrca, *Michael Cusack and the GAA* (Dublin: Anvil Books, 1989), p. 91.

3 Ibid., pp. 95–6.

4 *United Ireland*, 11 October 1884.

5 'Irish athletics', *United Ireland*, 18 October 1884, p. 2.

6 Dónal McAnallen, '"The greatest amateur association in the world"? The GAA and amateurism', in Mike Cronin, William Murphy and Paul Rouse (eds), *The Gaelic Athletic Association, 1884–2009* (Dublin: Irish Academic Press, 2009), p. 157.

7 Ibid., p. 158.

8 Michael Cusack and A. Morrison Millar (eds), *The Celtic Times, Michael Cusack's Gaelic games newspaper* (reprint Ennis: CLASP, 2003), 6 August 1887, p. 5.

9 M.A. Speak, 'Social Stratification and Participation in Sport in Mid-Victorian England with Particular Reference to Lancaster, 1840–70', in J.A. Mangan (ed.), *Pleasure, Profit, Proselytism: British culture and sport at home and abroad, 1700–1914* (London: Frank Cass, 1988), p. 59.

10 Norman Baker, 'Whose Hegemony? The origins of the amateur ethos in nineteenth century English society', *Sport in History*, vol. 24, no. 1 (Summer 2004), p. 3.

11 *Tipperary Free Press*, 24 August 1875.

12 Cormac Ó Gráda, 'The Wages Book of a Fethard Farmer, 1880–1905', in Marcus Bourke (ed.), *Tipperary Historical Journal 1994*, pp. 69–71.

13 *Freeman's Journal*, 21 May 1877, p. 2; *Irish Times*, 21 May 1877, p. 3.

14 Crump, 'Athletics', p. 51.

15 Pat Davin, *Recollections of a Veteran Irish Athlete: the memoirs of Pat Davin, world's all-round athletic champion* (Dublin: The Juverna Press, 1938), p. 15.

16 For an insight into the development of pedestrianism in the eighteenth and early nineteenth centuries see Walter Thom, *Pedestrianism; or an account of the performances of celebrated pedestrians during the last and present century* (Aberdeen: A. Brown & A. Frost, 1813).

17 *Tipperary Free Press*, 8 June 1842. The men were drawn from the Royal Artillery, 5th Dragoons, and 46th Depot, all garrisoned in Clonmel.

18 As pedestrianism became popular in the United Kingdom, large sums of money were wagered on the ability of a pedestrian to complete a specific task in the required time. As Thom has shown, there were several men who would bet on themselves to complete the task once there was another gambler willing to bet against him. Thom, *Pedestrianism*, pp. 47–8, 51–4; *Tipperary Free Press*, 19 October 1850.

19 Thom, *Pedestrianism*, pp. 33–5.

20 Neil L. Tranter, 'The Chronology of Organised Sport in Nineteenth-century Scotland: a regional study. I – patterns', *The International Journal of the History of Sport*, vol. 7, no. 2 (1990), p. 191.

21 Jim Sharlott, *On the Starting Line: a history of athletics in Leicester* (Leicester: Leicester City Council, 1994), p. 12.

22 *United Ireland*, 11 October 1884.

23 Colm Farry, 'Popular Sport in Ireland: the codification process, 1750–1885', unpublished MA thesis, Dublin City University, 2001, pp. 43–4; Joe Coyle, *Athletics in Drogheda, 1861–2001* (Victoria, Canada: Trafford 2003), p. 7.

24 Coyle, *Athletics in Drogheda*, pp. 8–10.

25 *Clonmel Chronicle*, 23 October 1861, 26 October 1861.

26 *Nenagh Guardian*, 7 July 1857.

27 Sharlott, *Athletics in Leicester*, pp. 13–4.

28 Mason and Reidi, *Sport and the Military*, p. 7.

29 *Clonmel Chronicle*, 23 June 1869, 2 September 1871.

30 *Tipperary Free Press*, 9 June 1868.

31 Finn, 'Trinity Mysteries', p. 2274.

32 *Clonmel Chronicle*, 28 September 1870.

33 Ibid., 3 July 1872.

34 *Nenagh Guardian*, 2 May 1868.

35 Ibid.

36   See Davin, *Recollections of a Veteran Irish Athlete* and Séamus Ó Riain, *Maurice Davin (1842–1927): first president of the GAA* (Dublin: Geography Publications, 1994) for further insights into their careers.

37   *Tipperary Advocate*, 12 July 1873, 26 July 1873, 9 August 1873; *Nenagh Guardian*, 13 August 1873.

38   Bassett, *Tipperary: a guide and directory, 1889*, p. 319.

39   Ibid.

40   *Nenagh Guardian*, 13 August 1873, 23 August 1873, 24 September 1873, 24 June 1874, 28 August 1875, 15 September 1875; *Tipperary Advocate*, 18 July 1874; John Lawrence, *Handbook of Cricket in Ireland, 1871–72*, vol. 7 (Dublin: John Lawrence, 1872), p. 208; John Lawrence, *Handbook of Cricket in Ireland, 1872–73*, vol. 8 (Dublin: John Lawrence, 1873), pp 181–2; John Lawrence, *Handbook of Cricket in Ireland, 1873–74*, vol. 9 (Dublin: John Lawrence, 1874), p. 154; John Lawrence, *Handbook of Cricket in Ireland, 1875–76*, vol. 11 (Dublin: John Lawrence, 1876), p. 167; John Lawrence, *Handbook of Cricket in Ireland, 1876–77*, vol. 12 (Dublin: John Lawrence, 1877), p. 120; John Lawrence, *Handbook of Cricket in Ireland, 1877–78*, vol. 13 (Dublin: John Lawrence, 1878), p. 129.

41   *Kilkenny Journal*, 29 September 1879.

42   Holt, *Sport and the British*, p. 138.

43   Ibid.

44   *Clonmel Chronicle*, 3 April 1872, 24 September 1873.

45   Ibid., 20 August 1873.

46   *Tipperary Advocate*, 20 July 1878.

47   *Clonmel Chronicle*, 3 April 1872, 7 August 1872.

48   Ibid., 20 August 1873; *Tipperary Free Press*, 26 September 1873, 24 September 1875.

49   *Clonmel Chronicle*, 28 June 1873, 20 August 1873, 24 September 1873.

50   Ibid., 28 June 1873, 20 August 1873.

51   *Tipperary Free Press*, 24 September 1875, 3 October 1876.

52   Rouse, *Sport and Ireland*, p. 139.

53   Littleton athletic sports programme of events, September 1877: *Clonmel Chronicle*, 15 September 1877; *Nenagh Guardian*, 15 September 1877.

54   Tony O'Donoghue, *Irish Championship Athletics, 1873–1914* (Dublin: Tony O'Donoghue, 2005), p. 7.

55   *Clonmel Chronicle*, 28 June 1873.

56   *Tipperary Advocate*, 10 June 1876.

57   Ibid., 31 May 1879.

58   Ibid., 17 July 1875.

59   Ibid., 10 June 1876; *Nenagh Guardian*, 17 June 1876.

60 *Tipperary Advocate*, 17 June 1876.

61 Ibid., 9 October 1880, 16 October 1880.

62 'Minute book – Carrick-on-Suir Athletic, Cricket and Football Club. Established August 1879'.

63 *Tipperary Free Press*, 23 September 1873.

64 *Clonmel Chronicle*, 18 June 1873. Italics as in the original text.

65 St Stephen's Day is the common Irish definition of 26 December, its English counterpart is Boxing Day.

66 *Clonmel Chronicle*, 16 December 1874.

67 Tranter, 'Scotland: a regional study. I – patterns', *The International Journal of the History of Sport*, p. 189.

68 *Census of Ireland 1871*; James Gray (ed.), *Scottish Population Statistics including Webster's 'Analysis of Population 1755'* (Edinburgh: Scottish Historical Society, 1952), p. xxix.

69 Ó Riain, *Maurice Davin*, p. 31.

70 Tranter, *Sport, Economy and Society*, p. 42; Jeremy Crump, 'Athletics', in Tony Mason (ed.), *Sport in Britain: a social history* (Cambridge: Cambridge University Press, 1989), p. 50.

71 de Búrca, *Michael Cusack*, p. 45.

72 Ibid., p. 46; Ó Riain, *Maurice Davin*, pp. 22–6.

73 *Tipperary Free Press*, 9 August 1872.

74 *Clonmel Chronicle*, 28 June 1873.

75 Ibid., 28 June 1873, 20 August 1873, 29 September 1875, 13 October 1875, 26 September 1877; *Freeman's Journal*, 21 May 1877; *Kilkenny Moderator*, 28 July 1877; *Nenagh Guardian*, 15 September 1877; *Tipperary Free Press*, 23 September 1873, 26 September 1873, 8 October 1875.

76 O'Donoghue, *Irish Championship Athletics*, p. 7.

77 Peter Swain, 'Cultural Continuity and Football in Nineteenth-century Lancashire', *Sport in History*, vol. 28, no. 4 (December 2008), p. 572.

78 Carrick-on-Suir athletic sports, *Clonmel Chronicle*, 3 April 1872; Powerstown athletic sports, *Clonmel Chronicle*, 17 July 1872; Killusty athletic sports, *Tipperary Free Press*, 1 August 1873.

79 *Clonmel Chronicle*, 20 August 1873.

80 Tom Hunt, 'Tipperary Hurlers, 1895–1900: a socio-economic profile', *Tipperary Historical Journal 2009*, pp. 119–21.

81 This contradicts Ó Riain who stated that athletic sports meetings 'were usually held on a Sunday': Ó Riain, *Maurice Davin*, p. 31. No meetings have been identified from Tipperary which took place on a Sunday.

82 Neal Garnham, 'Accounting for the Early Success of the Gaelic Athletic Association', *Irish Historical Studies*, vol. 34, no. 133 (May 2004), pp. 71–4.

Farry, 'Popular Sport in Ireland', p. 79.

83 Dennis Brailsford, *British Sport: a social history* (Cambridge: Lutterworth Press, 1992), p. 68; Holt, *Sport and the British*, p. 61.

84 Tranter, *Sport, Economy and Society*, p. 41.

85 Guttman, *From Ritual to Record*, p. 31.

86 Charles J. Kickham, *Knocknagow, or The Homes of Tipperary* (Dublin: James Duffy, 1887), p. 461. In this fictional account of a village in rural Tipperary, Matt the Thresher competed in local sports meetings throwing the hammer, which he did 'for the credit of the little village'. Kickham was from Mullinahone.

87 Ó Riain, *Maurice Davin*, p. 26.

88 *United Ireland*, 18 October 1884, p. 2.

89 *Clonmel Chronicle*, 26 June 1861.

90 Eric Halladay, *Rowing in England: a social history. The amateur debate* (Manchester & New York: Manchester University Press, 1990), p. 15.

91 *Clonmel Chronicle*, 10 July 1871, 12 August 1874, 11 August 1875; *Tipperary Free Press*, 12 September 1876.

92 *Clonmel Chronicle*, 23 August 1871, 30 August 1871.

93 Ibid., 10 April 1872.

94 Conor Curran, 'Why Donegal Slept: the development of Gaelic games in Donegal, 1884–1934', unpublished PhD thesis, De Montfort University, Leicester, 2012, p. 151. Seumas MacManus moved to the United States and by 1907 the GAA structure in Donegal started to collapse once he had departed as an administrator.

95 *Clonmel Chronicle*, 23 August 1865, 27 April 1870.

96 Ibid., 23 August 1865, 1 August 1866, 3 April 1872, 7 August 1872.

97 Ibid., 30 July 1870, 30 August 1871.

98 Ibid., 30 August 1871.

99 Halladay, *Rowing in England*, p. 17.

100 *Clonmel Chronicle*, 23 August 1871.

101 Ibid., 9 September 1871. The club has 1869 as the date of its foundation but evidence of this date was not identified in the contemporary press.

102 Ibid., 13 September 1871.

103 *Slater's Directory of Ireland, 1870* (Manchester and London: Slater's Directory Co., 1870), p. 36.

104 Bassett, *Tipperary: a guide and directory, 1889*, p. 103.

105 *Clonmel Chronicle*, 13 June 1877, 19 January 1878.

106 Ibid., 23 March 1872.

107 Ibid., 18 May 1872.

108 Ibid., 13 July 1872.

109 Ibid., 27 July 1872, 10 August 1872.

110 Ibid., 24 August 1872, 28 August 1872.

111 Ibid., 28 August 1872.

112 *Tipperary Free Press*, 17 August 1875.

113 Later in the century when shop assistants' unions sought to introduce a half-day holiday, employers resisted vigorously.

114 *Clonmel Chronicle*, 9 August 1879.

115 Neil Wigglesworth, *The Social History of English Rowing* (London and New York: Frank Cass, 1992), p. 3.

116 *Tipperary Free Press*, 13 August 1875; *Clonmel Chronicle*, 12 June 1878.

117 *Clonmel Chronicle*, 12 August 1874, 11 August 1875; *Tipperary Free Press*, 14 May 1875; 13 August 1875, 12 September 1876.

118 *Clonmel Chronicle*, 27 April 1872; 11 May 1872.

119 Ibid., 13 May 1876.

120 Wigglesworth, *English Rowing*, p. 81.

121 *Tipperary Free Press*, 20 July 1875.

122 *Clonmel Chronicle*, 15 January 1876.

123 *Tipperary Free Press*, 24 August 1875.

124 Ibid., 3 September 1875; *Clonmel Chronicle*, 4 September 1875.

125 Gerald Lindner, personal communication, 7 January 2014.

126 Wigglesworth, *English Rowing*, p. 81.

127 *Clonmel Chronicle*, 28 June 1876.

128 Ibid., 13 June 1877.

129 *Irish Times*, 11 August 1879.

130 Raymond Blake, *In Black and White: a history of rowing at Dublin University* (Dublin: University Boat Club, 1991), pp. 15, 36.

131 *Irish Times*, 22 March 1872.

132 *Clonmel Chronicle*, 9 August 1879.

133 *Tipperary Free Press*, 20 July 1880.

134 *Clonmel Chronicle*, 9 April 1879. In 1858 Taylor, a professional rower and boat-builder, was described as 'combining the practical skill of the waterman with the mental intelligence of the amateur': Halladay, *Rowing in England*, p. 9.

135 *Irish Times*, 26 May 1873, 11 July 1877.

136 Blake, *In Black and White*, p. 22.

137 *Clonmel Chronicle*, 3 July 1878.

138 Ibid., 9 April 1879.

139 Ibid., 26 July 1879.

140 Ibid., 13 April 1878. £350 equates to £31,180 (€36,977.53) in 2016 when calculated on MeasuringWorth.com website, https://www.measuringworth.com/ukcompare/relativevalue.php (Accessed 9 May 2017).

141 *Tipperary Free Press*, 21 September 1875.

142 Neil Tranter, 'The Chronology of Organised Sport in Nineteenth-century Scotland: a regional study. II – causes', *The International Journal of the History of Sport*, vol. 7, no. 3 (1990), p. 376.

143 The Mullingar spring meeting of 1903 was the first sporting event to impose a general admission fee of 6*d*: Hunt, *Sport and Society*, p. 223.

144 *Clonmel Chronicle*, 9 August 1879, 17 July 1880.

CHAPTER 6 BALL GAMES

1 Rouse, *Sport and Ireland*, pp. 93–4.

2 While some rugby and lawn tennis clubs have histories which commence in the 1870s, the majority of the books on sport in Tipperary are GAA-related and they start in the years after 1884. Golf did not feature at this time.

3 Fogarty, *Tipperary's GAA*, pp. 13–17.

4 Bob Stakelum, *Gaelic Games in Holycross-Ballycahill, 1884–1990* (Holycross: Bob Stakelum, 1992), p. xi.

5 Neal Garnham, *Association Football and Society in Pre-partition Ireland* (Belfast: Ulster Historical Foundation, 2004), pp. 2–4.

6 Emma Griffin, *England's Revelry: a history of popular pastimes, 1660–1830* (Oxford: Oxford University Press, 2005), pp. 104–7; Richard Sanders, *Beastly Fury: the strange birth of British football* (London: Bantam, 2009), pp. 6–8.

7 Griffin, *England's Revelry*, p. 106.

8 Rouse, *Sport and Ireland*, p. 94.

9 Griffin, *England's Revelry*, p. 107.

10 Ibid.; National Archives of Ireland. Clonmel: Court Service: Petty Sessions Order Book, 1/2850, no. 228, 28 October 1856.

11 *Freeman's Journal*, 9 August 1792, 11 August 1792.

12 *Kilkenny Moderator*, 12 August 1829.

13 Ibid., 11 June 1831.

14 *Harrow School Register*, p. 133.

15 *Tipperary Constitution*, 5 August 1836.

16 *Tipperary Free Press*, 20 June 1846; *Tipperary Vindicator*, 19 May 1849.

17 *Rugby School Register: Volume I, from 1675–1849 inclusive* (Rugby: A.J. Lawrence (late Billington), 1881), pp. 156, 267.

18 Tony Collins, *A Social History of English Rugby Union* (London: Routledge, 2013), p. 5.

19 *Harrow School Register*, p. 16.

20 Sean Reid, 'Ireland's Wisden: the handbook of cricket in Ireland and the golden age of Irish cricket, 1865–1885', unpublished MA dissertation, University of Bristol, 2006.

21 These teams are listed in the appendices.

22 Mike Cronin and Brian Ó Conchubhair, 'Ní Cothram na Féinne É Sin: cricket, lexicography and cultural purity in Ireland', *Journal of Historical Sociology*, vol. 24, no. 4 (December 2011), p. 496.

23 *Tipperary Free Press*, 22 April 1840.

24 *Freeman's Journal*, 10 October 1876, p. 8.

25 *Tipperary Free Press*, 16 August 1864.

26 *Cashel Gazette*, 15 August 1874; *Tipperary Advocate*, 23 June 1877, 4 August 1877; *Nenagh Guardian*, 18 August 1877.

27 Neal Garnham, 'The Roles of Cricket in Victorian and Edwardian Ireland', *Sporting Traditions*, vol. 9, no. 2 (May 2003), p. 27.

28 The skill level or ability of specific players cannot be quantified, and neither can it be proved that this was one's sole income.

29 Ashbrook Union Cricket Club scorebook, 1846–9: 'Rules and regulations for the season 1847', no. 3.

30 Ibid. 'Rules and regulations for the season 1847', no. 5.

31 This is equal to labour earnings of £13,390.00 (€15,873.65) in 2016 when compared on MeasuringWorth website, https://www.measuringworth.com/ukcompare/relativevalue.php (Accessed 9 May 2017)

32 Underdown, *Start of Play*, pp. 69–72.

33 Hunt, 'The Development of Sport in County Westmeath', p. 183.

34 Ibid., p. 184.

35 Reid, 'Cricket in Victorian Ireland', p. 2.

36 Kevin Whelan, 'The Geography of Hurling', *History Ireland*, vol. 1, no. 1 (Spring 1993), p. 28.

37 Eoin Kinsella, 'Riotous Proceedings and the Cricket of Savages: football and hurling in early modern Ireland', in M. Cronin, W. Murphy and P. Rouse, *The Gaelic Athletic Association, 1884–2009* (Dublin: Irish Academic Press, 2009), p. 30.

38 *Tipperary Free Press*, 2 May 1873.

39 *Nenagh Guardian*, 23 July 1873.

40 Mike Huggins, 'Second-class Citizens? English middle-class culture and sport, 1850–1910: a reconsideration', *The International Journal of the History of Sport*, vol. 17, no. 1 (March 2000), p. 28.

41 *1849 (45) Offences (Ireland). A bill for the more speedy trial and punishment of offences in Ireland. Highways (Ireland) 1853, a bill to consolidate and amend the laws relating to highways in Ireland.*

42   Fethard, Court Service: Petty Sessions Order Book, 1/5413, No. 292-310, 26 June 1854.

43   Bansha, Court Service: Petty Sessions Order Book, 1/9265, No. 5-18, 14 January 1856.

44   Wray Vamplew, *Pay Up and Play the Game: professional sport in Britain, 1875–1914* (Cambridge: Allen Lane, 1988), p. 54.

45   Kelly, *Sport in Ireland*, p. 258.

46   Ibid., p. 259.

47   *Tipperary Free Press*, 23 May 1852.

48   Kelly, *Sport in Ireland*, p. 246.

49   *Irish Times*, 19 December 1862.

50   Fogarty, *Tipperary's GAA*, p. 16.

51   de Búrca notes that 'amongst the major casualties of the Famine were the field games and other traditional pastimes of rural Ireland, which in many areas suffered an irreversible decline': de Búrca, *The GAA*, p. 5; Seamus J. King, *A History of Hurling* (Dublin: Gill & Macmillan, 1996), p. 40.

52   Stakelum, *Gaelic Games in Holycross-Ballycahill*, p. xi; Kinsella, 'Riotous Proceedings', pp. 15–31.

53   Seamus J. King, *The Clash of the Ash in Foreign Fields: hurling abroad* (Cashel: Seamus J. King, 1998), p. 42.

54   This is based on research conducted by this writer of contemporary Australian newspapers.

55   *The Argus*, 17 April 1878, p. 5. There was a great desire among hurling men to establish a hurling organisation in Victoria. On Monday, 15 April 1878 the meeting took place with 'delegates from the various hurling clubs' attending at Dillon's Hotel, 'for the purpose of adopting one code of laws for the regulation of the game for the whole of the colony, and also for the formation of a Hurling Club Association. Representatives from Melbourne, Kyneton, Collingwood, Brighton, Prahran and Richmond clubs were present. It was decided to form an association, to be called the Victorian Hurling Club Association, and a provisional committee was appointed to carry out the revision of the laws, and submit them to the various clubs for approval.' This was an important development for hurling in Australia and it was, in all but name, a prototype for the future foundation of the GAA, six years later.

56   See, for example, Tranter, *Sport, Economy and Society*, pp. 8–11.

57   *Irish Times*, 23 January 1968. The author of the letter subsequently acknowledged that he 'was relying on hearsay when he pointed out that Webb Ellis had learned the game of cad from his cousins in Tipperary'; Edmund Van Esbeck, *Irish Rugby, 1874–1999: a history* (Dublin: Gill & Macmillan, 1999), p. 9.

58   *Tipperary Free Press*, 16 August 1845; *Nenagh Guardian*, 17 February 1866; *Clonmel Chronicle*, 19 September 1863, 23 December 1865.

59   *Clonmel Chronicle*, 16 January 1869.

60   Tony Collins, personal communication, 21 January 2012.

61   Rita M. Boswell (Archivist, Harrow School), personal communication, 27 January 2012.

62   *The Harrow School Register, 1800–1911* (Harrow, 1911), pp. 266, 357.

63   J.A. Mangan, *Athleticism in the Victorian and Edwardian Public School* (London: Frank Cass, 2000), p. 3.

64   Rouse, *Sport and Ireland*, p. 126.

65   H.E.C. Stapylton, *The Eton School Lists from 1791 to 1877, with notes and index* (Eton: R. Ingalton Drake, 1884), pp. 278, 314.

66   Ibid., p. 364.

67   Edward Liddle, *Irish Cricketers, 1855–1980* (Cleethorpes: The Association of Cricket Statisticians, 1980), p. 23.

68   *Nenagh Guardian*, 9 April 1884.

69   *1849 (45) Offences (Ireland). A bill for the more speedy trial and punishment of offences in Ireland* (London, 1849), pp. 2–3.

70   *Highways (Ireland) 1853, a bill to consolidate and amend the laws relating to highways in Ireland* (London, 1853), pp. 42–3.

71   *Tipperary Free Press*, 16 August 1845.

72   *Clonmel Chronicle*, 13 August 1862, 16 August 1862, 4 July 1863, 19 September 1863, 13 November 1872; *Nenagh Guardian*, 28 January 1865, 10 February 1877.

73   Tranter, *Sport, Economy and Society*, p. 4; Sanders, *Beastly Fury*, p. 11.

74   *Nenagh Guardian*, 17 February 1866.

75   *Tipperary Free Press*, 18 November 1856.

76   Mike Huggins, *The Victorians and Sport* (London and New York: Hambledon & London, 2004), p. 45.

77   R.J. Holt, 'Football and the Urban Way of Life in Nineteenth-century Britain', in J.A. Mangan (ed.), *Pleasure, Profit, Proselytism: British culture and sport at home and abroad, 1700–1914* (London: Frank Cass, 1988), p. 71.

78   See, for example, the study carried out by J.A. Mangan, *Athleticism in the Public School.*

79   Holt, 'Football and the Urban Way of Life', p. 71; Tony Mason, 'Football', in Tony Mason (ed.), *Sport in Britain: a social history* (Cambridge: Frank Cass, 1989), p. 150.

80   Puirséal, *The GAA in Its Time*, p. 31.

81   Marcus de Búrca, *The GAA: a history of the Gaelic Athletic Association* (Dublin: Cumann Lúthchleas Gael, 1980), p. 6.

82   Tony Collins, 'History, Theory and the "Civilizing Process"', *Sport in History*, vol. 25, no. 2 (August 2005), pp. 294–5.

83   *Cork Examiner*, 26 February 1878, 12 March 1878.

84   *Clonmel Chronicle*, 14 February 1880, 5 May 1880.

85   Joe Lennon, *The Playing Rules of Football and Hurling, 1602–2010* (Gormanstown, Co. Meath: Northern Recreation Consultants, 2001), p. 10.

86   The club histories of Templemore, Thurles, Moycarkey and Two-Mile-Borris make no reference to these games.

87   Neal Garnham, *The Origins and Development of Football in Ireland, Being a Reprint of R.M. Peter's Irish Football Annual of 1880* (Belfast: Ulster Historical Foundation, 1999), p. 3.

88   Sean Diffley, *The Men in Green: the story of Irish rugby* (Dublin: Pelham Books, 1973), pp. 13–14.

89   Van Esbeck, *Irish Rugby*, p. 327.

90   Ibid., pp 26, 37.

91   National Library of Ireland, Ms. 9515, Account book and records of Kilruane Football Club, 1876–80.

92   *Clonmel Chronicle*, 15 November 1879; 14 January 1880, 11 October 1882.

93   Account book and records of Kilruane Football Club, 1876–80.

94   *Nenagh Guardian*, 29 March 1884, 12 April 1884. See also Donal A. Murphy, *Nenagh Ormond's Century 1884–1984: a rugby history* (Nenagh: Relay Publications, 1984).

95   *Clonmel Chronicle*, 11 October 1882.

96   *Nenagh Guardian*, 29 December 1875.

97   Ibid., 10 June 1876.

98   *Census of Ireland for the Year 1871: province of Munster: County Tipperary* (Dublin: A. Thom for Her Majesty's Stationery Office, 1872), p. 774.

99   Collins, *English Rugby Union*, p. 9.

100   Cronin, 'A Chaotic Reading of Irish History', p. 2757.

101   *Clonmel Chronicle*, 29 October 1879, 5 November 1879, 15 November 1879, 22 November 1879, 13 March 1880.

102   Garnham, *Origins and Development of Football in Ireland*, p. 65; Liam O'Callaghan, *Rugby in Munster: a social and cultural history* (Cork: Cork University Press, 2011), p. 30.

103   *Clonmel Chronicle*, 11 December 1878, 29 November 1879.

104   *Nenagh Guardian*, 29 December 1875.

105   Ibid., 16 August 1876, 20 February 1886; *Tipperary People*, 1 September 1876; *Tipperary Advocate*, 6 July 1878.

106   For Clanwilliam cricket see *Clonmel Chronicle*, 27 July 1878, 30 July 1879, 12 June 1880. For Clanwilliam rugby see *Clonmel Chronicle*, 14 January

1880, *Sport*, 22 April 1882.

107 Bassett, *Tipperary: a guide and directory, 1889*, p. 241.

108 Denis G. Marnane, *Clanwilliam Football Club, 1879–1979: centenary history* (Tipperary: Clanwilliam RFC, 1980), p. 11.

109 *Tipperary Constitution*, 10 January 1840.

110 There has been some debate as to the exact number of people who were in attendance at the foundation meeting of the GAA. A figure of seven men has long been given as the number present. T.K. Dwyer, grandson of a local contemporary athlete, Tim (T.K.) Dwyer, and Jimmy Fogarty put the figure for those in attendance at thirteen: T.K. Dwyer and James Fogarty, *Moycarkey Borris GAA Story* (Thurles: Moycarkey Borris GAA Club, 1984), pp. 10–11. J.M. Tobin also places the number of those present at thirteen in an article entitled 'Who Was Present at the Founding of the GAA at Thurles in 1884?' in *History Ireland*, vol. 23, no. 5 (September/October 2015), pp 32–4.

111 *Irish Independent*, 16 March 1943, p. 3.

112 Garnham, *Origins and Development of Football in Ireland*, p. 19.

113 David Toms, *Soccer in Munster: a social history, 1877–1937* (Cork: Cork University Press, 2015).

114 In his study of the association game in Ireland, Neal Garnham notes, in poetic form in the preface, that 'Much has been written about the history of football, although the game in Ireland remains somewhat aloof. No great chronicler, or even studious amateur, has given the game its deserved memorial.' Garnham, *Association Football*, preface.

115 Dublin and Belfast were seen as the central areas for the initial growth of the association game. Garnham, *Association Football*, pp. 4–7.

116 *Clonmel Chronicle*, 26 November 1879.

117 Ibid., 20 December 1879.

118 Ibid., 10 March 1880.

119 Ibid., 1 May 1880.

120 Minute book, Carrick-on-Suir Athletic, Cricket and Football Club: 'Committee meeting Monday 17th April 1882'.

121 *Clonmel Nationalist*, 21 April 1897. See also Garnham, *Origins and Development of Football in Ireland*, p. 18.

122 Garnham, *Association Football*, pp. 4–7.

123 Jack Mahon, *A History of Gaelic Football* (Dublin: Gill & Macmillan, 2000), pp. 2–3.

124 *Census of Ireland for the Year 1851. Part III: Report on the statues of disease* (Dublin: A. Thom for Her Majesty's Stationery Office, 1851).

125 *Census of Ireland, 1851*, pp. 60–1.

126 For instance at Clonmel Petty Sessions, on 10 November 1857, John McGrath was charged with causing a 'nuisance on the street by kicking a football' (Court Service: Petty Sessions Order Book, 1/2853, no. 100), while on 29 August 1858, Michael Mullins was charged with 'ball playing in the public street' (Court Service: Petty Sessions Order Book, 1/2855, no. 256).

127 Military Archives, Dublin. Detail of skittle alley and fives-court at Tipperary barracks, *c.*1876 (IE/MA/MPD/AD119275-006). Detail of ball courts at Templemore Barracks, *c.*1873 (Templemore Barracks WO78-2870).

128 *Clonmel Chronicle*, 3 June 1874.

129 Clonmel, Court Service: Petty Sessions Order Book, 1/2852, no. 221-226, 29 June 1857.

130 *Tipperary Free Press*, 2 October 1850.

131 *Tipperary Free Press*, 21 September 1858; *Tipperary Examiner*, 22 September 1858.

132 *Clonmel Chronicle*, 7 September 1868.

133 Tom McElligott, *Handball: the game, the players, the history* (Dublin: Wolfhound Press, 1984), p. 158.

134 *Tipperary Free Press*, 15 October 1872; *Clonmel Chronicle*, 16 October 1872.

135 Detail of skittle alley and fives-court at Tipperary barracks, *c.*1876 (source: Military Archives IE/MA/MPD/AD119275-006).

136 *Nenagh Guardian*, 2 September 1871.

137 *Clonmel Chronicle*, 14 June 1876.

138 Ordnance Survey town plan for Clonmel 1874, sheet 7 and sheet 15. Surveyed in 1874 and zincographed in 1876 under the direction of Lt Colonel Wilkinson R.E. at the Ordnance Survey Office, Phoenix Park. On the 1905 Ordnance Survey six-inch map for Clonmel, five ball courts are identified.

139 Rouse, *Sport and Ireland*, p. 109.

CONCLUSION

1 Brigadier A.G. Hewson, M.C., *Memoirs of a Regimental Officer* (London: Greenaways, 1970), p. 19.

2 Hunt, *Sport and Society*, pp. 171–3; Mason and Riedi, *Sport and the Military*, pp. 35–7.

3 Mason and Riedi, *Sport and the Military*, p. 52.

4 *Return of Owners of Land*, p. 172.

5 Tranter, 'The Chronology of Organized Sport. II – causes', p. 365.

6 Huggins, *The Victorians and Sport*, p. 19.

7   For example see Brian Griffin, 'Cycling and Gender in Victorian Ireland', *Éire-Ireland*, vol. 41, no. 1 (Spring 2006), pp. 213–41.

8   Hayes, 'From Ludicrous to Logical', p. 265.

9   Guttman, *From Ritual to Record*, p. 59.

10   Holt, *Sport and the British*, p. 240.

11   Hunt, 'The Development of Sport in County Westmeath', p. 307.

12   *Clonmel Chronicle*, 22 September 1880, 30 August 1882; *Tipperary Leader*, 25 August 1883.

13   Charles Landon, *Classic Moments of Wimbledon* (Frome: Moorland Publishing, 1982), p. 13.

14   R.V. Comerford, *Ireland: inventing the nation* (London: Hodder Arnold, 2001), p. 218.

15   'Royal Sport of Cock Fighting' was how an advertisement for a cock fight in Wexford in 1778 for 200 guineas was promoted: *Finn's Leinster Journal*, 6 June 1778; 'Cock fight in Durrow, Co. Laois for 40 guineas', *Finn's Leinster Journal*, 19 July 1794. For an overview of cock fighting in the eighteenth century see Chapter 3, 'Cockfighting', in Kelly, *Sport in Ireland*, pp. 157–206.

Appendix 1
Matches played by Tipperary cricket combinations, 1840–1869

NAME	YEARS
Ballinderry CC	1863, 1866
Ballinderry Invincibles CC	1868
Ballylanigan CC	1868
Borrisoleigh CC	1851
Cahir & Clonmel Garrison CC	1849–50
Cahir & Fethard CC	1849
Cahir CC	1843, 1846, 1864–9
Cahir Garrison CC	1843, 1846, 1850, 1866–9
Cahir, Clonmel & Carrick Garrison CC	1867
Carrick-on-Suir CC	1864, 1868
Carrick-on-Suir Garrison CC	1866, 1868
Carrick-on-Suir Mechanics CC	1863
Carrig CC	1866
Cashel Cathedral School CC	1863, 1868
Cashel CC	1868
Cashel Deanery School CC	1869
City of the Kings CC, Cashel	1869
Clogheen CC	1865
Cloneaska CC	1866
Clonmel & Cahir CC	1850
Clonmel CC	1849–52, 1864–9
Clonmel Commercial CC	1864–5
Clonmel Garrison CC	1849, 1851–2, 1856, 1864–5, 1867–9
Cloughjordan & Mr Thwaites XIII	1862
Cloughjordan CC	1858, 1860, 1862–3
Co. Tipperary CC	1864, 1869
Dovea CC	1865
Dundrum CC	1866–9
Dundrum School CC	1866–9
Emill CC, Cloughjordan	1862
Fethard Garrison CC	1867
Killenaule CC	1864

NAME	YEARS
Knockavilla School CC	1866–7
Lower Ormond CC	1867
Master Pennefeather XI	1867
Mr A.C. Newell XI	1867–8
Mr Andrews XI	1865
Mr Baker XI, Tipperary	1865–6
Mr D'Alton XI	1864, 1865, 1868
Mr E. Bayly XI, Dundrum	1866
Mr E. Piper XI	1866
Mr Fosberry XI	1866
Mr Gough XI	1865, 1868–9
Mr H. Munster XI	1869
Mr H.A. Wood XI	1866
Mr J Bayly XI, Dundrum	1866
Mr J. Greene XI, Dundrum	1866
Mr J. O'Brien XI, Cashel	1868
Mr J. Thompson XI	1866
Mr O'Reilly XI	1864
Mr Seymour XI	1864
Mr T. Gough XI	1868
Mr Thwaites XI	1862
Mr Waller XI	1864
Mr White XI, Cashel	1863
Nenagh CC	1849, 1852, 1867–9
Newcastle CC	1869
Newport CC	1868
Ormond CC	1857, 1859–60, 1862–9
Poulacapple CC	1867–8
Priory CC, Templemore	1862
RIC Dundrum & Schoolboys XI	1868
RIC Dundrum CC	1867–9
RIC Nenagh CC	1851
Rock CC, Cashel	1868–9
Rockwell College CC	1869
Shanbally CC	1867

NAME	YEARS
South Tipperary CC	1864–5
St John's College CC, Newport	1868–9
Templemore & Barnane CC	1868
Templemore CC	1847–50, 1861–2, 1868–9
Templemore Garrison CC	1849–52, 1860–3, 1865, 1868
Templemore Shamrock CC	1862
The Abbey CC, Tipperary	1864, 1867–9
Thurles & Templemore CC	1869
Thurles CC	1869
Tipperary CC	1867
Tipperary United CC	1865
United Service XI, Cashel	1868
Upham CC, Killenaule	1864
Upper Ormond CC	1867

Appendix 2

Matches played by Tipperary cricket combinations, 1870–1880

NAME	YEARS
Ardmayle CC	1875
Ballinahow CC, Ballycahill	1875
Ballinard CC	1873
Ballinderry CC	1870
Ballintemple CC	1877
Ballinware CC	1874, 1877
Ballyanny CC	1877
Ballycapple CC	1876, 1878
Ballykisteen CC	1873–4, 1876–7
Ballymackey CC	1874
Barna CC	1875–6
Barnane CC	1876, 1878
Bawn CC	1876–9
Beechwood CC	1875–6, 1878

NAME	YEARS
Beechwood Park XI	1873
Borrisokane CC	1880
Borrisoleigh Boot Makers CC	1878
Borrisoleigh CC	1878
Borrisoleigh Commercial CC	1878
Boulera CC, Roscrea	1880
Boulthenny CC	1875
Cahir CC	1870–4, 1876–8
Cahir Garrison CC	1870, 1873, 1874, 1880
Captain Morton XI	1876
Carney CC	1872–3
Carrick-on-Suir CC	1873, 1875–7, 1879–80
Carrick-on-Suir Garrison CC	1870
Carrick-on-Suir Shamrock CC	1871
Cashel CC	1871, 1875, 1878
Cashel Deanery School CC	1870
Cashel Excelsior CC	1875
Cashel Rovers CC	1875
Cashel Shamrock CC	1871, 1875
Clanwilliam CC	1878–80
Claremont CC	1872
Clashnevin CC	1874–7
Clogheen CC	1871, 1873, 1876, 1878
Cloneen CC	1873
Clongour CC, Thurles	1875
Clonmel CC	1870, 1873–4, 1880
Clonmel Endowed School CC	1877
Clonmel Garrison CC	1870–1, 1873, 1875–6, 1880
Clonmel School CC	1874–6, 1878, 1880
Cloughjordan CC	1872–6
Compsey CC	1875–7
Congor CC	1874
Coolagoran CC	1874, 1876
Dovea & Barnane CC	1872
Dovea CC	1874–6, 1880

NAME	YEARS
Driminure CC	1880
Dundrum CC	1870–6
Dundrum School CC	1870
Emerald CC, Thurles	1875, 1877
Emill CC, Cloughjordan	1877–8
Fantane CC	1878
Garrengrena CC, Borrisoleigh	1879
Glenahilty CC	1874
Gortagarry CC	1878
Grange CC, Holycross	1875
Gregavine Shamrocks CC	1875
Grennanstown CC	1878, 1880
Holycross CC	1880
Kilcash CC	1876
Killeen CC, Borrisoleigh	1879
Killoskehane CC	1876
Knockenroe CC, Templemore	1877
Liscarode CC	1878
Longfield CC, Boherlahan	1875
Marlfield CC	1879–80
Mobarnane CC	1877
Mr Baker XI, Tipperary	1876
Mr Bell XI, Tipperary	1876
Mr Blake XI	1873
Mr Bourchier XI	1870, 1873, 1875
Mr Bourke XI, Tipperary	1879
Mr Budd XI, Nenagh	1874
Mr C.H. D'Alton XI	1870–1
Mr Cooper Chadwick XI	1873
Mr C.P. Coote XI	1874
Mr E. O'Brien XI, Cashel	1877
Mr E.W. Murphy XI, Cashel	1873
Mr H. Brougham VIII, Cashel	1870
Mr H. Gordon XI	1870
Mr H. Thompson XI, Barnane	1876–7

NAME	YEARS
Mr Hamilton XI	1877
Mr Hanly XI, Drom	1875–6
Mr Harry Poe XI	1877
Mr J. Murphy XI, Cashel	1873
Mr MacAuliffe XI, Cashel	1871
Mr Newport White XI	1873
Mr O'Reilly XI, Tipperary	1878
Mr R. Hewson XI, Tipperary	1877
Mr R.J. Arthur VIII, Cashel	1870
Mr Stokes XI, Tipperary	1876
Mr Trant XI, Dovea	1876
Mr Waller XI	1879
Mr Walter Ryan XI	1873
Mr W.H. Bennett XI, Tipperary	1877
Mullinahone CC	1873, 1875
Mullinahone Shamrock CC	1879
Nenagh Borderers CC	1874
Nenagh CC	1870–9
Nenagh Garrison CC	1870, 1872–4, 1876–7
Nenagh Olla Podridas CC	1877–8
Nenagh Wanderers CC	1872, 1877–8
New Street CC, Carrick-on-Suir	1880
Newport CC	1874
Newtown CC, Carrick-on-Suir	1874–6
Noan CC, Ballinure	1877
Nodstown CC	1875
North Tipperary Light Infantry CC	1880
Ormond CC	1870–3, 1875
Ormond Wanderers CC	1879
Rev Ross-Lewin XI, Tipperary	1879
Rock CC, Cashel	1873–8
Rockwell College CC	1871–8, 1880
Roscrea Borderers CC	1872, 1874–80
Roscrea CC	1871, 1877–8
Roscrea CYMS CC	1873–8

NAME	YEARS
Roscumroe CC	1876
Shanakill CC, Roscrea	1880
Shanbally CC	1871–3
Silvermines CC	1877
Sir William Osborne XI	1872–5, 1877
Solsborough CC	1877–8, 1880
Sopwell Hall XI	1873–4
Sorrell Hill CC, Templemore	1877–8, 1880
South Tipperary CC	1871, 1873–6, 1878
Springfield CC, Templemore	1877
Springmount CC	1872
St John's College CC, Newport	1870, 1872–7, 1879
St Patrick's College CC, Thurles	1871–2, 1875
Strogue CC, Castleiney	1877
Templemore Astonishers CC	1878, 1880
Templemore CC	1875–8, 1880
Templemore Commercial CC	1878
Templemore Garrison CC	1871–4, 1876, 1878, 1880
The Abbey CC, Tipperary	1870–80
The Bankers CC, Tipperary	1873, 1875–7
The Commercials CC, Roscrea	1876
The Lily Ballyboe CC	1876–7
The Millparks CC, Roscrea	1875
The Wanderers CC	1874–5
Thurles CC	1870–6, 1878
Tipperary CC	1872–4, 1878–9
Tipperary Commercial CC	1878
Tipperary Garrison CC	1875, 1879–80
Tipperary Silurian CC	1870
Tipperary XXII	1874
Toomevara CC	1875–7
Tubberadora CC	1875
Turtulla CC	1874–8
Tyone CC, Nenagh	1874

BIBLIOGRAPHY

Primary Sources
Archival Sources

Córas Iompair Éireann Archives, Dublin
Great Southern and Western Railway minute book, no. 5, 1849–50

Durrow Castle, County Laois
Ashbrook Union Cricket Club scorebook, 1846–8

National Archives of Ireland, Dublin
Bansha, Court Service: Petty Sessions Order Book. 1/9265, 14 January 1856
Clonmel, Court Service: Petty Sessions Order Book. 1/2849, 6 July 1856
Clonmel, Court Service: Petty Sessions Order Book. 1/2850, 28 October 1856
Clonmel, Court Service: Petty Sessions Order Book. 1/2852, 13 June 1857
Clonmel, Court Service: Petty Sessions Order Book. 1/2853, 10 November 1857
Clonmel, Court Service: Petty Sessions Order Book. 1/2855, 29 August 1858
Clonmel, Court Service: Petty Sessions Order Book. 1/2857, 6 February 1860
Fethard, Court Service: Petty Sessions Order Book. 1/5413, 26 June 1854
Templemore, Court Service: Petty Sessions Order Book. 1/9117, 7 December 1859
Templemore, Court Service: Petty Sessions Order Book. 1/9118, 15 August 1860

National Library of Ireland, Dublin
Ms 9515. Account book and records of Kilruane Football Club, 1876–1880

Private Collections
The chronicles of Ashley Park, commenced AD 1866 by James N. Atkinson A diary
   from 2 Apr. 1866 to 29 April 1871
Littleton athletic sports programme of events, September 1877
Minute book – Carrick on Suir Athletic, Cricket and Football Club. Established
   August 1879

Tipperary Studies, Tipperary County Council Library Service, Thurles
Ordnance Survey of Ireland, 1840. Tipperary County, scale: six inches to one mile
Ordnance Survey of Ireland, 1874. Clonmel Town, scale: 1:500

Newspapers

Cashel Gazette, 1864–66; 1868–80

Celtic Times, 1887

Clonmel Chronicle, 1848–84

Cork Examiner, 1878

Finn's Leinster Journal, 1769–72

Freeman's Journal, 1788–92; 1850–99

Kilkenny Journal, 1879

Kilkenny Moderator, 1829–31; 1877

Nationalist (Clonmel), 1897

Nenagh Guardian, 1840–80

Sport, 1882–3

The Argus (Australia), 1878

The Irish Times, 1872–79; 1968

Tipperary Advocate, 1858–80

Tipperary Constitution, 1840–48

Tipperary Examiner, Apr. to Dec. 1858

Tipperary Free Press, 1840–80

Tipperary Leader, 1883

Tipperary Vindicator, 1844–9

Tipperary Weekly News, Jan. to Feb. 1858

United Ireland, 1884

Acts of Parliament

'An act for the protection and improvement of the salmon, trout, and other inland fisheries of Ireland [31 August 1848]', in *A collection of the public general statutes, passed in the eleventh and twelfth year of the reign of her majesty Queen Victoria* (London: George E. Eyre and William Spottiswoode, 1848), pp. 518–28

'1849 (45) Offences (Ireland). A bill for the more speedy trial and punishment of offences in Ireland', vol. IV, p. 387. *Parliamentary papers: List of the bills, reports, estimates and accounts and papers. Printed by order of the House of Commons, and of the papers presented by command, session 1849* (London: House of Commons, 1849)

'Highways (Ireland) 1853. A bill to consolidate and amend the laws relating to highways in Ireland', vol. III, p. 273. *Parliamentary papers: List of the bills, reports, estimates and accounts and papers. Printed by order of the House of Commons, and of the papers presented by command, session 1852–53* (London: House of Commons, 1853)

Directories and Works of Reference

Auden, Rev. J.E. (ed.), *Shrewsbury School Register 1734–1908* (Owestry: Caxton Press, 1909)

Bannerman Wainewright, John (ed.), *Winchester College, 1836–1906: a register* (Winchester: P. & G. Wells, 1907)

Bassett, George Henry, *County Tipperary One Hundred Years Ago: a guide and directory, 1889* (reprint Belfast: Friar's Bush Press, 1991)

Borwick, F. (ed.), *Clifton College Annals and Register, 1862–1925* (Bristol: J.W. Arrowsmith Ltd., 1925)

Census of Ireland for the Year 1851, Part III: Report on the statues of disease (Dublin: Alexander Thom for Her Majesty's Stationery Office, 1851)

Census of Ireland for the Year 1871: Province of Munster: County Tipperary (Dublin: Alexander Thom for Her Majesty's Stationery Office, 1872)

Census of Ireland 1871, Part 1: Area, houses and population: also the ages, civil condition, occupations, birthplaces, and education of the people, vol. II, province of Munster, no. 5, county of Tipperary (Dublin: Alexander Thom for Her Majesty's Stationery Office, 1874)

Census of Ireland 1881, Part 1: Area, houses and population: also the ages, civil or conjugal condition, occupations, birthplaces, and education of the people, vol. II, province of Munster, no. 5, county of Tipperary (Dublin: Alexander Thom for Her Majesty's Stationery Office, 1882)

Courtenay Welch, R. (ed.), *The Harrow School Register 1800–1911* (London, New York and Bombay: Longmans, Green & Co., 1911)

Debrett's Illustrated Peerage and Baronetage of the United Kingdom of Great Britain and Ireland, 1864 (London: Bosworth & Harrison, 1864)

Garnham, Neal, The Origins and Development of Football in Ireland, being a reprint of R.M. Peter's Irish Football Annual of 1880 (Belfast: Ulster Historical Foundation, 1999)

General alphabetical index to the townlands and towns, parishes and baronies of Ireland (Baltimore: Genealogical Publishing Co., Inc., 1984)

Griffith, Richard, *General Valuation of Rateable Property in Ireland. County of Tipperary, south riding, Barony of Middlethird* (Dublin: Valuation Office, 1851)

————, *General Valuation of Rateable Property in Ireland. County of Tipperary, north riding, Barony of Eliogarty* (Dublin: Valuation Office, 1852)

Hunter, R.J., *The Racing Calendar* (Dublin: R.J. Hunter, yearly from 1840 to 1880)

Lawrence, John, *Handbook of Cricket in Ireland* (Dublin: John Lawrence, yearly from 1866 to 1882)

Messiter, G.S. (ed.), *Repton School Register, 1557–1905* (Repton: A.J. Lawrence,

1905)

Return of owners of land of one acre and upwards in the several counties, counties of cities, and counties of towns in Ireland (Dublin: A. Thom for H.M. Stationery Office, 1876)

Ruff, W., *Guide to the Turf for 1847: spring edition* (London: R. Ackermann, 1847)

_____, *Guide to the Turf for 1848* (London: R. Ackermann, 1847)

Rugby School Register: volume 1, from 1675–1849 inclusive (Rugby: A.J. Lawrence (Late Billington), 1881)

Slater's Directory of Ireland, 1870 (Manchester and London: Slater's Directory Co., 1870)

Stapylton, H.E.C., *The Eton School Lists from 1791 to 1877, with notes and index* (Eton: R. Ingalton Drake, 1884)

Walford, Edward, *The County Families of the United Kingdom* (London: Robert Hardwicke, 1860)

Weatherby, James, *Racing Calendar: containing an account of the plates, matches, and sweepstakes run for in Great Britain and Ireland in the year 1775*, vol. 3 (London: James Weatherby, 1775)

_____, *Racing Calendar: containing and account of the plates, matches and sweepstakes run for in Great Britain and Ireland in the year 1786*, vol. 14 (London: James Weatherby, 1786)

_____, *Racing Calendar: containing and account of the plates, matches and sweepstakes run for in Great Britain and Ireland in the year 1797*, vol. 25 (London: James Weatherby, 1798)

Contemporary Works

Davin, Pat, *Recollections of a veteran Irish athlete: the memoirs of Pat Davin, world's all-around athletic champion* (Dublin: The Juverna Press, 1938)

Delmé Radcliffe, F.P., *The Noble Science: a few general ideas on fox-hunting, for the use of the rising generation of sportsmen, and more especially those of the Hertfordshire Hunt Club* (London: Rudolph Ackermann, 1839)

A Hunting Journal of Henry, Third Marquess of Waterford from the date of his taking the Tipperary hounds in 1840, to April, 1849 (Dublin: Browne & Nolan, 1901)

Hussey de Burgh, U.H., *The Landowners of Ireland* (Dublin: Hodges, Foster & Figgis, 1878)

Lewis, Samuel, *A Topographical Dictionary of Ireland*, 2 vols (London: S. Lewis & Co., 1837)

Murray, John, *Handbook for Travellers in Ireland* 2nd revised edn (London: John Murray, 1866)

Stokes, William, *Pictorial Survey and Tourists' Guide to Lough Derg and the River Shannon* (London: Schulze & Co., 1842)

Thom, Walter, *Pedestrianism; or an account of the performances of celebrated pedestrians during the last and present century* (Aberdeen: A. Brown & A. Frost, 1813)

Secondary Sources

Books and Articles

Aalen, F.H.A., Whelan, Kevin and Stout, Matthew (eds), *Atlas of the Irish Rural Landscape*, 2nd edn (Cork: Cork University Press, 2011)

Armstrong, W.A., 'The Use of Information about Occupations', in E.A. Wrigley (ed.), *Nineteenth Century Society* (Cambridge: Cambridge University Press, 1992), pp. 191–310

Bacon, Peter, *Land, Lust and Gun Smoke: a social history of game shoots in Ireland* (Dublin: The History Press Ireland, 2012)

Baker, Norman, 'Whose Hegemony? The origins of the amateur ethos in nineteenth century English society', *Sport in History*, vol. 24, no. 1 (Summer, 2004), pp. 1–16

Barry, Albert (CSSR), *The Life of Count Moore* (Dublin: M.H. Gill & Son Ltd., 1905)

Bateman, John, *The Great Landowners of Great Britain and Ireland* (reprint New York: A.M. Kelley, 1970)

Bell, Eileen, 'Lena Rice of New Inn: the only Irish ladies Wimbledon champion', *Tipperary Historical Journal 1988*, pp. 13–14

Bence-Jones, Mark, *Burke's Guide to Country Houses: volume 1: Ireland* (London: Burke's Peerage, 1978)

———, *Twilight of the Ascendancy* (reprint London: Constable, 1993)

Blake, Raymond, *In Black and White: a history of rowing at Dublin University* (Dublin: Dublin University Boat Club, 1991)

Bonsall, Penny, *The Irish RMs: the resident magistrates in the British administration of Ireland* (Dublin: Four Courts Press, 1997)

Bouchier, Nancy B., *For the Love of the Game: amateur sport in small-town Ontario, 1838–1895* (Montreal: McGill Queen's University Press, 2003)

Bowen, Muriel, *Irish Hunting* (Tralee: The Kerryman, 1954)

Boyle, John W., 'A Marginal Figure: the Irish rural labourer', in Samuel Clark and James J. Donnelly Jnr, *Irish Peasants: violence and political unrest, 1780–1914* (Dublin: Gill & Macmillan, 1983), pp. 311–38

Bracken, Patrick, *Foreign and Fantastic Field Sports: cricket in Co. Tipperary* (Thurles: Liskeveen Books, 2004)

Brailsford, Dennis, *British Sport: a social history* (Cambridge: Lutterworth Press, 1992)

British Hunts and Huntsmen in England (North), Scotland and Ireland: compiled in conjunction with The Sporting Life (London: Biographical Press, 1911)

Burke, Sir Bernard, *A Genealogical and Heraldic History of the Landed Gentry of Ireland* (London: Burke's Peerage, 1904)

Burke, Bernard, *A Genealogical and Heraldic History of the Landed Gentry of Ireland* (London: Burke's Peerage, 1912)

Campbell, J.D., 'Training for Sport is Training for War': sport and the transformation of the British Army, 1860–1914', *The International Journal for the History of Sport*, vol. 17, no. 4 (December 2000), pp. 21–58

Carville, Geraldine, *The Heritage of Holycross* (Belfast: Blackstaff Press, 1973)

Clark, Samuel and Donnelly Jnr., James J. (eds), *Irish Peasants: violence and political unrest 1780–1914* (Manchester: Manchester University Press, 1983)

Collins, Tony, 'History, Theory and the "Civilizing Process"', *Sport in History*, vol. 25, no. 2 (August 2005), pp. 289–306

————, *A Social History of English Rugby Union* (London: Routledge, 2009)

————, *Sport in Capitalist Society* (London: Routledge, 2013)

Comerford, R.V., *The Fenians in Context: Irish politics and society, 1848–82* (reprint Dublin: Wolfhound Press, 1998)

————, *Ireland: inventing the nation* (London: Hodder Arnold, 2001)

Costello, Con, *A Most Delightful Station: the British Army on the Curragh of Kildare, Ireland, 1855–1922* (Cork: The Collins Press, 1996)

Coyle, Joe, *Athletics in Drogheda, 1861–2001* (Victoria, Canada: Trafford, 2003)

Cronin, Mike, *Sport and Nationalism in Ireland: Gaelic games, soccer and Irish identity since 1884* (Dublin: Four Courts Press, 1999)

————, '"Trinity Mysteries": responding to a chaotic reading of Irish history' *The International Journal of the History of Sport*, vol. 28, no. 18 (December 2011), pp. 2753–60

Cronin, Mike and Higgins, Roisín, *Places We Play: Ireland's sporting heritage* (Cork: The Collins Press, 2011)

Cronin, Mike and Ó Conchubhair, Brian, 'Ní Cothram na Féinne É Sin: cricket, lexicography and cultural purity in Ireland', *Journal of Historical Sociology*, vol. 24, no. 4 (December 2011), pp. 494–518

Crossman, Virginia, 'Irish Barracks in the 1820s and 1830s: a political perspective', *The Irish Sword*, vol. XVII, no. 68 (1989), pp. 210–13

Crump, Jeremy, 'Athletics', in Tony Mason (ed.), *Sport in Britain: a social history* (Cambridge: Cambridge University Press, 1989), pp. 44–77

Curtis Jr., L.P., 'Stopping the Hunt, 1881–1882: an aspect of the Irish Land War', in C.H.E. Philpin (ed.), *Nationalism and Popular Protest in Ireland* (Cambridge: Cambridge University Press, 2002), pp. 349–402

D'Arcy, Fergus A, *Horses, Lords and Racing Men: the Turf Club, 1790–1990* (The Curragh: The Turf Club, 1991)

Daly, John A, 'A New Britannia in the Antipodes: sport, class and community in colonial South Australia', in J.A. Mangan, (ed.), *Pleasure, Profit, Proselytism: British culture and sport at home and abroad 1700–1914* (London: Frank Cass, 1988), pp. 163–174

Daly, Mary E., 'The Development of the National School System, 1831–40', in Art Cosgrove and Donal McCartney (eds), *Studies in Irish History, Presented to R. Dudley Edwards* (Dublin: University College, Dublin, 1979), pp. 150–63

————, *Social and Economic History of Ireland since 1800* (Dublin: The Educational Company, 1981)

Davis, Richard, 'Irish Cricket and Nationalism', *Sporting Traditions: Journal of the Australian Society for Sports History*, vol. 10, no. 2 (1994), pp. 77–96

de Burca, Marcus, *The GAA: a history of the Gaelic Athletic Association* (Dublin: Cumann Lúthchleas Gael, 1980)

————, *Michael Cusack and the GAA* (Dublin: Anvil Books, 1989)

Diffley, Sean, *The Men in Green: the story of Irish rugby,* (Dublin: Pelham Books, 1973)

Donnelly, J.S. and Miller, Kerby A., *Irish Popular Culture, 1650–1850* (Dublin and Portland: Irish Academic Press, 1999)

Dooley, Terence, *The Decline of the Big House in Ireland* (Dublin: Wolfhound Press, 2001)

Drücker, Nicola, 'Hunting and Shooting: leisure, social networking and social complications', in Terrence McDonough (ed.), *Was Ireland a Colony? Economics, politics and culture in nineteenth-century Ireland* (Dublin: Irish Academic Press, 2005), pp. 117–144

Ellison, Rev. C.C., 'Going of Munster', *The Irish Ancestor*, vol. IX, no. 1 (1977), pp. 21–43

Finn, G.P.T., 'Trinity Mysteries: university, elite schooling and sport in Ireland', *The International Journal of the History of Sport*, vol. 27, no. 13 (Sept. 2010), pp. 2255–87

Fogarty, Canon Philip, *The Tipperary GAA Story* (Thurles: The Tipperary Star, 1960)

Garnham, Neal, 'The Roles of Cricket in Victorian and Edwardian Ireland', *Sporting*

Traditions, vol. 9, no. 2 (May 2003), pp. 27–48

_____, 'Accounting for the Early Success of the Gaelic Athletic Association', *Irish Historical Studies*, vol. 34, no. 133 (May 2004), pp. 65–78

_____, *Association Football and Society in Pre-partition Ireland* (Belfast: Ulster Historical Foundation, 2004)

Gillmeister, Hiner, *Tennis: a cultural history* (London: Leicester University Press, 1998)

Gray, James (ed.), *Scottish Population Statistics Including Webster's Analysis of Population, 1755* (Edinburgh: Scottish Historical Society, 1952)

Griffin, Brian, 'Cycling and Gender in Victorian Ireland', *Éire-Ireland*, vol. 41, no. 1 (Spring 2006), pp. 213–41

_____, 'The Big House at Play: archery as an elite pursuit from the 1830s to the 1870s', in Ciaran O'Neill (ed.), *Irish Elites in the Nineteenth Century* (Dublin: Four Courts Press, 2013), pp. 153–71

Griffin, Emma, *England's Revelry: a history of popular sports and pastimes, 1660–1830* (Oxford: Oxford University Press, 2005)

_____, *Blood Sport: hunting in Britain since 1066* (New Haven and London: Yale University Press, 2007)

Griffin, Padraig, *The Politics of Irish Athletics, 1850–1990* (Dublin: Marathon Publications, 1990)

Grubb, Geoffrey Watkins, *The Grubbs of Tipperary: studies in heredity and character* (Cork: Mercier Press, 1972)

Guha, Ramachandra, *A Corner of a Foreign Field: the Indian history of a British sport*, (London: Picador, 2002)

Guttman, Allen, *From Ritual to Record: the nature of modern sports* (New York: Columbia University Press, 1978)

Hall, T.F., *History of Boat-racing in Ireland* (Dublin: Irish Amateur Rowing Union, 1939)

Halladay, Eric, *Rowing in England: a social history. The amateur debate* (Manchester and New York: Manchester University Press, 1990)

Hayes, Joseph C., 'Guide to Tipperary newspapers 1770–1989', *Tipperary Historical Journal* (1989), pp. 1–16

Hayes, Tom, 'God Save the Green, God Save the Queen and the Usual Loyal Toasts: sporting and dining for Ireland and/or the Queen', Peter Gray (ed.), *Victoria's Ireland? Irishness and Britishness, 1837–1901* (Dublin: Four Courts Press, 2004), pp. 81–7

Hayes, William and Kavanagh, Art, *The Tipperary Gentry*, vol. 1 (Dublin and Bunclody, Co. Wexford: Irish Family Names, 2003)

Hayes, William J., 'Church, Land and Politics at the End of the 19th Century', in W.J. Hayes (ed.), *Moyne-Templetuohy: a life of its own. The story of a Tipperary parish*, vol. II (Thurles: Moyne-Templetuohy History Group, 2001), pp. 182–337

Heaton, Peter, *Yachting: a history* (London: B.T. Batsford, 1955)

Heckerman, David L., 'King of Kings', *The Blood-horse* (19 July 1997), pp. 3822–6

Hewson, Brigadier A.G., *Memoirs of a Regimental Officer* (London: Greenaways, 1970)

Higgins, Noreen, *Tipperary's Tithe War, 1830–1838: parish accounts of resistance against a church tax* (Tipperary: St Helen's Press, 2002)

Higgins, Tom, *The History of Irish Tennis* (Sligo: Sligo Tennis Club, 2006)

Holt, Richard, *Sport and the British: a modern history* (Oxford: Clarendon Press, 1989)

Holt. R.J., 'Football and the Urban Way of Life in Nineteenth-century Britain', in J.A. Mangan (ed.), *Pleasure, Profit, Proselytism: British culture and sport at home and abroad, 1700–1914* (London: Frank Cass, 1988), pp. 67–85

Hone, Patrick, *Cricket in Ireland* (Tralee: The Kerryman, 1955)

Huggins, Mike, 'Second-class Citizens? English middle-class culture and sport, 1850–1910: a reconsideration', *The International Journal of the History of Sport*, vol. 17, no. 1 (March 2000), pp. 1–35

———, *Flat Racing and British Society, 1790–1914: a social and economic history* (London: Routledge, 2000)

———, *The Victorians and Sport* (London and New York: Hambledon & London, 2004)

———, 'Sport and the Upper Classes: introduction', *Sport in History*, vol. 28, no. 3 (Sept. 2008), pp. 351–63

Hunt, Tom, *Sport and Society in Victorian Ireland: the case of Westmeath* (Cork: Cork University Press, 2007)

———, 'Women in Sport in Victorian Westmeath', *Irish Economic and Social History*, vol. xxxiv (2007), pp. 29–46

———, 'Tipperary Hurlers, 1895–1900: a socio-economic profile', *Tipperary Historical Journal 2009*, pp. 115–28

Hyland, Francis P.M., *History of Galway Races* (London: Robert Hale, 2008)

Itzkowitz, David C., *Peculiar Privilege: a social history of English fox hunting, 1753–1885* (Hassocks: Harvester Wheatsheaf, 1977)

Johnes, Martin, 'Archery, Romance and Elite Culture in England and Wales, c.1780–1840', *History*, vol. 89 (2004), pp. 193–208

Jones, J. Philip, *Gambling Yesterday and Today: a complete history* (Newton Abbot:

David & Charles, 1973)

Jones Hughes, T., 'Landholding and Settlement in County Tipperary in the Nineteenth Century', in William Nolan (ed.), *Tipperary: history and society* (Dublin: Geography Publications, 1985), pp. 339–66

Judd, Denis, *Empire: the British imperial experience from 1765 to the present* (London: HarperCollins, 1996)

Kelly, James, 'The Pastime of the Elite: clubs and societies and the promotion of horse racing', in James Kelly and Martyn J. Powell (eds), *Clubs and Societies in Eighteenth-century Ireland* (Dublin: Four Courts Press, 2010), pp. 409–24

―――――, *Sport in Ireland, 1600–1840* (Dublin: Four Courts Press, 2014)

Kerrigan, Paul M., 'Barracks in Ireland, 1847', *The Irish Sword*, vol. XIX, no. 77 (Summer 1995), pp. 227–8

Kickham, Charles J., *Knocknagow, or The Homes of Tipperary* (Dublin: James Duffy, 1887)

King, Seamus J., *A History of Hurling* (Dublin: Gill & Macmillan, 1996)

―――――, *The Clash of the Ash in Foreign Fields: hurling abroad* (Cashel: Seamus J. King, 1998)

Kinsella, Eoin, 'Riotous Proceedings and the Cricket of Savages: football and hurling in early modern Ireland', in Mike Cronin, William Murphy and Paul Rouse (eds), *The Gaelic Athletic Association, 1884–2009* (Dublin: Irish Academic Press, 2009), pp. 15–31

Laffaye, Horace A., *Polo in the United States: a history* (Jefferson, NC: McFarland & Company, Inc., 2011)

Lalor, Brian (ed), *The Encyclopaedia of Ireland* (Dublin: Gill & Macmillan, 2003)

Landon, Charles, *Classic Moments of Wimbledon* (Frome: Moorland Publishing, 1982)

Lanigan, Anne, 'The Workhouse Child in Thurles, 1840–1880', in William Corbett and William Nolan (eds), *Thurles: the cathedral town* (Dublin: Geography Publications, 1989), pp. 55–80

Lee, Joseph, *The Modernisation of Irish Society, 1848–1918* (reprint Dublin: Gill & Macmillan, 1989)

Lee, Rawdon B., *A History and Description of the Modern Dogs of Great Britain and Ireland, Sporting Division*, vol. 1 (London: Horace Cox, 1897)

Lennon, Joe, *The Playing Rules of Football and Hurling, 1602–2010* (Gormanstown, Co. Meath: Northern Recreation Consultants, 2001)

Lewis, Colin A., *Hunting in Ireland: an historical and geographical analysis* (London: J.A. Allen, 1975).

Liddle, Edward, *Irish Cricketers, 1855–1980* (Cleethorpes: The Association of

Cricket Statisticians, 1980)

Loft, Martin, *Lieutenant Harry Loft of Louth and the 64th Regiment of Foot (Second Staffordshire)* (Leek: Churnet Valley Books, 2003)

Lyons, F.S.L., *Ireland since the Famine* (London: Weidenfeld & Nicolson, 1971)

Lyons, Mary Cecelia, *Illustrated Incumbered Estates* (Whitegate, Co. Clare: Ballinakella Press, 1993)

MacDonnell, Randall, *The Lost Houses of Ireland* (London: W&N, 2002)

MacEwan, Michael, *Tipperary: the people, the horses, the hounds* (Dublin: Bookconsult, 2003)

Magee, Jonathan, 'The Legacy of Master McGrath: coursing and sporting heroes in Ireland', *Sport in History*, vol. 25, no. 1 (April 2005), pp. 77–97

Maher, Pat, 'The Cashel Racecourse Stand House', *Boherlahan Dualla Historical Journal 2000*, pp. 40–5

Mahon, Jack, *A History of Gaelic Football* (Dublin: Gill & Macmillan, 2000)

Mandle, W.F., *The Gaelic Athletic Association and Irish Nationalist Politics, 1884–1924* (London and Dublin: Gill & Macmillan, 1987)

Mangan, J.A., *Athleticism in the Victorian and Edwardian Public School* (London: Frank Cass, 2000)

Marnane, Denis G., *Clanwilliam Football Club, 1879–1979: centenary history* (Tipperary: Clanwilliam RFC, 1980)

_____, 'The Coming of the Railway to County Tipperary in 1848', *Tipperary Historical Journal 1998*, pp. 138–49

_____, 'John Davis White's Sixty Years in Cashel', *Tipperary Historical Journal 2001*, pp. 57–81

_____, *Cashel: history and guide* (Dublin: Nonsuch Publishing, 2007)

Mason, Tony and Reidi, Eliza, *Sport and the Military: the British armed forces, 1880–1960* (Cambridge: Cambridge University Press, 2010)

McAnallen, Dónal, Hassan, David and Hegarty, Roddy, *The Evolution of the GAA: Ulaidh, Éire agus eile* (Belfast: Ulster Historical Foundation, 2009)

McAnallen, Dónal, '"The greatest amateur association in the world"? The GAA and amateurism', in Mike Cronin, William Murphy and Paul Rouse (eds), *The Gaelic Athletic Association, 1884–2009* (Dublin: Irish Academic Press, 2009), pp. 157–81

McCormack, Stan, *Against the Odds: Kilbeggan races, 1840–1994* (Westmeath: The Author, 1994)

McElligott, Tom, *Handball: the game, the players, the history* (Dublin: Wolfhound Press, 1984)

Mehigan, P.D., *Fifty Years of Irish Athletics* (Dublin: Gaelic Publicity Services, 1943)

Metcalfe, Alan, 'Organised Sport in the Mining Communities of South Northumberland, 1800–1889' in *Victorian Studies*, vol. 25, no. 4 (Summer 1982), pp. 469–95

Middleton, Iris M., 'The Origins of English Fox Hunting and the Myth of Hugo Meynell and the Quorn', *Sport in History*, vol. 25, no. 1 (April 2005), pp. 1–16

Mokyr, Joel, *Why Ireland Starved: a quantitative and analytical history of the Irish economy, 1800–1850* (London: Allen & Unwin, 1983)

Muenger, Elizabeth A., *The British Military Dilemma in Ireland* (Dublin: Gill & Macmillan, 1991)

Murphy, David, '"The Battle of the Breeches": the Nenagh mutiny, July 1856', *Tipperary Historical Journal 2001*, pp. 139–45

———, *Ireland and the Crimean War* (Dublin: Four Courts Press, 2002)

Murphy, Donal A., *Nenagh Ormond's Century, 1884–1984: a rugby history* (Nenagh: Relay Publications, 1984)

Murphy, William, 'Sport in a Time of Revolution: Sinn Féin and the hunt, Ireland, 1919', *Éire-Ireland*, vol. 48, nos 1 & 2 (Spring/Summer 2013), pp. 112–47

Murray, K.A. and McNeill, D.B., *The Great Southern and Western Railway* (Dublin: Irish Railway Record Society, 1976)

Nolan, William, 'Patterns of Living in County Tipperary from 1770 to 1850', in William Nolan (ed.), *Tipperary: history and society* (Dublin: Geography Publications, 1985), pp. 288–324

O'Callaghan, Liam, *Rugby in Munster: a social and cultural history* (Cork: Cork University Press, 2011)

O'Connor, Kevin, *Ironing the Land: the coming of the railways to Ireland* (Dublin: Gill & Macmillan, 1999)

O'Donnell, Patrick D., *The Irish Faction Fighters of the 19th Century* (Dublin: Anvil Books, 1975)

O'Donnell, Seán, *Clonmel, 1840–1900: anatomy of an Irish town* (Dublin: Geography Publications, 1999)

———, 'John Bagwell: politician and landlord (1811–1883)' in *Tipperary Historical Journal 2017*, pp. 26–35

O'Donoghue, Tony, *Irish Championship Athletics, 1873–1914* (Dublin: Tony O'Donoghue, 2005)

O'Flaherty, John, *Listowel Races, 1858–1991* (Listowel: John O'Flaherty, 1992)

Ó Gráda, Cormac, *Ireland: a new economic history, 1780–1939* (Oxford: Oxford University Press, 1994)

———, 'The Wages Book of a Fethard Farmer, 1880–1905', in Marcus Bourke (ed.), *Tipperary Historical Journal 1994*, pp. 69–71

O'Hara, M.M., *Chief and Tribune: Parnell and Davitt* (Dublin and London: Maunsel & Co., 1919)

Ó Maolfabhail, Art, *Camán: 2,000 years of hurling in Ireland* (Dundalk: Dundalgan Press, 1973)

Ó Riain, Séamus, *Maurice Davin (1842–1927): first president of the GAA* (Dublin: Geography Publications, 1994)

O'Shea, James, *Priest, Politics and Society in Post-famine Ireland: a study of County Tipperary, 1850–1891* (Dublin: Wolfhound Press 1983)

O'Shea, Walter S., *A Short History of Tipperary Military Barracks (Infantry), 1874–1922* (Rosegreen: Phoenix Publishing, 1999)

O'Sullivan, Donal, *Sport in Cork: a history* (Dublin: The History Press Ireland, 2010)

O'Sullivan, Thomas F., *The Story of the GAA* (Dublin: Thomas F. O'Sullivan, 1916)

Phillips-Birt, Douglas, *The History of Yachting* (London: Elm Tree Books, 1974)

Polo: players Edition, vol. 15, no. 4 (December 2011)

Power, Patrick C., *Carrick-on-Suir and Its People* (Dun Laoghaire: Anna Livia Books [for] the Carrick Society, 1976)

————, *Carrick-on-Suir: town and district* (Carrick on Suir: Carrick Books, 2003)

Power, Thomas, *Land, Politics and Society in Eighteenth-century Tipperary* (Oxford: Clarendon Press, 1993)

Prim, J.G.A., 'Olden Popular Pastimes in Kilkenny', *Transactions of the Kilkenny Archaeological Society*, vol. II, 1852–53 (Dublin, 1855), pp. 319–35.

Puirséal, Pádraig, *The GAA in Its Time* (Dublin: Ward River Press, 1982)

Quarton, Marjorie, *The North Tipperary Foxhounds: hunting in north Tipperary over two centuries* (Nenagh: Marjorie Quarton, 2010)

Reilly, Ciarán, *The Irish Land Agent, 1830–60: the case of King's County* (Dublin: Four Courts Press, 2014)

Rouse, Paul, *Sport and Ireland: a history* (Oxford: Oxford University Press, 2015)

Sanders, Richard, *Beastly fury: the strange birth of British football* (London: Bantam, 2009)

Sharlott, Jim, *On the Starting Line: a history of athletics in Leicester* (Leicester: Leicester City Council, 1994)

Shepherd, Ernie, *Waterford, Limerick and Western Railway* (Hersham, Surrey: Ian Allan Ltd., 2006)

Smyth. J.G., *Lawn Tennis* (London: B.T. Batsford Ltd., 1953)

Solow, B.L., *The Land Question and the Irish Economy, 1870–1903* (Cambridge, MA.: Harvard University Press, 1971)

Speak, M.A., 'Social Stratification and Participation in Sport in Mid-Victorian

England with Particular Reference to Lancaster, 1840–70', in J.A. Mangan (ed.), *Pleasure, Profit, Proselytism. British culture and sport at home and abroad, 1700–1914* (London: Frank Cass, 1988), pp. 42–66

Spiers, E.M., 'Army Organisation and Society in the Nineteenth Century', in Thomas Bartlett and Keith Jeffrey (eds), *A Military History of Ireland* (Cambridge: Cambridge University Press, 1996), pp. 335–57

Stakelum, Bob, *Gaelic Games in Holycross-Ballycahill, 1884–1990* (Holycross: Bob Stakelum, 1992).

Swain, Peter, 'Cultural Continuity and Football in Nineteenth-century Lancashire', *Sport in History*, vol. 28, no. 4 (December 2008), pp. 566–82.

Tierney, Andrew, 'Architecture of Gentility in Nineteenth-century Ireland' in Conor O'Neill (ed.), *Irish Elites in the Nineteenth Century* (Dublin: Four Courts Press, 2013)

Tierney, Mark, *Croke of Cashel: the life of Archbishop Thomas William Croke, 1823–1902* (Dublin: Gill & Macmillan, 1976)

Tolson, John and Vamplew, Wray, 'Derailed: railways and horse-racing revisited', *The Sports Historian*, no. 18 (November 1998), pp. 34–49

————, 'Facilitation not Revolution: railways and British flat racing, 1830–1914', *Sport in History*, vol. 23, no. 1 (Summer 2003), pp. 89–106

Tranter, Neil L., 'Organised Sport and the Middle-class Woman in Nineteenth-century Scotland', *The International Journal of the History of Sport*, vol. 6, no. 1 (1989), pp. 31–48

————, 'The Patronage of Organised Sport in Central Scotland, 1820–1900', *Journal of Sport History*, vol. 16, no. 3 (Winter 1989), pp. 227–47

————, 'The Chronology of Organised Sport in Nineteenth-century Scotland: a regional study. I – patterns', *The International Journal of the History of Sport*, vol. 7, no. 2 (1990), pp. 188–203

————, 'The Chronology of Organised Sport in Nineteenth-century Scotland: a regional study. II – causes', *The International Journal of the History of Sport*, vol. 7, no. 3 (1990), pp. 365–87

————, *Sport, Economy and Society in Britain, 1750–1914* (Cambridge: Cambridge University Press 1998)

Underdown, David, *Start of Play: cricket and culture in eighteenth-century England* (London: Penguin Books, 2000)

Vamplew, Wray, *The Turf: a social and economic history of horse racing* (London: Allen Lane, 1976)

————, *Pay Up and Play the Game: professional sport in Britain, 1875–1914* (Cambridge: Cambridge University Press, 1988)

Van Esbeck, Edmund, *Irish Rugby, 1874–1999: a history* (Dublin: Gill & Macmillan, 1999)

Vaughan, W.E. and Fitzpatrick, A.J., *Irish Historical Statistics: population, 1821–1971* (Dublin: Royal Irish Academy, 1978)

Vaughan, W.E., *Landlords and Tenants in Mid-Victorian Ireland* (Oxford: Oxford University Press, 1994)

Wade, Virginia and Rafferty, Jean, *Ladies of the Court: a century of women at Wimbledon* (London: Pavilion, 1984)

Waller, Hardress, 'Lough Derg Yacht Club', *Cois Deirge* (Summer 1980), pp. 8–10

Watson, Col. S.J., *Between the Flags: a history of Irish steeplechasing* (Dublin: Allen Figgis, 1969)

Welcome, John, *Irish Horse-racing: an illustrated history* (London: Gill & Macmillan, 1982)

Whelan, Kevin, 'The Geography of Hurling', *History Ireland*, vol. 1, no. 1 (Spring 1993), pp. 27–31

Wigglesworth, Neil, *The Social History of English Rowing* (London and New York: Frank Cass, 1992)

Williams, G. St J. and Hyland, F.P., *The Irish Derby, 1866–1979* (London: J.A. Allen, 1980)

_____, *Jameson Irish Grand National: a history of Ireland's premier steeplechase* (Dublin: The Organisation, 1995)

Wynne-Thomas, Peter, *The History of Cricket: from the weald to the world* (Norwich: Stationery Office, 1997)

Unpublished Theses

Curran, Conor, 'Why Donegal Slept: the development of Gaelic games in Donegal, 1884–1934'. Unpublished PhD thesis, De Montfort University, Leicester, 2012

Farry, Colm, 'Popular Sport in Ireland: the codification process, 1750–1885'. Unpublished MA thesis, Dublin City University, 2001

Fogarty, Catherine, 'The Disenfranchisement of the Boroughs of Cashel and Sligo'. Unpublished MA thesis, National University of Ireland, Maynooth, 2000

Hayes, Thomas, 'From Ludicrous to Logical: the transformation of sport in north Munster, 1850–90'. Unpublished PhD thesis, Mary Immaculate College/University of Limerick, 2009

Hunt, Tom, 'The Development of Sport in County Westmeath, 1850–1905'. Unpublished PhD thesis, De Montfort University, Leicester, 2005

Middleton, Iris Maud, 'The Developing Pattern of Horse Racing in Yorkshire, 1700–1749: an analysis of the people and the places'. Unpublished PhD thesis,

De Montfort University, Leicester, 2000

Reid, Sean, 'Ireland's Wisden: the handbook of cricket in Ireland and the golden age of Irish cricket, 1865–1885'. Unpublished MA dissertation, University of Bristol, 2006

Tolson, John, '"The railway myth": flat racing in mainland Britain, 1830–1914'. Unpublished PhD thesis, De Montfort University, Leicester, 2000

INDEX